Liberating Words

Liberating Words

PAUL'S USE OF RHETORICAL MAXIMS IN 1 CORINTHIANS 1–10

Rollin A. Ramsaran

TRINITY PRESS INTERNATIONAL
Valley Forge, Pennsylvania

Trinity Press International, P.O. Box 851, Valley Forge, PA 19482-0851
Trinity Press International is part of the Morehouse Publishing Group

Library of Congress Cataloging-in-Publication Data
Ramsaran, Rollin A.
    Liberating words : Paul's use of rhetorical maxims in 1
Corinthians 1-10 / Rollin A. Ramsaran.
        p. cm.
    Includes bibliographical references and index.
    ISBN 1-56338-164-8 (pbk. : alk. paper)
    1. Bible. N.T. Corinthians, 1st, 1-10 – Quotations. 2. Bible.
N.T. Corinthians, 1st, 1-10 – Criticism, interpretation, etc.
I. Title.
BS2675.2.R36 1996
227'.2066 – dc20   96-24733
                                             CIP

Printed in the United States of America

96   97   98   99   00   01   10   9   8   7   6   5   4   3   2   1

Contents

Preface

The title of this book, *Liberating Words*, is suggestive of two different perspectives. First, in the fascinating world of first-century rhetoric and maxim appropriation, Paul's own maxims were open to *mis*appropriation — to being taken captive! — by the moral reasoning of others. In 1 Corinthians 1–10, Paul sought to liberate those words and himself, in the sense of being fully and correctly understood. Second, Paul the apostle, even when misunderstood, remained committed to a new reality of freedom based in the gospel of God through Jesus Christ. Hence, within Paul's own religious worldview, any larger clarification of his moral reasoning and example, any attempt to unpack the tight, memorable packaging that maxims provided, took the idiom of freedom — liberating words. The story of Paul and the Corinthians is a debate and a reckoning of judgments that are important even in our own time: How is freedom defined, and how are individuals to flourish in true freedom vis-à-vis the larger community?

I am very appreciative of two fine scholars of 1 Corinthians who have read this manuscript in its entirety. J. Paul Sampley has provided penetrating analysis, helpful discussion, and sound suggestions that have greatly improved the content, communication, and readability of my work. Richard A. Horsley, in addition to suggesting various improvements, challenged me to clarify further a number of important issues. Despite their best efforts, the mistakes and errors in judgment that remain are mine alone.

Thanks are due also to S. Scott Bartchy, who first introduced me to the social world of early Christianity and how this information was relevant to the interpretation of all the New Testament documents, including 1 Corinthians. And finally my gratitude is extended to Howard Clark Kee, who deepened my understanding of early Christian origins, especially with respect to evaluating methodological perspectives with some acumen.

This book is dedicated to my parents, James and Jo-Carol Ramsaran. They have taught me responsible freedom constrained by love from my first day until now. I remain in their debt.

Introduction

All cultures, indeed, all religious movements, have their traditional sayings; most have a stock of religious maxims. This study provides one building block in a larger comparative study whose goal is determining by whom, for whom, and for what purposes maxims are used to provide internal ordering, stability, and a general stock of teaching material for religious movements. The study, therefore, contributes to the larger investigation of religion by providing a comparative example of how a nascent and developing religious tradition (the Pauline believing community in Corinth) must simultaneously argue and persuade from the symbol system of its larger culture while adapting, shaping, transforming, and even creating from that culture's inherited traditions its own new symbolic universe.

In coming to terms with the role played by Greco-Roman cultural traditions in the development, preservation, and propagation of early Christianity's teachings, the various influences and techniques of rhetoric merit serious attention. Greco-Roman rhetorical conventions provide the broader cultural context for the earliest Christian writers and presumably the early preachers of oral tradition before them.[1] Hence, a clear understanding of the influence of rhetoric at the turn of the eras further contributes to the modern interpreter's understanding of the social, rhetorical, literary, theological, and ethical aspects of the New Testament writings.[2]

That the apostle Paul and his congregations also participated in the Greco-Roman rhetorical conventions of their time appears clear, and recent studies on Paul's use of rhetoric and his audiences' response to that rhetoric abound.[3] Few sustained attempts have been made, however, to evaluate Paul's use of a particular rhetorical device; of those studies that do make the attempt, fewer still have shown how such devices shed light on Paul's argumentation for a new worldview designated the gospel of God through Jesus Christ (see Rom 1:9; Gal 1:12; 1 Thess 2:2) and Paul's right to be a minister of that gospel.[4] The careful, systematic investigation of one particular rhetorical device in one of his letters will illuminate Paul's level of mastery with respect to rhetorical conventions and will highlight some of the subtleties of his argumentation.

In this study I invite the reader to consider the full and proper context that stands behind the social interaction of Paul and the believing community in Corinth. I contend that this context is incomplete without a recognition of the rhetorical conventions of maxim usage found in Paul's world. To understand Paul's use of maxim argumentation *and* to realize that it is motivated, in part,

1

by his response to the maxim argumentation of some Corinthians is to open up an approach to these texts that has not been previously explored. As of yet, no sustained treatment of the various forms and functions that maxims took in the first-century world of the apostle Paul has been made. I have found it necessary, therefore, to cover that ground myself in chapter 1. In so doing, I must beg the pardon of my readers for not getting to the Pauline texts more quickly. A firm grasp, however, of the developing and dynamic maxim traditions to be found within the Greco-Roman milieu will greatly aid the interpretive endeavor ahead.

Greeks called proverb-like, pithy, and epigrammatic sayings *gnōmai;* Romans called them *sententiae.* The content of these gnomic sentences is drawn largely from recurrent, observable, and taken-for-granted experiences common to the world of the intended hearers.[5] I use the English term "maxims" to refer to the *gnōmai* and *sententiae* as found in the rhetorical handbooks at Paul's time. Most translations of the rhetorical handbooks use "maxim" to designate *gnōmē* and *sententia.* In addition, the standard dictionary definition of "maxim"[6] best exemplifies the identifying boundaries of *gnōmē* and *sententia* material as portrayed in these handbooks.

That Paul used maxims in his writings has been mentioned by many but studied in-depth by few. Hans Dieter Betz has commented on gnomic sentences or *sententiae* in his work[7] but summarily suggests that, on the whole, "[t]he investigation of Paul's gnomic sentences remains a *desideratum* of New Testament scholarship."[8] Recently, Betz's student Walter T. Wilson has written extensively on the background of the "gnomic saying" and Paul's use of a Hellenistic-Jewish *gnomologia* paradigm in Rom 12:9–21.[9] In an important way, Wilson's study partially fills this desideratum. Wilson portrays Paul as a "gnomic poet," but while remarking that Paul composes and uses isolated maxims,[10] he does not investigate them. For the interested reader, Appendix A provides a more extensive survey of maxim investigation in Pauline studies.

My purpose in this study is to extend the understanding of Paul's use of maxims by (1) critically examining the diverse and dynamic social spheres out of which maxim usage emerged and coalesced at Paul's time, (2) suggesting and applying preliminary criteria for identifying isolated embedded maxims in 1 Corinthians, and (3) elaborating on how Greco-Roman rhetorical conventions concerning the maxim undergird Paul's argumentation. I limit my close work to 1 Corinthians because this letter provides a variety of information on "practical conduct"—the type of material that is conducive to maxims. Information from the other undisputed Pauline letters reinforces findings from the investigation of 1 Corinthians 1–10.[11]

The identification of embedded maxim material in 1 Corinthians will not be sufficiently established by either a *static* comparative theory or a *static* definition from the sources—whether those sources be ancient, modern, comparative, or some combination of the above. I seek, therefore, to understand maxims within the social sphere of rhetoric in Greco-Roman education and life as a whole and within the rhetorical handbooks in particular. An adequate social understanding is *dynamic* — it analyzes transformations and conflicts that lead to a variety of options with respect to social knowledge and action.[12] As social conditions changed from the classical period (ca. 380 B.C.E.) to the time of Quintilian (ca. 85 C.E.), rhetoricians developed the maxim into three distinct forms: the gnomic maxim, the gnomic sentence, and the moral *sententia*. As a result, there were a number of options open to Paul in his usage of maxims.

No consensus exists, however, about what constitutes recognizable maxims in Paul's writings. The identification of what is or is not a maxim is not a simple matter. Only the "maxim stacks" or *gnomologia* can be identified with relative ease.[13] Our selected passages must, therefore, be substantiated as texts that contain persuasive linguistic patterns that may very well have functioned as Greco-Roman rhetorical maxims. Rhetoricians and philosophic moralists considered it a sign of maturity and stature to compose their own rules or maxims for proper living. They, like other ancient writers, commonly neither cited their sources nor prefaced their created wisdom outright. This produced what may be called "embedded" maxim material. The identification of maxims in 1 Corinthians is derived from a variety of criteria such as formal characteristics, direct identification by Paul, recognized attestation of the maxim or the general wisdom it encompasses in outside sources, and the inherent power of the language used.

A near consensus of folklorists, anthropologists, and biblical scholars[14] acknowledges that simple classification of traditional sayings (including maxims) is not nearly as informative as understanding the broad range of factors that bring a traditional saying into use in any given social situation. This study, therefore, has as its principal goal the elucidation of Paul's dealings with the Corinthians — Paul's persuasiveness, his argumentation as it is constructed through the rhetorical device of the maxim. To that end, selected passages (1 Corinthians 1–4; 7; 8–10) show how Paul carefully crafts his rhetorical use of maxims to protect his leadership integrity and mission, to establish a foundation for expanding ethical counsel, to correct the misunderstanding and misuse of his own counsel, and to encourage the continued strengthening of the believing community within a context of freedom.

Paul's maxim argumentation, then, properly helps us determine the forms, divisions, and strategy used by Paul in his persuasive constructions. How Paul proceeds with his rhetorical argument and maxim argumentation in 1 Corinthians 1–10 indicates how he conducts his moral counsel among the Corinthians: with a high regard for the reasoning processes of his audience, with a fundamental restraint in exercising absolute authority, and with a genuine concern for both preserving the individual's freedom and promoting community sensitivity. All the while, Paul's pastoral style provides a number of models by which this believing community in Corinth can more effectively do their own moral reasoning together. These insights provide a window through which the rest of the letter should be read.

Many pressures and currents in modern society socialize people away from true community. Conflicts abound. Paul belongs to a group of ancient authors who gave hard, deliberate, and focused thought to how the individual and community could thrive together. I will argue in the conclusion to this book that Paul's counsel to the Corinthians has applicability for fractured communities today.

Chapter 1

Maxims in Paul's World

Every level of the Greco-Roman educational system was directed to transmitting and reinforcing *paideia*, in the sense of a moderately uniform culture (laws, customs, moral values) based on a traditional stock of knowledge.[1] To that end, Greco-Roman education (primary, secondary, and rhetorical training) was a process that advanced in stages. Movement from one stage to the next was dependent not only on accomplishment but also upon an intermingling of factors among which were social status, finances, leisure (as opposed to being needed for labor), and available resources. Rhetoric and/or philosophy were studied at the higher levels,[2] though elements of each influenced the lower stages.

Education focused on conduct and how to speak effectively. Once formal schooling was complete, learning continued in various areas of social life by exercising *imitatio* or mimesis in the private and public spheres.[3] Opportunities for social intercourse in the private sphere included debates, symposia, and private conversations. In the public sphere, there were demonstrations such as debates or declamations, speeches connected with civic duties or religious festivals, and, of course, local assembly meetings.[4] If pupils stopped formal education in the earlier stages, they still had the opportunity to learn by observation and imitation in public.

How does the maxim fit into the various levels of Greco-Roman education, and how does it support the overall goal of *paideia*? Why were the forms and usages of the rhetorical maxim highly valued as a means of persuasive speech in the Greco-Roman world? In this chapter I examine the role of the maxim in primary and secondary education as the appropriate background to the rhetorical handbooks. Then from Quintilian's *Institutio oratoria* 8.5, I explain three maxim forms current in first-century Greco-Roman rhetoric. Finally, I consult the rhetorical handbooks for counsel on maxim usage and effectiveness. By following these steps, an important and neglected component of Paul's world comes into view with sharpened clarity.

The Maxim in Primary and Secondary Education

The rhetorical handbooks do not give complete information on maxims.[5] These handbooks assume a certain general knowledge and familiarity with maxims and their usage. Therefore, an examination of maxim usage in the Greco-Roman

5

primary and secondary education levels that preceded rhetorical training is help-ful and sometimes necessary. Such consideration allows us to read the rhetorical handbooks with the background and insight into maxims presumed by the ordi-nary student, to appreciate fully the weighty stature given to the maxim despite its (somewhat misleading) appearance as only one of many figures of speech during the imperial period, and to evaluate the maxim's role as an identifying marker for those who are wise and of cultural and social distinction.

Maxims in Primary Education and Early Home Life

The maxim always held a prominent place in Greco-Roman education. At the primary level of training,[6] the maxim's wide usage in instruction was due to its brevity. As short sentences, maxims fit nicely as a transition from the learning of letters and words to the learning of short, continuous passages.[7] Under the guidance of the grammatist, pupils learned to read and write maxims through dictation, memorization, and recitation exercises.[8] Continued work with maxims produced, in some cases, a lifetime memory of their content, as attested by writers of the time.[9]

In addition to brevity of form, teachers selected maxims for use at the primary level because of their moral value. As noted, a firm principle of Greco-Roman education was the continual implementation of *paideia* that produced moral education.[10] Simple maxims such as "Honour your parents and treat well your friends" and "No liar undetected is for long" indicate that even at this early stage of training, there were no delivered mechanics without a view to delivered morals.[11] The memorization and internalization of these simple maxims pro-vided the students with a modest base of material from which to judge their behavior or that of others.

Outside the schoolroom proper, the social realm of the home provided the beginning student an additional (and probably more directly influential) context for moral training through maxims. The Roman father took a direct role in a child's moral education, sometimes administering the "paternal precepts" (*"prae-cepta paterna, . . . given . . . usually in succinct and sententious form"*) to the son as early as the age of eleven.[12] Plutarch's notation of the involvement of mother, nurse, father, and pedagogue in a child's moral upbringing should be considered characteristic of wider Greco-Roman culture.[13]

Not to be overlooked is the pedagogue's use of maxims to reinforce the moral development of his charge. It was the Greek custom, and one adopted by de-veloping Greco-Roman education, to assign an older, wiser slave to a child as pedagogue (Gr. *paidagogos;* Lt. *paedagogus*).[14] The task of the pedagogue was to accompany, care for, protect, and upbraid the child as he went about his activi-ties, including going back and forth to school.[15] The pedagogue, in other words, was really in charge of the child's moral upbringing. "Thus the 'pedagogue' took over from the parents the general training in manners, and inculcated the traditional proprieties of behaviour in the home and out of doors."[16]

In summary, from very early in the life of a child, the maxim played an important role both in the schooling situation and in wider social life. Maxims were effective teaching material in the primary school curriculum because of (1) their suitability in moving students from the learning of individual letters and words to short, continuous passages and (2) their inherent moral character that contributed initial building blocks in the impartation of the traditional values of *paideia*. The moral value of maxims played a significant role in familial life as well as the other realms of social life, always under the watchful care of the pedagogue.[17] By the end of primary education the child conceivably had an ingrained knowledge of a variety of maxims, an acquaintance knowledge of many more, and an understanding that maxims were the material of moral counsel. These emphases were continued and developed in secondary education.

Maxims in Secondary Education

Maxims were examined in classical texts or collections during secondary education. The grammarian[18] tutored pupils in the appropriate use of a variety of literary devices and figures, of which the maxim was one.[19] In a given text, was a maxim (or other literary device) well chosen as to content and context? Was it well placed in relation to the whole? What attributed to its persuasive power?[20] Tutoring helped students to see poetical texts as sources for imitation. On a very rudimentary level, students began to consider maxims in regard to matters of invention, arrangement, and style.[21]

In literary education students equated maxims with the wise. Teachers presented the poetical works of Homer, Hesiod, Pindar, Euripides, Virgil, Horace, and other revered figures as the chosen materials from which Greco-Roman identity was shaped; maxims were abundant within them.[22] Students' study of *gnomologia* or maxim collections reinforced and heightened the distinction of maxims.[23] Maxims as wise sayings were deemed valuable, and this estimation led to exceptional efforts at collection, preservation, and attribution to wise and famous individuals.

Secondary education progressed from exposition of textual features to the composition of preliminary exercises or *progymnasmata*.[24] Each preliminary exercise, of which the maxim was one, developed a rhetorical device in a variety of ways for use in speech.[25] The extant rhetorical exercise handbooks[26] record the elaboration or the argumentation patterns of the maxim as a *progymnasma*.

The rhetorical exercise handbooks of Theon and Hermogenes are most important for this study.[27] From their counsel the student learned what features were appropriate to maxims and what linguistic shapes distinguished them. Theon describes the maxim as a speech form of general content about matters useful in life.[28] Hermogenes considers the maxim to be a summary statement of general application, having either deliberative or declarative value: it persuades or dissuades in moral behavior, or it "makes a declaration concerning the nature of a thing."[29] Hermogenes gives a technical categorization for maxims: those that are true or plausible; those that are simple, compound, or hyperbolic.[30]

The maxim *progymnasma* incorporated a pattern of ancillary exercises for elaboration and argumentation. From these exercises students learned to add clarification and detail to maxims and then to adapt maxims to support a speech in a variety of ways.[31] For the maxim Theon gives the following exercises: recitation, inflection, comment, objection, expansion and condensation, and refutation and confirmation.[32] Hermogenes suggests a more structured pattern for maxim elaboration designed to reinforce the saying with a number of elements of argumentation: "The working out [of the maxim] is similar to that of the chria; for it proceeds by (1) brief encomium of him who made the saying, as in the chria; (2) direct exposition; (3) proof; (4) contrast; (5) enthymeme; (6) illustration; (7) example; (8) authority."[33] This suggests that when one encounters a maxim in rhetorical usage, it may be developed in one of the variety of ways suggested by Theon and Hermogenes.

One of the ancillary exercises connected with the maxim *progymnasma* deserves closer treatment. Refutation and confirmation of maxims needs explication due to its lack of treatment in the rhetorical handbooks.[34] According to Theon, a list of commonplace arguments familiar to deliberative contexts establishes the refutation or confirmation of a maxim:[35] "[O]ne must refute chreiai [and maxims]:[36] (a) for obscurity, (b) for excess, (c) for incompleteness, (d) for impossibility, (e) for implausibility, (f) for falsity, (g) for disadvantageousness, (h) for uselessness, (i) for shamefulness."[37] Hence, like a deliberative proposal before an assembly, a maxim's proposal of "truth" is evaluated with concern for good sense and proper application to contextual factors governing the situation.[38]

Finally, we note that the thesis *progymnasma* of Theon promotes the confirmation of a thesis by a maxim: "We will get the introductions of theses by confirming the thesis with a maxim, a proverb, a chreia, a useful saying, a story, an encomium, or a denunciation of the subject matter which the investigation concerns."[39] Hence, students were taught that bracing or supporting a thesis with a maxim was an appropriate argumentation pattern. This is to be kept in mind because the rhetorical handbooks fail to make this point.[40]

In summary, the maxim was important in the literary studies and the *progymnasmata* exercises of secondary education. The knowledge and use of a good maxim were equated with wise individuals, whether the source was one of the poets or a person to whom a *gnomologium* was attributed. Literary studies provided a rudimentary appreciation for literary devices like the maxim as they were read in context. The maxim was one of the early *progymnasmata* exercises that allowed students to compose their own argumentative material. The rhetorical exercise handbooks of Theon and Hermogenes indicate that students learned an extensive number of techniques to elaborate or strengthen the counsel of a maxim. Some of these techniques supplement or give us information not available in the rhetorical handbooks of advanced training. The continued attention paid to the maxim in secondary education demonstrates that students were well aware of the wisdom, persuasion, and prestige an effective and well-developed maxim lent to rhetorical speech.

Three Maxim Forms at the Time of Quintilian

Rhetoric was the crowning achievement of Greco-Roman *paideia;* rhetoric provided an ongoing means of the acquisition of *paideia,* a clear voice for the propagation of *paideia,* and finally an active means for participation in the development and adaptation of *paideia* itself.[41] At the time of the early empire, rhetorical training under the rhetor[42] combined three stages in sequence or combination: rhetorical theory, imitation, and applied exercises.[43] This sequence is reflected in the extant rhetorical handbooks, which provide the bulk of our available information and guidance on maxim forms and usage in the first century C.E.[44]

Quintilian's *Institutio oratoria* gives us the best information on the forms of the rhetorical maxim used at the time of Paul.[45] Quintilian's discussion of the maxim in 8.5.3–34 shows a keen perception of the maxim's assortment of forms and its varied roles in rhetorical practice. It is not possible or necessary to discuss *Institutio oratoria* 8.5 in detail here.[46] The passage raises a number of technical issues and has long been recognized as difficult and ambiguous at some points.[47]

We can be clear, however, as to the basic forms of the maxim. Quintilian acknowledges that all maxims go by the name *sententia* in his Latin context. His consideration of maxims from a developmental and historical perspective recognizes two distinct classes: the Greek *gnōmē,* from which Latin rhetoric inherited two forms, and the subsequent Latin *sententia.*[48] This helps to identify three forms: the gnomic maxim, the gnomic sentence, and the moral *sententia.*[49] What holds the various forms together as a group is their perception as encapsulated wisdom focused on moral conduct. We now discuss each of these forms in turn, noting the appropriate evidence from the other rhetorical handbooks.

The Gnomic Maxim

The *gnōmē* should not be perceived as "purely rhetorical in origin or usage."[50] The gnomic maxim is an expression of general, traditional, moral truth as found in a variety of poetical and prose genres. Quintilian's counsel in *Institutio oratoria* 8.5.3–8 does not explicate the gnomic maxim in any detail,[51] but some examples reflect the form.[52] Undoubtedly, Quintilian presumes the reader has it in mind, for the gnomic maxim is the maxim material well known to the student from primary and secondary training.[53]

Homer's careful rhetorical formulation of gnomic maxims provided exemplary material for later imitation throughout antiquity. This is the assessment of Quintilian in 10.1.46–50. J. Villemonteix has undertaken a study of Homeric maxims that reveals that those attributed to the characters in the *Iliad* and *Odyssey* are not the "sayings" of individuals; they are common rather than individual wisdom.[54] In Homer, gnomic maxims are stylized and moralistic expressions ("*gnōmē*-maximes") of general perceptions about human nature or the human worldview as determined by and inclusive of the gods.[55]

Gnomic maxims can be found within a variety of early Greek literature prior to the fourth century B.C.E., though the word *gnōmē* is not used directly to describe these maxims.[56] The term *gnōmē* may refer directly to the faculty of a person in the sense of "reasoned judgment"; "mind, personality"; or "comprehension divinely inspired."[57] The exercise of *gnōmē* has a moral quality characterized by assessment or judgment that is attentive to prudence, justice, and doing of the good.[58] Given *gnōmē*'s attention to quality of thought and moral evaluation, it is not difficult to see how later Greek education and rhetoric adopted *gnōmē* as a designation for general, traditional, and moral truths.

The handbooks vary in their consideration of the gnomic maxim. Aristotle's definition of a maxim as general and pertaining to matters of practical conduct is broad enough to include the gnomic maxim. His examples are drawn from Euripides and Epicharmus when discussing what is self-evident[59] and from Homer when noting common and frequently quoted maxims.[60] These traditional, general, moral quotations from well-known poets are gnomic maxims. There is no discussion and no evidence of gnomic maxims in *Ad Alexandrum*.[61] *Ad Herennium*, however, prefers the gnomic maxim, emphasizing the general over the specific nature as a maxim criterion.[62]

The Gnomic Sentence

Analysis suffers when we overgeneralize from wide and disparate sources about what a maxim *must* be, not differentiating what type or form of maxim is being considered.[63] To appreciate fully the role of the gnomic sentence in deliberative contexts requires a brief examination of the transformation from gnomic maxim to gnomic sentence. This transformation occurred as part of the social-historical shift in early Greek rhetoric during the fifth and fourth centuries B.C.E.[64]

The Sophists paved the way in creating and using gnomic sentences. According to Villemonteix, the Sophists coined the adjective *gnōmotupos* (coiner of sentences) as a self-description.[65] The sophistic usage of the *gnōmē* as a "saying" or "sentence" emphasized the formulation of human judgments.[66] These judgments were made persuasive by eristic reasoning and stylistic expression, characterized by the sophistic perspective of "man as the measure of all things." The Sophists treated the *gnōmē* as they treated all aspects of rhetoric — as a means to an end, with that end being the winning of the case. Human wisdom should be shaped, even manipulated, to support the case.[67]

According to J. P. Levet, Isocrates sought to establish gnomic usage in a way that was philosophically attentive to a morally centered mind pursuing justice and truth. Isocrates knows of this newer use of the *gnōmē*,[68] but he does not agree with current sophistic employment.[69] Isocrates, from a sophistic background himself, knows that gnomic sentences can be, when abused, simply human opinion.[70] It is precisely for this reason that Isocrates' approach to the *gnōmē*, as well as to rhetoric as a whole, draws its conception and usage into a true philosophy based on earlier Greek moral values. The *gnōmē* maintains its characteristic heritage; it is no mere opinion (possibly even one contrived to mislead) but a true assessment based on one's moral posture.[71]

The attribution of a positive moral value to the use of *gnōmai* had repercussions for the teaching of rhetoric. Isocrates connects the *gnōmē* not only with technique but also with the proper appropriation of moral counsel through technique: "Now, in Isocrates' system of *philosophia*, the true teacher prepares his students not at all to have good opinions, but personally to formulate just opinions by reckoning from the nature of real circumstances."[72] Therefore, in teaching his students to be functional citizens for life, Isocrates was concerned for the discernment of true and responsible *gnōmai*. Given the changing social, political, and intellectual patterns of his time, Isocrates took the consideration of words seriously. He taught that the *gnōmē* did not warrant immediate agreement and acceptance but careful reflection and discussion with final approval in light of additional considerations, discussions, and discoveries.[73]

Given this social-historical transformation, the gnomic sentence is the individual's spoken expression of recognized wisdom, based on general observations or decrees of judgment, applied to particular circumstances of the moment as moral counsel.[74] It is a move from the universal to the particular. Speakers shape their utterances with words particular to the present context.[75] The gnomic sentence is not simply traditional, but it is rhetorical. It brings recognized wisdom to bear in a deliberative context and as such must be framed in light of one's stature, one's ability to move the audience, and the coherency of the counsel given with the particulars of the situation.[76]

The fourth-century rhetorical handbooks of Aristotle and Anaximenes illuminate and show considerable interest in the gnomic sentence.[77] Quintilian's knowledge of this counsel shows a continuation of the traditions into the first century.[78] Here I review briefly some key elements of the gnomic sentence according to the handbooks.

Rhetoricians create their own gnomic sentences based on traditional and widely held knowledge.[79] While they may closely resemble traditional wisdom or even the maxims of another person, the gnomic sentences are perceived as having been created by the one using them. A gnomic sentence may bear the stamp of that individual through a first-person introduction.[80] In addition or instead, the maxim may attach itself to the individual by that individual's more complex formulation of deliberative counsel directed to a specific situation or set of circumstances.[81] Unlike the more general gnomic maxim, the gnomic sentence is particularized to both the speaker and the situation.

The acceptance of an individual's gnomic sentence as created counsel was not always the same as the acceptance of a tradition-bound gnomic maxim. The gnomic maxim and the gnomic sentence, while both being spoken by the rhetor, differed in their perceived sources of truth. Gnomic maxims containing general, traditional, moral truths firmly planted in a common *paideia* were generally regarded by all parties as "indisputable." The gnomic sentence, however, as general wisdom formulated to particulars for a deliberative context, was often in need of confirmation and was always open to refutation.

A prominent means of confirming maxims was by one's *ēthos* or character. A speaker's reputation for strong moral character added weight to the acceptance of created moral wisdom.[82] A second means for confirmation was setting forth the gnomic sentence in a clear and logical way. This could be accomplished by anticipating obscurity, paradox, or any other element of imperfect reasoning and adding a supplement for clarification.[83] Of course in situations where confirmation is necessary, the possibility of refutation and deliberative debate will occur. Hence we find in Aristotle a discussion of maxim disagreement or refutation with regard to gnomic sentences.[84]

The Moral *Sententia*

Quintilian spends the greater part of *Institutio oratoria* 8.5 speaking of the "new" (*nova*) *sententia* (8.5.9–34). The rise and popularity of declamation in the early empire (8.5.13–14; 24; 27; see 12.10.45–48) clearly account for the attention given to this *sententia*. Again, a social-historical shift has occurred that provides a new form for the maxim. I begin, therefore, with a brief discussion of declamation practices before considering more closely the "new" *sententia*.

In rhetorical training the declamation was a fully composed speech exercise debating one or the other side of an issue. The *suasoria* was a deliberative speech based on a historical or partly historical situation. The *controversia* was a judicial speech about invented legal cases.[85] Once again, the method of instruction was by imitation. Initially the rhetor declaimed a theme, often stopping to explain the division of parts, figures used, and techniques of development. With specific themes assigned and lines of argument provided, each student would compose a speech, present it to the teacher for correction, memorize the corrected piece, and then deliver it orally for critique by fellow classmates and teacher.[86]

The declamation exercises formed a bridge from education to active social life, whether rhetorical training was to lead to a profession or not. The *suasoriae* produced speaking and evaluating skills for debate, public or private discussion, and private conversation. For those not holding a high political or a professional position, the *controversiae* still provided a background from which to weigh declamation displays or court cases.

A leading factor in the rise of declamation was the ease with which educational training and the ability to speak persuasively fed into social life. Declamation exercises moved out of the schoolrooms and private homes into a larger social sphere in the first centuries B.C.E. and C.E.[87] Rhetoricians who operated on a fee-paying basis opened up declamation exhibitions as a means of attracting potential students in an increasingly competitive market.[88] In addition, as declamation became more popular, rhetoricians — notoriously low in status — had an opportunity to raise their status through declamation display or hosting others of noteworthy position.[89]

Declamation sessions became "an entertaining and stimulating social activity in their own right," offering recreation, entertainment,[90] intellectual excitement, friendly competition, and the practice, maintenance, and improvement of oratorical skills and criticism.[91] The ability to speak well in competition or to associate oneself with those who did became a major means of status conferral from the early empire onward.

Critiques of the usefulness and the abuse of declamation were widespread.[92] The critiques of Seneca the Elder and Quintilian best reflect the period under study. Both warn against showy abuse, yet they highlight the advantageousness of moderate, restrained declamation exercises.[93] As we will see, moderation also characterizes their approach to the *sententiae,* a major component of these newer declamations.

The Orator's and Rhetor's Sententiae, Divisions, and Colors, by Seneca the Elder, provides valuable information on how *sententiae* were taught, used, and valued at the turn of the first century c.e.[94] Seneca "considered *sententiae,* divisions, and colors to be the crucial mechanical features of declamation as he understood it."[95] In Seneca's opinion, chief among these features were the *sententiae,* which come first in the explication and make up 45 percent of the overall content of *Controversiae* and *Suasoriae.*[96] Despite declamation abuse during his day, Seneca nonetheless accepts the use of *sententiae* as an important stylistic and persuasive technique. The catalog of *sententiae* presented in his work tends toward the noticeable and stunning as he "admittedly [selects] the more striking purple patches, both good and bad."[97]

In the *sententiae* sections, Seneca provides quotations only. Hence, our understanding of Seneca's presentation of *sententiae* is dependent on observations. Lewis A. Sussman, following Stanley F. Bonner's analysis, notes that *sententiae* fall into two categories: those that are "gnomic, proverbial, universal in application" and those that "pertain expressly to the specifics of the individual speech."[98] *Sententiae* are not limited to the area of practical conduct in either category. Often they simply state the way things are to be perceived properly.[99] Hence, Bonner describes the *sententia* as a "brief pointed comment, aptly summing up some aspect of life or the case."[100]

The use of *sententiae* and their functions expanded greatly in the declamation speeches. Encouraged by the pleasure brought to an audience by an appropriate *sententia,* rhetoricians appear to have increased the variety of functions and placements of *sententiae* in the different parts of their speeches. In Seneca, *sententiae* may function as commonplaces (*Controversiae* 1.pr.23; 2.4.4), proverbs (*Controversiae* 7.3.8–9), exempla (*Controversiae* 2.2.17), colors, stylistic ornaments, and comparisons (*Controversiae* 9.4.5) in the narration portion of the speech (*Controversiae* 2.5.1–2) and in argumentation.[101] In addition, declaimers were especially fond of using terse *sententiae* for transitions from one part of a speech to another (see *Controversiae* 1.1.25) and to close off a periodic sentence.[102]

A closer investigation of the preface to book 1 reveals other considerations pertaining to maxims. First, Seneca stresses the *ēthos* of the rhetor and speaks with conviction about the *vir bonus* tradition "which stated that only morally good men could attain eloquence."[103] But beyond propriety, Seneca suggests that powerful *sententiae* may take different forms and be suited to different temperaments:

> Seneca especially admires the qualities of liveliness and spirit, and thus praises Cassius Severus for his animated *sententiae* (3.pr.2; cf. 2.6.12). Even with his non-technical vocabulary, Seneca effectively points out which *sententiae* work, but rarely how or why. His standard is the total effect upon the listener, and this he can only express in generalities, though picturesque and evocative. There are, however, some coherent themes in his criticism; the attraction of brevity, liveliness, and force, coupled with dislike of the inappropriate, the hyperbolic, the foolish, and the cute. Seneca also believed that there were certain imponderables of style which allowed *sententiae* of dissimilar qualities to achieve success. Thus Clodius Turrinus, a talented but not great declaimer, authored *sententiae* which Seneca esteems because they are "lively, wily, and pointed" (10.pr.15). But Albucius, who enjoyed the respect of Seneca and Pollio, authored *sententiae* of a totally different sort: they were "straightforward and clear, adding nothing hidden or unexpected; but were resounding and brilliant" (*Controversiae* 7.pr.2).[104]

The use of stylish and proper maxims increased the *ēthos* of the speaker even to the point that "an exceptionally good one passed swiftly among the declaimers and could confer an instant reputation upon its author" (see *Controversiae* 2.4.9; 7.6.15; 9.2.23; 10.1.14; 10.2.10).[105]

Second, in a passage describing Porcius Latro's rhetorical-training regime, Seneca introduces material that sheds light on the usage of maxims:

> He practised another sort of exercise: one day he would write only "exclamations" [*epiphonemata*], one day only enthymemes, one day nothing but traditional passages we properly call *sententiae,* that have no intimate connection with the particular *controversia,* but can be quite aptly placed elsewhere too, such as those on fortune, cruelty, the age, riches. This type of *sententia* he called his "stock." (*Controversiae* 1.pr.24)

According to this passage, *sententiae* still operate in a general manner and may be identified by their ability to function in a variety of different situations ("can be quite aptly placed elsewhere too"). Also of note: Latro keeps a "stock" of *sententiae* ready at hand. In other words, Latro has a set of *sententiae* to fit accepted commonplaces (*loci communes*) in an argumentative situation.[106]

In *Institutio oratoria* 8.5.8–34, Quintilian makes explicit the characteristics of this new *sententia* form. Like the examples in Seneca, these *sententiae* are brief, pointed statements. In contrast to Seneca's more general and broad descriptions, Quintilian categorically describes the *sententiae*. Three appear to be better established and worthy of Quintilian's fuller comment: the *enthymema ex contrariis,*[107] or proposition in which the conclusion is drawn from contraries;[108]

the *noema,* or proposal in the form of innuendo or allusion;[109] and the *clausula,* or proposition forming the conclusion or final cadence of a period.[110]

The fourth type of *sententia* is labeled *magis nova sententiarum* (even more modern) and is more a grouping than a single type. As D. M. Kriel points out from close examination of the examples given, they are "pithy expressions" or *"any* pointed expression which relies for its effect on antithesis, word-play, hyperbole or mere witticism."[111] Quintilian discusses these "more modern" or "newer" *sententiae* in the context of overuse, a practice he attributes to the growing interest in declamation (see 12.10.45–48).

Quintilian divides the "newer" *sententiae* into two groups: those that may be either good or bad and those that are always bad. The first group consists of those *sententiae* fashioned from surprise, allusion, citation, and doubling of a phrase, especially with comparison. The second group, always bad, are fashioned from play on words, that which is hard to imagine, an artificial antithesis, superficial wit, or forced hyperbole.[112] The abuse and overuse of both good and bad have promoted the breakdown of unity in style, the acceptance of mediocrity over brilliance, and absurdity in particulars. Some rhetoricians employ *sententiae* exclusively, while others in reaction avoid them completely.

Quintilian agrees with Seneca the Elder on three key points. First, Quintilian's discussion of the *magis nova sententiarum* confirms that *sententiae* began to develop the shape of any pointed expression notable for its "Silver Age" characteristics: brief, well rounded, memorable, employing a striking figure, having an aesthetic-emotional appeal, and often placed as a *clausula.*[113]

Second, Quintilian (*Institutio oratoria* 8.5.30) indirectly attests to an expansion of *sententiae* usage in forming the various parts of a speech[114] — a development carefully noted in Seneca. These expanded elements of usage[115] focused declamation on drawing crowd approval and applause. Hence, unlike all *gnōmai,* some uses of the new *sententia* showed no moral content. Bonner notes a shift that would have occurred in training:

> Moralizing is most concise when presented in the form of a maxim (*sententia*), as, for instance, when Alexander is advised that "the sign of a great spirit is moderation in success." With this kind of aphorism, or gnomic *sententia,* boys had been familiar from primary-school days. But now they learnt, from listening to their teachers of declamation, that the most effective kind of *sententia* was not a general truth, but an apt and pithy comment on a particular situation.[116]

This later, broader usage reflects a time when audience expectation and appreciation for a well-formulated *sententia* were high. Regardless of their function in the speech, the brilliant new *sententiae* conferred character and status on the first-century C.E. rhetorician.

This shift, however, was not strong enough to eliminate the *sententia*'s usage as a maxim. Kriel's outright insistence, based on evidence in Quintilian, that newer *sententiae* could not be classified as maxims oversteps his own findings and the analysis of evidence from Seneca the Elder.[117] Moral general truth could be shaped in the form of a "newer" *sententia:* that is, it could be given a brief, well-rounded, memorable, aesthetically and emotionally appealing, and possibly "final" form. The concerns of the speaker or writer and the classification of oratory being used are far better barometers for determining the precise function of any *sententia.*

By its very nature the Greco-Roman rhetorical maxim concerns itself with moral conduct or "questions of practical conduct."[118] Hence, this study concerns itself with the "moral *sententia*" that should be properly classed as a subset of *sententiae* in general.[119] As moral counsel the *sententia* qualifies as a maxim; when functioning in a different capacity, it can appropriately be labeled according to that function — as a division, commonplace, exemplum, color, stylistic ornament, comparison, and so forth. By studying the *sententiae* as a whole, we have determined some of the identification markings and usage patterns for the moral *sententia.*

Finally, both Seneca the Elder and Quintilian are aware of the possibility of overuse and abuse of *sententiae.* Both, however, advance moderate positions that are cautious yet retain an opportunity for brilliance. In Quintilian's own words:

> Rhetoricians are divided in opinion on this subject: some devote practically all their efforts to the elaboration of *reflexions* [*sententiae*], while others condemn their employment altogether. I cannot agree entirely with either view. . . . If they are crowded too thick together, such *reflexions* merely stand in each other's way . . . [and may break] up our speeches into a number of detached sentences; every *reflexion* is isolated, and consequently a fresh start is necessary after each. . . . What sin is there in a good epigram? Does it not help our case, or move the judge, or commend the speaker to his audience? . . . But a middle course is open to us here no less than in the refinements of dress and mode of life, where there is a certain tasteful elegance that offends no one. Therefore, let us as far as possible seek to increase the number of our virtues, although our first care must always be to keep ourselves free from vices. (*Institutio oratoria* 8.5.25–34)

Quintilian opts for a mediating view: a moderate use that aims at brilliance in expression.

In summary, at the time of Paul the maxim appeared in three forms. What holds the various forms together as a group is their perception as encapsulated wisdom focused on moral conduct. The gnomic maxim was taken from poetical or prose genres as an expression of general, traditional, and moral truth. The gnomic sentence was the individual's spoken expression of recognized wisdom, based on general observations or decrees of judgment, applied to particular circumstances of the moment. The moral *sententiae* comprise a subset of the "new" *sententiae* that had reached great popularity with the rise in declamation. Moral *sententiae* share the same stylistic markers as all other *sententiae,* but they form a separate and distinctive category as statements of moral counsel.

Maxim Usage and Effectiveness

I now consider how the three forms of the maxim were used and how their effectiveness was enhanced. The advice of the rhetorical handbooks on usage and effectiveness is applicable to all three types. This advice for contextualizing moral guidance forms a flexible and ongoing common background as maxim options increased from gnomic maxim to gnomic sentence to moral *sententia.* Elements are considered under three areas: speaker and audience, expressive technique, and elaboration. Of course, the various elements worked in concert to make the maxim as effectual as possible.

Speaker and Audience

The *ēthos* of a rhetorician or moralist[120] greatly affected a maxim's reception by an audience. A maxim by definition concerned moral guidance,[121] and it was therefore natural that the speaker's own moral character (*ēthos*) was an evaluative factor in its acceptance as truth. With the development of the gnomic sentence and its potential for ill-use, the viability of a speaker's created wisdom was more closely evaluated with his *ēthos.*[122] Maxim usage was best suited to the *ēthos* of older men and those with recognized experience in the subject under consideration.[123]

Suitable usage of maxims in a speech provided a further opportunity to enhance a rhetorician's *ēthos.* Audiences responded well to clearly and (sometimes) cleverly expressed maxim forms.[124] If the maxims were judged as good, the speaker was esteemed as one who embodied good moral conduct, and the whole content of the speech, too, was seen as a source for moral guidance.[125] A rhetorician might even create a maxim that was contrary to "the most popular sayings, such as 'Know thyself' and 'Nothing in excess,' " if this use might somehow enhance character.[126] Using too many maxims in a speech, however, could bring about a negative evaluation.[127] One might be perceived as "preaching morals,"[128] or the speech might appear fragmented, lacking continuity.[129]

Carefully and properly gauging one's audience can improve a maxim's desired effect. Attention to and familiarity with the audience's shared social stock of knowledge are helpful.[130] This knowledge might suggest the use of "common and frequently quoted maxims" that have the semblance of being true because of long-held cultural acceptance.[131] But the rhetorician need rely only on an accurate perception of "how his hearers formed their preconceived opinions and what they are" and not on the availability of ready-made common maxims. For an effective rhetorician can appropriately fashion maxims with which "[hearers] are pleased if an orator, speaking generally, hits upon the opinions which they specially hold."[132]

Expressive Technique

A good rhetorician expresses maxims in a way that focuses clarity. Some maxims are self-evident. Aristotle describes these as "already known": "[N]o sooner are they uttered than they are clear to those who consider them."[133] Some maxims are in need of a supplement (*epilogos*) or reason: those "contrary to general opinion," "disputable," or "paradoxical" and those in which the statement is "obscure."[134] In such cases the counsel of a maxim benefited from being constructed as an enthymeme (proof).[135] There are two kinds of proof: (1) maxims that form part of an enthymeme as either a premise or a conclusion;[136] (2) maxims that are "enthymematic, but are not part of an enthymeme," having their reason stated as part of or embedded in the statement itself.[137]

In addition, a supplement may be added to focus the interpretation of a maxim's more general truth to the particular situation in which it is offered as a guide for moral conduct. In this way the supplement may clarify the motivations of the speaker and the response desired.[138] If the language of the proposed maxim is very general, a supplement should be offered to pinpoint "the moral purpose."[139]

Maxim usage may also be considered in terms of positioning. Strictly speaking, the maxim may appear in any position in argumentation, but placement at the beginning or the end highlights particular usage patterns. The rhetorical exercise handbook of Theon points to the use of the maxim to confirm a thesis.[140] Hence, in advancing argumentation for or against a thesis, the maxim may be the guide from which argumentation is introduced. In that case, it would occupy the lead position in the argument. The use of the moral maxim in the final (end) position was a popular characteristic of the new *sententia* usage from at least the time of Seneca the Elder. The maxim in final position provides summation, reiteration, and emphasis.[141]

The maxim finds its power to draw attention, distinguish itself as a rhetorical and poetic form, and become memorable through its stylistic markings. This has been most noticeable with the moral *sententia* that we have already described as brief, well rounded, memorable, employing a striking figure, having an aesthetic-emotional appeal, and often placed as a *clausula*.[142] Gnomic maxims, however, were also singled out and appreciated for presenting wisdom in an aesthetically pleasing way with poetic figures.[143] And rhetoricians took exceptional care to catalog stylistic markings that would aid in formulating gnomic sentences, as evidenced in *Ad Alexandrum*, *Ad Herennium*, Hermogenes' *Progymnasmata*, and Quintilian's *Institutio oratoria*.[144] Brevity and the employment of a figure of speech or thought characterize most maxims.

Elaboration

The rhetorical exercise handbooks of Theon and Hermogenes give evidence that schoolboys were taught to elaborate maxims. Maxims, then, may have a variety of accompanying supplemental information that reinforce and reiterate their message. Good rhetoricians bolstered their maxim argumentation with, among other things, expansion or condensation, illustrations, examples, contrast, enthymeme proof, objection, and refutation.[145] We do not have specific instructions for using all of these methods of elaboration with the maxim. Presumably some methods were taught in the course of education and required little explanation for use.[146] I now examine those rhetorical strategies where some specific counsel is given (refutation, refining, and commonplace preparation).

Patterns for confirming the maxim with a supplement or reason have been discussed above and will not be reviewed again here. The opposite of the confirmation of a maxim, which is its refutation, does, however, now warrant further comment. Theon tells us that refutation of the maxim was an important *progymnasma* for schoolboys. Theon's counsel offers a list of commonplace arguments (for example, for obscurity, for incompleteness, for impossibility) from which the refutation of a maxim might be established.[147]

Aristotle discusses the refutation of maxims in his *Rhetorica*. A short section on refutation in 2.21.13–14 follows upon his advice about confirmation by supplement or reason. Aristotle notes that maxims should be used "even when contrary to the most popular sayings."[148] Success is gained when doing so makes one's character appear better or when the contrary maxim is spoken with passion.[149] In using a maxim for refutation, the response should have its moral purpose made clear by the language; otherwise a reason should be added.[150]

Aristotle gives us a clear example of a maxim being used to refute another maxim in *Rhetorica* 2.21.14. In response to the maxim, "Love as if one were bound to hate," Aristotle's suggested reply is, "The maxim does not please me, for the true friend should love as if he were going to love for ever."[151] Two things are of note here. First, Aristotle signals clearly his disagreement — "It does not please me."[152] Second, Aristotle's maxim disagreement is a reformulation using common vocabulary of the maxim in dispute (*dei; philein*).[153]

In *Ad Herennium* 4.42.54–43.56, we find a remarkable discussion of *expolitio* (refining) that uses a maxim[154] for its illustration. According to *Ad Herennium*, this rhetorical practice exercise, expanding on and combining the secondary-level *progymnasmata* of "expansion" and "confirmation" (see Theon above), is

> [a figure of thought that] not only gives force and distinction to the speech when we plead a cause, but it is by far our most important means of training for skill in style. It will be advantageous therefore to practise the principles of Refining in exercises divorced from a real cause, and in actual pleading to put them to use in the Embellishment of an argument. (4.44.58)

Expolitio, or refining, takes two argumentative patterns. In the first place, it "consists in dwelling on the same topic and yet seeming to say something ever new." It is accomplished by repetition with changes in words, in delivery, and in treatment by "form of dialogue" or "form of arousal" (4.42.54).[155]

In the second place, refining is, as a fuller argumentative pattern, the discoursing on a theme with a treatment in seven parts: simple pronouncement, reason(s), second expression in new form, statement of the contrary, comparison, use of example, and conclusion (4.42.54–44.58).[156] Of course, this second pattern is an appropriation of the maxim *progymnasma* as seen in Theon and Hermogenes. We find, then, in *Ad Herennium* a clear pattern of training for speech ("our most important means of training for skill in style") that clearly includes the development of the maxim.

Finally, Porcius Latro's training regime is instructive for maxim use and elaboration.[157] Prepared rhetoricians had a set of moral *sententiae* that were their "stock." These moral *sententiae* were of a general nature and truth, forming a repertoire of commonplaces to fit a variety of moral questions, deliberations, or topoi. A supply of moral maxims readily at hand was impressive, especially in spontaneous situations such as debate or declamation displays.

Conclusion

The young person who came through the Greco-Roman educational system was very knowledgeable and competent with respect to maxims and their usage. Primary education instilled a knowledge and stock of maxims in the memory through the teaching of letters. Secondary and rhetorical training furthered knowledge of maxim material through reading and discussion; more importantly this training began a process of guidance in the function and value of maxims as sources for or supporting elements of argumentation. *Progymnasmata* and rhetorical handbook theory provided specific practice exercises and helpful counsel for maxim use in speech composition, whether for the establishment of proof or rebuttal. At all levels maxims were equated with esteemed moral counsel and viewed as a source of *paideia*.

Rhetoric in the first-century C.E. Greco-Roman world combined older and newer traditions. The forms of the maxim varied. On the one hand, there were gnomic maxims and gnomic sentences applied to matters of practical conduct, as described by Aristotle and followed by others. On the other hand, moral *sententiae* as brilliant, witty, and short statements of practical conduct or general observation developed from the milieu of declamatory exercises and popular declamation exhibitions. Quintilian recognizes and desires a return to the values of the older traditions, but he nevertheless perceives the power of the newer ones:

> But with regard to those passages to which we give the name of *reflexions* [*sententiae*], a form of ornament which was not employed by the ancients and, above all, not by the Greeks, although I do find it in Cicero, who can deny their usefulness, provided they are relevant to the case, are not too diffuse and contribute to our success? For they strike the mind and often produce a decisive effect by one single blow, while their very brevity

makes them cling to the memory, and the pleasure which they produce has the force of persuasion. (*Institutio oratoria* 12.10.4)

Caught in the middle, Quintilian finds common ground and approval for both.

We should view the apostle Paul against this background — an era of shifting and combining traditions and an era of choices to be made with regard to style and the use of devices such as maxims. Paul, like other rhetoricians and moralists, knew that the effectiveness of maxim usage is relative to a number of factors: the perceived *ēthos* of the maxims' initiator; proper identification with one's audience; the clarity, form, and applicability of formulated wisdom to particular situations; and finally the confirmation, refutation, and embellishment of maxims through elaboration patterns. A rhetorician's attention to these factors constitutes maxim argumentation.

Beyond the sphere of Greco-Roman education proper, rhetoric and its use of maxims moved out among a variety of social spheres. Debates, symposia, public speeches, private conversations, private meetings, and local assembly meetings were all arenas for the use and display of and the status approval connected with rhetoric in general and maxims in particular. This larger social context is properly applied to the believing community in Corinth where Paul functioned as founder, teacher, and moral counselor. As we move on to consider maxim identification and argumentation, the social context, the forms of the maxim, and its usage patterns are now clear.

Chapter 2

Identifying Paul's Maxims and Reading Them within a Rhetorical Context

Maxim Identification in 1 Corinthians

Rhetoricians and moralists, like other ancient writers, neither regularly cited their sources nor prefaced their created wisdom. In most cases, we encounter "embedded" maxim material; therefore, identification is made more difficult. Conceptually we are dependent on matching the moral core of a maxim, whether directly appropriated, adapted, or creatively configured, with the general and recognizable wisdom within a particular culture.[1]

A new social movement forms a subset within the larger culture as a whole. Paul and his Corinthian followers operated in an emerging symbolic universe (within Greco-Roman culture) specific to their new movement.[2] Thus Paul and the Corinthians had an additional reservoir of developing "in-group" social knowledge from which to fashion and comprehend maxims. With respect to the creation of maxims by Paul and some of the Corinthians, then, due attention is to be given to general wisdom as it may be appropriated from the larger Greco-Roman culture, from the belief structure (marked by the influence of Hellenistic-Jewish traditions) of Paul and his believing community in Corinth, or from a combination of both.[3]

In some cases, the citation of moral wisdom does appear to be indicated. In most of these instances, the citations appear to be maxim positions advanced by certain Corinthian groups rather than by Paul himself.[4] Paul appears to quote Corinthian positions as a point of reference from which to launch his own counsel.[5] In at least one case, however, Paul, knowing the appreciation and credence the Corinthians give to maxims, evidently states that he too is advancing a maxim (7:25–26).[6] Thus the identification of maxims in 1 Corinthians extends from Paul's embedded maxim counsel to his knowledge and engagement of Corinthian maxims. This maxim exchange is a relational element in the early stages of the ongoing correspondence between Paul and the believing community in Corinth.[7]

General Indicators for Maxim Identification

What makes the maxim recognizable to hearers and clues them in to the available functions the maxim may provide for the argument or *ēthos* of the speaker? The rhetoricians thought of the maxim as an item of traditional moral material that was brief and figured.[8] This general description by the rhetoricians is a foundational point from which to consider proposed maxims in 1 Corinthians.

1. *Traditional Moral Content.* Is the proposed maxim directly or indirectly concerned with moral matters? Is the moral content of a proposed maxim derived from either (1) the social stock of knowledge recognizable in the wider Greco-Roman society or (2) the common (in-group) social stock of knowledge recognizable to a participant of a Pauline community? Is this moral content nuanced strongly enough to be easily recognizable to a first century hearer?[9] Directed to an audience invested with decision-making responsibility,[10] does the maxim originate from the stance of the speaker as wise person?

2. *Brevity or Conciseness.* Does the proposed maxim maintain a brief form of one to two lines? While the brevity of maxims is often relative in the handbook examples, generally the longer maxims are the exception.[11] The moral *sententiae* are usually quite short. Gnomic sentences, while concise, tend to be longer with the addition of particularizing characteristics such as the supplement or reason. Gnomic maxims vary with the types of stylistic features chosen.

3. *Figured Form.* Does the proposed maxim exhibit one or more figures or stylistic markers (for example, comparison, antithesis, *epanaphora*, interrogation, etc.) that attract the hearer's attention and mark it off from everyday speech? Rhetors seem to have been very keen on describing maxims from this perspective.[12] One caveat: sometimes brevity itself, in the sense of simplicity, straightforwardness, or directness, functions as the "figure" that heightens the emotive power of a maxim.[13]

In the final analysis, with traditional moral content as a given, both the relative brevity and the type and number of figures used with maxims may vary slightly from rhetor to rhetor according to stylistic preferences.[14] These three general aspects, taken together with the features of the gnomic maxim, gnomic sentence, and moral *sententia*, form an appropriate guide for identification of Pauline maxims.

Features of the Three Specific Categories: Gnomic Maxim, Gnomic Sentence, and Moral *Sententia*

Before encountering the text of 1 Corinthians directly, it is appropriate to review in a more compact manner the features of the three gnomic types. Selected Pauline examples are given for consideration.[15]

1. *The Gnomic Maxim.* The gnomic maxim is an expression of a general, moral truth as taken from or modeled upon formulated traditional wisdom as found in a variety of poetical and prose genres. Rhetors use a gnomic maxim

either by direct citation or by recasting the wording of a citation or traditional wisdom in general. Direct citation of gnomic maxims from epic poetry, plays, or *gnomologia* of revered individuals or philosophers was characteristic of Greco-Roman maxim usage. For a Hellenistic-Jewish figure like Paul, the pool of sources for gnomic-maxim citations included Israel's scriptures and their accompanying oral traditions.[16] A Pauline example of a gnomic maxim from scripture is 1 Cor 1:31, "Let the one who boasts, boast in the Lord" (cf. Jer 9:24).[17] In one instance Paul knows (and is willing to use) a citation of the poet Menander, "Bad company ruins good morals" (1 Cor 15:33).

Recasting the wording of a gnomic maxim or simply fashioning traditional wisdom in poetical style allows a rhetor to integrate the maxim more persuasively into a specific section of speech. It might be given particular thematic words, an interrogative form, or any number of other techniques that also serve to link larger parts of the discourse together.[18] Examples are 1 Cor 4:2, "Moreover, it is required of stewards that they be found trustworthy," and 1 Cor 9:7, "Who plants a vineyard and does not eat any of its fruit?" The gnomic maxim always retains a high level of generality; it can be moved from context to context without difficulty.

2. *The Gnomic Sentence.* The gnomic sentence is a spoken expression of recognized wisdom, applied to particular circumstances of the moment as moral counsel. The gnomic sentence is closely connected with the speaker's creativity, and it may employ a recognizable configuration such as the *Tobspruch* (an *A* is better than *B* saying), comparison (*symphoresis*), *parallelismus membrorum*, antithesis, or some other figured pattern.[19]

The gnomic sentence is a particularizing of general wisdom. There are at least three indicators of this particularizing process that may occur independently or together: a first-person introductory formulation; address in the second person or specific third person (for example, "Caesar," as in Quintilian *Institutio oratoria* 8.5.7); and an added supplement or reason.[20] With these types of indicators, the gnomic sentence is more closely tied to its immediate context than the gnomic maxim. However, the readily identifiable core of general wisdom from which the gnomic sentence originates can conceivably be reemployed in another context. An example of the gnomic sentence is 1 Cor 7:26, "I think that in light of the present distress, it is well for a person to remain as he or she is" (my trans., based on RSV).[21]

3. *The Moral* Sententia. Moral *sententiae* share the same stylistic markers as all other *sententiae*, but they form a separate and distinctive category as statements of moral counsel. In summary fashion, the identifying markers of moral *sententiae* may be categorized as brevity, pointedness, memorability, and sometimes placement in a final position.

The brevity of the *sententia* is consistent when compared with the slight ambiguity noticed in maxims as a group.[22] Often used as summary statements in the final position that drive a point home, the *sententiae* generally are unencumbered with reasons and supplements — a factor contributing to succinctness. A *sententia* is described as pointed because it employs one of a variety of figures or is simply strikingly straightforward.[23]

Both brevity and pointedness, along with an attention-getting emotive or aesthetic appeal, contribute to a *sententia* being memorable. Admittedly, there is a type of "feel" or "shape" to the *sententia* that is subjectively encountered where these factors are in place. The ancients called it "brilliance."[24] Examples of *sententiae* in 1 Corinthians are, "For the kingdom of God depends not on talk but on power" (1 Cor 4:20); "There is no God but one" (1 Cor 8:4); and "All things are permissible" (1 Cor 10:23a; my trans.).

Two Supporting Factors: Argumentation and Recurrence

The maxim is moral counsel found in deliberative contexts; it is an identifiable but fluid form[25] whose function can be attributed to the argumentative procedures of its time.[26] The identification of a proposed maxim is strengthened when the maxim is shown to be argued according to the known patterns for maxim usage in the rhetorical handbooks. In order to avoid repetition here and later in the analysis, these argumentative parallels are illuminated in the next major section where the text of 1 Corinthians is encountered directly. Argumentative parallels argued below include maxim usage (1) for the establishment of the rhetor's *ēthos*, (2) for refutation, (3) for elaboration, and (4) according to diatribal style.

Recurrence of a maxim through commonplace usage in 1 Corinthians or among other letters in the Pauline corpus strengthens its identification. Rhetoricians to some degree treated their maxims as commonplaces.[27] Useful maxims were ready at hand for certain moral situations, and they could be flexibly applied according to the nuances of the particular circumstances.[28] Moral *sententiae* that reflect this commonplace usage in 1 Corinthians are, "It is to peace that God has called you" (7:15); and "For God is a God not of disorder but of peace" (14:33).[29] Examples of recurrence of maxim usage between different letters of the authentic Pauline corpus include: "For whatever a person sows, that will he or she also reap" (Gal 6:7; my trans. based on RSV); and "The one who sows sparingly will also reap sparingly, and the one who sows bountifully will reap bountifully" (2 Cor 9:6). Again, "Circumcision is nothing, and uncircumcision is nothing; but obeying the commandments of God is everything" (1 Cor 7:19); and "For neither circumcision nor uncircumcision is anything; but a new creation is everything!" (Gal 6:15; see Gal 5:6).

Conclusion

The description of maxims and their usage in Greco-Roman rhetorical traditions provides valuable clues for maxim identification in 1 Corinthians. A number of features, both general and specific, have been proposed as guidelines for establishing proposed maxims. Identifying Paul's maxims is complicated because Paul constructs "embedded" maxims from both the broader Greco-Roman traditions *and* those traditions more specific to the nascent believing communities. In addition, the maxim as a rhetorical form maintains a certain fluidity and great variety in expression. It is conceivable, then, that despite the guidelines given, there may very well be some disagreement on identifications. This disagreement, however, may ultimately sharpen the discussion of what is at present a developing area of inquiry.

Much discussion has taken place recently about the proper boundaries and usage of rhetorical criticism. The debate over important subjects, such as genre recognition, authorial intent, propriety of "new rhetoric" approaches, and literary criticism versus practical criticism, need not be fully rehearsed here.[30] It is, however, important that I convey a sense of how I intend to proceed with rhetorical analysis in this study.

Reading Paul's Argumentation in Rhetorical Context

This study is about Paul's rhetoric, not simply because it incorporates rhetorical criticism but because its subject — the relationship between Paul and his followers at Corinth — takes place in a "rhetorical culture." The study presumes, with a growing number of scholars, that rhetoric was a pervasive social convention in Greco-Roman society and that rather than being the sole possession of an elite class, its customs, techniques, and practices had filtered down to all levels of society.[31]

This study is concerned with social-rhetorical criticism in which an emphasis is placed on the social histories of both author and audience.[32] It asks how Paul and groups within the Corinthian congregations interact rhetorically, how they seek to persuade one another about moral counsel with words, and more specifically how they do this by using maxims.

This approach does not devalue historical criticism or social-historical criticism of texts,[33] but it does acknowledge the difficulties caused by scant information, referential fallacy, and undervaluing the perspective of the reader. An ahistorical literary approach cannot be accepted, however, for certainly texts are in some sense historically grounded.[34] Rather, with George A. Kennedy, I consider rhetorical criticism as a means to bridge this hermeneutical impasse:

> Rhetorical criticism can help to fill a void which lies between form criticism on the one hand and literary criticism on the other.... [It] takes the text as we have it, whether the work of a single author or the product of editing, and looks at it from the point of view of the author's or editor's intent, the unified results, and how it would be perceived by an audience of near contemporaries.[35]

Hence, rhetorical criticism may take seriously the author's intent *and* the hearer/reader's response, evaluating both in terms of the social, historical, and rhetorical conventions of the time. A social-rhetorical criticism acknowledges that Paul's intent is also a response in an ongoing conversation and interaction of social histories. The social history of some Corinthians is to value highly a wisdom associated with rhetoric as moral counsel. They use maxims to convey this wisdom and to enhance its persuasion. As this study demonstrates, this Corinthian social history prompts Paul's response in 1 Corinthians 1–4, 7, and 8–10.

Rhetorical criticism or rhetorical analysis of New Testament texts seeks to understand the persuasive value of a document's composition and expression. The method generally consists of determining (1) the rhetorical unit, (2) the rhetorical situation or exigence[36] of the unit, (3) the one overriding problem, (4) the species of rhetoric,[37] (5) the arrangement of the material (through an analysis of the text), and (6) the success of meeting the rhetorical exigence.[38] The process is circular — each part contributes to the understanding and refinement of the whole.[39] Precisely because the methodological elements are circular in movement, I point out the order of engagement that works best for the goals of this investigation.

The consideration of the text of 1 Corinthians as a whole should be taken up first and kept in mind throughout. The rhetorical species of 1 Corinthians is deliberative oratory within an epistolary framework.[40] Because there is no reason to believe that Paul changed his course of argumentation midstream in the document,[41] the deliberative nature of the argumentation is presumed throughout.[42] Paul argues for moral positions and behavioral guidelines with regard to a number of issues, advancing proofs that support concord in the community (countering the one major problem: divisions within the community).

Subsections of the larger document are best treated as supporting proofs to the thesis statement (an address to the one overriding difficulty: divisions and lack of concord in the Corinthian community) advanced in 1 Cor 1:10. This is preferable to identifying subsections as individual speech segments that each contain their own *exordium, narratio, probatio,* and *peroratio.*[43] Although the rhetorical genre of 1 Corinthians is deliberative oratory, the argumentation may make use of the elements of judicial and epideictic oratory in its construction.[44]

The rhetorical unit should be determined by analyzing beginning and closing points of argumentation, textual and conceptual evidence for likely division, and preliminary consideration of the rhetorical situation addressed in the pericope chosen. Within a given selected unit a main deliberative question is determined (for example, in 1 Corinthians 7, "Is it appropriate to continue or enter into marital relations?").[45] Then the analysis of the text is undertaken to highlight Paul's maxim argumentation as a response to a moral position advanced by a Corinthian group. My understanding of Greco-Roman rhetoric from the handbooks and other sources guides the illumination of Paul's argumentation in general and his maxim argumentation in particular.

In analyzing a rhetorical unit, we can speak of a pattern of Paul's argumentation (a method of arrangement). This pattern may be closely connected to a pattern found within the handbooks themselves (for example, 1 Cor 10:23–30),[46] or it may be a complex and integrated pattern designed by Paul himself (1 Corinthians 1–4).[47] The rhetor made use of prevailing traditions but was never bound by them (see Quintilian *Institutio oratoria* 2.13.6–7, 17; Cicero *De oratore* 2.25).[48] Hence, the focus is on how Paul's pattern of argumentation meets and addresses the rhetorical situation[49] — and how the use of maxims plays a significant role in this process.

The evaluation and analysis of Paul's argumentation in the individual unit may suggest a more complete rhetorical situation behind the text. What can we learn about the Corinthians' interaction with one another? What can we learn about their interaction with Paul, especially in terms of their participation in defining proper moral behavior for this nascent believing community? What, if anything, makes Paul's response appropriate, persuasive, and possibly successful? Because the examination of selected texts moves along with Paul's overall argument, the rhetorical situation may be further illuminated as the investigation proceeds.

Given the identifying features of Greco-Roman rhetorical maxims as presented above, I now consider 1 Corinthians, a document replete with maxims. The concluding goal of this study is to understand *the function of maxims in Paul's argument*, not simply to identify and catalog the maxims within the letter. This goal imposes length and time limitations and necessitates restricting the study to one larger section (1 Corinthians 1–10) rather than the letter in its entirety.

For three reasons, 1 Corinthians 1–10 provides a manageable context for accomplishing the goals of this study. First, this larger section contains a number of examples from each of the three maxim types: gnomic maxim, gnomic sentence, and moral *sententia*. Paul's knowledge of the various maxim types and his skillfulness in utilizing them within a number of argumentative patterns (covert allusion, refutation, elaboration, diatribal style, refining) can be sufficiently demonstrated.[50]

Second, 1 Corinthians 1–4, with its indication of rhetorical issues (1:17; 2:1, 4), and 1 Cor 6:12–11:1, with its high number of Corinthian quotations,[51] furnish exceptional material for connecting maxim use and argumentation to the social histories of *both* Paul and some Corinthian members. I ask how Paul and groups within the Corinthian congregations interact rhetorically, how they seek to persuade one another about moral counsel with words, and more specifically how they do this by using maxims. A social-rhetorical study of 1 Corinthians 1–10 adequately demonstrates that some strong members of the believing community in Corinth had the capacity to advance moral positions in the form of maxims; that other weaker members in the community may not have had the capacity or voice to disagree; and that Paul's appropriate and persuasive maxim argumentation aimed to restore concord to all parts of the community.

Third, a consistent theme of "freedom" in 1 Corinthians 1–10 marks the rhetorical argument as a whole and the maxim argumentation in particular. Indeed, 1 Cor 6:12–11:1 forms a connected section of text begun with the Corinthian freedom maxim in 6:12a: "All things [*panta*] are permissible for me" (cf. 1 Cor 10:23). Yet, as this study will show, Paul *has already* anticipated the discussion of freedom in 6:12–11:1 with his own maxims in 1 Cor 1:31 ("Let the one who boasts, boast in the Lord") and 3:21–23 ("All things [*panta*] are yours, . . . and you belong to Christ"). This connection between "freedom" and Paul's use of maxim argumentation throughout 1 Corinthians 1–10 has yet to be carefully demonstrated.[52]

The selection of texts within 1 Corinthians 1–10 is determined in the first instance by a consideration of Paul's own use of the term *gnōmē* (1:10) in 1 Corinthians 1–4. Maxim argumentation plays a key role in shaping Paul's efforts to heal divisions in the community and secure a position of leadership for himself. After bridging 1 Corinthians 5–6, a second usage of *gnōmē* by Paul in 7:25 directs the investigation to maxim usage in 1 Corinthians 7 as a mode of developing moral counsel. Maxim argumentation is an exchange between some Corinthians and Paul, as members of the community determine how to treat one another in light of their freedom. My analysis of 1 Corinthians 8–10 examines a number of maxims from which Paul strives to define the behavior of some individuals vis-à-vis others. The serial movement from chapters 1 through 10 allows maxim usage to be evaluated in light of Paul's overall and developing rhetoric.

In sum, this study moves conceptually on three levels: (1) identification of the maxims used in the selected texts, (2) discussion of how each individual maxim functions in its own context, and (3) examination of how this function contributes to the overall argument of 1 Corinthians 1–10. With this procedure as a guide, we now turn to the selected texts of 1 Corinthians.

Chapter 3

The Function of Maxims in Paul's Argumentation: 1 Corinthians 1–10

Paul's Use of Maxims in 1 Corinthians 1–4

Like the document as a whole, 1 Corinthians 1–4 is deliberative rhetoric from Paul to the believing community in Corinth.[1] Paul, the community's founder, seeks to influence the ethical decisions and moral behavior of the Corinthians who are characterized by intra-assembly conflict.[2] The letter's opening is marked by an early *parakaleō* statement in 1:10 that is restated in a different form in 4:16.[3] Both *parakaleō* statements point to the essential difficulty at Corinth: divisions among the members and the breakdown of the unity within the church. Paul in 1 Corinthians 1–4 discerns two problems: the attachment of community members to "leaders" and the elitist position of some members based on wisdom and other status claims. Paul's treatment of these two issues in 1 Corinthians 1–4 forms the basis for his counsel regarding more specific problems throughout the letter.[4]

The structure of Paul's rhetoric in 1 Corinthians 1–4 is based upon three factors. First, from 1:10–4:6 Paul chooses to advance his argument indirectly by using the rhetorical ploy of *logos eschēmatismenos,* or "covert allusion." Covert allusion is argument for reproach or correction in veiled form, using figurative examples that do not directly implicate the offenders. The audience is invited to learn from these examples and amend their own behavior.[5] As Paul constructs his covert allusion in 1 Cor 1:11–17, his illustration of divisions is centered on a disunity in spoken expressions. Paul figuratively portrays Corinthian groups as voicing slogans that identify them with apostolic leaders;[6] in reality the Corinthians have attached themselves to at least some leaders who are identified by moral positions advanced with maxims (see 6:12; 7:1; 8:1, 4; 10:23).[7] Thus the community is split over ethical matters and moral behavior.[8]

Paul designs his rhetoric to overcome the Corinthian divisions. In doing so, he constructs his argument to increase his chances of being heard by the entire community and to decrease the likelihood of divided groups taking a stance against his counsel. With the use of covert allusion, Paul is able (1) to approach the Corinthians gently as their concerned father,[9] (2) to avoid alienating his au-

30

dience from the beginning through harsh criticism, (3) to spare leaders and their followers direct humiliation and shame, and (4) to avoid cultural impropriety on his part by resorting to public censure.[10]

Second, Paul structures his argument in 1 Corinthians 1–4 around deliberative examples from which imitation is encouraged (see 4:16).[11] Paul does not directly engage at first those with whom he disagrees but rather provides exemplary models by which they may alter their behavior and receive commendation (4:4–5).[12] Paul continues his use of personal examples for instruction throughout the letter (see 11:1).[13]

Third, from beginning to end in 1 Corinthians 1–4, Paul's rhetoric shows the incompatibility of his gospel with rhetorical wisdom claims that have led some to inflate their sense of status,[14] to boast in knowledge and freedom,[15] and to encourage those in the community to denigrate one another (4:6).[16] The talk of some arrogant persons has challenged Paul's *ēthos* before the community (4:18–20).[17] Therefore, in 1 Corinthians 4, Paul moves to bolster his *ēthos*, the ground of his example and moral counsel,[18] prior to instructing the Corinthians about particular issues.

Fourth, Paul's maxim argumentation may be added to the analysis of the rhetorical structure of 1 Corinthians 1–4. In what follows I examine (1) the relationship between Paul's use of the word *gnōmē* in the exhortation statement in 1:10 and two rhetorical maxims at 1:31 and 3:21–23 that function to introduce, clarify, and censure boasting, and (2) Paul's use of a number of maxims to support his *ēthos* in 1 Corinthians 4.

What does Paul have in mind when he uses the word *gnōmē* in 1:10? The substance of Paul's appeal in 1:10 forms a chiasm. Paul makes his appeal in order that (*hina*) the Corinthians might (*A*) "speak the same thing" (*to auto legēte*), (*B*) have no divisions (*schismata*) among themselves, (*B'*) be united, and (*A'*) find this unification through the same mind and same *gnōmē*.[19] The center of the chiasm (*B, B'*) highlights the goal of Paul's appeal: unity of the group. The outer elements (*A, A'*) point to the means for the accomplishment of unity: accord in knowledge and spoken expression.[20] Paul may have intended a double meaning for *gnōmē* at this point in his argument: "judgment" and "maxim."[21]

In 1:11 Paul immediately illustrates Corinthian divisions through a disunity in spoken slogans ("I belong to Paul"; "I belong to Apollos . . ."). By setting up his illustration in this manner, Paul makes Corinthian unity (and the correction of divisions) dependent on the community finding commonality through another spoken expression that negates party slogans.[22] If in 1:10 Paul had in mind the idea of *gnōmē* as maxim, this would be confirmed by his offering a *gnōmē* to which the Corinthians could make common agreement. Of course, Paul's *gnōmē*, in order to be in accord with the exhortation of 1:10, must be a corrective to the prevailing attitudes of disharmony and dissension. In reality, Paul offers two *gnōmai*, at 1:31 and 3:21–23, respectively. These two *gnōmai* are closely interconnected so as to produce a judgment against boasting and the divisions in the community. These occurrences are now discussed in the context of Paul's argumentation.[23]

A Maxim on Proper Boasting: 1 Corinthians 1:31

Paul's consideration of the absurdity of divisions in 1:11–17 guides the structure and the content of 1:18–31. Paul's questions in 1:13 return the Corinthians to a consideration of the foundational aspects of their faith: "Was Paul crucified for you? Or were you baptized in the name of Paul?" Two subjects in 1:17 (Paul's preaching without human wisdom; the cross of Christ) form an outline for the division of 1:18–2:5. These subjects are taken up in reverse order: 1:18–31 (a digression[24] that amplifies the word of the cross as the basis of the Corinthians' call) and 2:1–5 (Paul's preaching example versus human wisdom).[25]

In 1:18–25, Paul reminds[26] the Corinthians of the character of the gospel he preached. Paul's gospel is the crucified Christ (1:18, 23) who is God's agent of salvation according to God's purposes ("wisdom of God" [1:21]). God's wisdom in Christ is antithetical to status-seeking ways of the world. God stands with the low and despised (1:28).[27] Indeed, according to Paul, God's wisdom struggles against the wise and clever. "Human wisdom," whether Jewish or Greek, cannot properly perceive how God works God's purposes through the cross of Christ.[28] The Corinthians, who are called (1:24; see 1:2, 9), however, have known the crucified Christ as the power and the wisdom of God. With a maxim Paul sums up the foundational basis of his preaching: "For God's foolishness is wiser than human wisdom, and God's weakness is stronger than human strength" (1:25).[29]

In 1:26–30, Paul argues on at least three fronts: "the many"[30] of the Corinthians are themselves proof of the working and the goal of God's purposes as defined in 1:18–25; the many of the Corinthians should align themselves with Paul's gospel of the crucified Christ and against those who continue to live on the basis of worldly standards of status (wisdom, power, nobility);[31] and the many should live in continuity with their call[32] and exercise their decision to rely on God's election, which brings about their full completion (1:30; see 1:4–9).

"Let the one who boasts, boast in the Lord" (1:31) is a gnomic maxim. It is not only a summation to 1:18–31 but also a caution to the Corinthians about their behavior. Paul quotes formulated traditional wisdom (Jer 9:22, LXX)[33] from a revered figure of Israel's traditions (cf. Matt 16:14) and applies it to an intracommunity problem of boasting. Paul has reformulated the LXX form of this wisdom, shaping it into a tight, memorable maxim that places a form of *kauchaomai* (to boast) around each side of the substituted phrase *en kyriō*.[34] That this became a common maxim of Paul's aimed at situations of improper boasting is evident from its (verbatim) recurrence in 2 Cor 10:17.

The maxim in 1:31 is well placed. To have begun with the maxim would have altered Paul's division of 1:18–31 based on the subjects delineated in 1:17 (see above). The maxim, however, benefits from the flow of Paul's moral counsel. He reminds the Corinthians of his message of weakness; their origin, status, and call out of weakness; and finally God's activity of power in their behalf. The maxim drives the point home and calls for consideration and response: coming-to-faith was all God's doing — maintain your weakness, allow the power of God to work through you, give up your attempts to gain strength through alignment into divisions, and (implicitly) do not boast in human beings. Spoken together in accord, the elements of the maxim in 1:31 would have functioned to block the boasting in status distinctions and human guides, therefore encouraging Corinthian unity.

In 2:1–5, Paul brings himself forth as an example of one who faithfully proclaimed God's message in a manner consonant with his maxim in 1:31. As a result, the faith of community members rests on God's power, and there is no place for any boasting but in the Lord.[35] In this way, Paul craftily aligns himself with the Corinthian weak and the power of God.[36] As a messenger, Paul did not claim the status features of a wise man, a rhetorician, one who would boast in wisdom claims.[37]

A Maxim on Proper Freedom: 1 Corinthians 3:21–23

In 1 Cor 2:6–3:4, the final verses once again focus the argument squarely on divisions by figuratively portraying individuals attached to Paul and Apollos (3:4). Paul has indicated the parameters of true wisdom, which is contrasted to the worldly wisdom sought by the Corinthians.[38] Paul is in a position to share a certain wisdom with the "mature," but the Corinthians do not qualify because of their "fleshly nature" manifested in jealousy and strife.

The logic of the following section, 3:5–4:5, moves from (1) Paul and Apollos as appropriate examples for the perception of community leaders (3:5–9), to (2) God's judgment of community leaders' work (3:10–17), to (3) a maxim exhortation for the community to avoid divisions (3:18–23), to (4) Paul's personal example as model for leaders (4:1–5). Paul's instruction to leaders is implicit; his instruction to the community in general is more direct.

Paul employs a metaphor of the Corinthian community as a field in 3:5–9. The goal for the community is growth (and therefore harmony). God provides the growth (see 1:28–30; 4:6–7). Human leaders (represented by Paul and Apollos) are given the role of equal fellow workers with apportioned tasks and due accountability (3:8). An apposite construction metaphor of the community as God's building (3:9) provides a transition to yet another description of building unity in the Corinthian community (3:10–15).[39]

Next, 1 Cor 3:10–17 unpacks 3:8b ("and each will receive wages according to the labor of each").[40] As a skilled master builder who lays the foundation, Paul is pivotal to the construction metaphor (see 4:14–16). Apollos, however, gives way as Paul's specified co-worker to the more general "anyone, any person" (*tis, tinos*).[41] Implicitly Paul is addressing leaders and those in the larger community who would attach themselves to these leaders' positions.[42] He encourages these people (leaders and followers) to consider their work carefully so that it might produce concord (structural integrity) in the community. In this way all might receive full compensation and commendation (cf. 4:5) from God rather than suffering loss (v. 15) or destruction (vv. 16–17).[43]

Paul brings his argumentation on divisions full circle in 3:18–23.[44] The themes of wisdom, boasting, and "belonging" are reintroduced. The form of Paul's argument is similar to that in 1:18–31: the argument is to the broad community,[45] and Paul reinforces it with scriptural proofs (1:19; 3:19–20) and maxims (1:25, 31; 3:21–23). In 3:18–23, however, the paraenesis is more direct as Paul employs imperatival directives at 3:18 and 21.[46] The imperative at 3:21a[47] and the concluding maxim now require explanation.

In 3:21–23, Paul twice employs a common Greco-Roman philosophical maxim, "All things are yours" (*panta hymōn estin; panta hymōn*). In its present form, the maxim is shorthand for ideas connected with either Cynic or Stoic self-definition: "All things are [permitted] to the wise man."[48] The maxim surely would have resonated with some of the Corinthians who had a stake in it as their foundation for moral conduct (6:12a with *moi;* 10:23a).

Paul employs the maxim twice in a highly stylized form with each usage being significant.[49] First the maxim in 3:21b forms an explanatory reason (*gar*) for the injunction at 3:21a ("Let no one boast about human leaders"). Paul offers a maxim that when spoken together as a community (see 1 Cor 1:10; *to auto legēte*) might eliminate the divisions because it turns the earlier slogans of belonging (figuratively expressed in 1:11 and 3:4: to Paul, to Apollos, to Cephas) upside down. How can these Corinthians belong to divisions represented by people or positions when all things fully[50] belong to them? The Corinthians are not to be enslaved to anything or anybody; rather they are to use freely all things to their benefit.[51] The positive claim of the maxim (like its counterpart in 1:31) negates any "boasting about human leaders."

Paul's second usage of the maxim (3:22b) is not a simple restatement but contains an important qualification: *hymeis de Christou, Christos de theou* ("and you, the community, belong to Christ, and Christ belongs to God") (3:23). This qualification is a foundational point from which Paul will launch his moral counsel throughout the letter: the Corinthians belong to Christ and to God.[52] Paul's maxim does not make a Cynic or Stoic claim: all things are to the wise. His maxim makes a claim pertinent to the believing community: all things are to the holy.[53] It asserts, through Christ, God's claim on believers who are set apart to acknowledge God (1:2, 17–18), who are to partake of the things of God's creation with thankfulness (10:30–31), and who are to participate in new community with love and acceptance (8:1b; 12:31b–14:1; 16:14).

Paul's maxim ("All things are yours...; all things [belong to] you...") presents an extensively crafted gnomic sentence.[54] Commonly ascribed cultural wisdom is reformulated, carefully qualified, and transformed in two particular respects. In the first instance, Paul's maxim caps off the argument on divisions by relativizing any attachment to leaders. In the second instance, the freedom of believers is proscribed within social relationships, life in the world, and the unique position of belonging and being set apart to Christ and to God. The proper use of one's individual freedom with a view to the well-being and unity of the community is precisely the issue of contention throughout the remainder of the letter. Paul's maxim in 1 Cor 3:21–23 sets a context for the discussion of freedom and its attendant issues and problems (esp. in 1 Corinthians 5–10).

Maxims and Paul's *Ēthos*: 1 Corinthians 4

The result of divisions in the Corinthian community is that members are becoming "puffed up [*physiousthe*] in favor of one against the other" (1 Cor 4:6).[55] In Paul's view, there is a problem of overestimation regarding self-importance. Paul has been informed by his sources that this overestimation has caused some to question his standing in the community (4:18–21). Some of these "arrogant" or "puffed up ones" (*ephysiōthēsan*) have advanced rhetorically constructed (some in the form of maxims [see 6:12; 7:1; 8:1, 4; 10:23]) moral counsel (*logos* [4:19]; cf. *sophia logou* [1:17 and 2:1])[56] in light of Paul's continuing absence. Presumably, these "arrogant" people feel their attempts to work out ways of living in the world as spiritual people are adequate, without continuing guidance from Paul and without regard to his known ways in the church (see 4:17). Paul begs to differ with these Corinthians about the effect and source of their wisdom and speech. He argues and appeals to the entire Corinthian community about their continued need for his guidance.

In 1 Corinthians 4, Paul's rhetoric moves along two lines: (1) the continuing advancement of his example (with Apollos or alone) as a corrective to divisive behavior and (2) the use of maxims to bolster his *ēthos* as a proper moral guide and himself as spokesman for the community.[57] In what follows, I keep both lines of argumentation in sight as I highlight Paul's use of maxims to support his character.

Rhetoricians and moralists enhanced their *ēthos* by interspersing moral maxims in their speeches. In this way they appeared to be people of good moral character and worthy of attention in matters of counsel.[58] In 1 Corinthians 1–3, Paul has used maxims at 1:25; 1:31; and 3:21–23. In 1 Corinthians 4, he employs maxims at 4:2; 4:15; and 4:20. The first two maxims directly support Paul's *ēthos*, and all three maxims focus on the ability to both guide and speak and on the appropriateness of doing so.

In 1 Cor 4:1–5,[59] Paul employs a gnomic maxim about household stewards:[60] "Moreover, it is required of stewards that they be found trustworthy" (4:2). The maxim is a common, self-evident summation of wisdom that is applicable in a variety of situations.[61] Paul's maxim functions as a check on behavior or as a warning (see 3:12–17; 4:5) for those who would perceive themselves as leaders counseling spiritual wisdom (*mystērion theou* [4:1]). These leaders/moral teachers should be *pistos* (trustworthy) with respect to God's (foolish) wisdom and God's purposes.[62] For God is also *pistos* (1:9) with respect to these things (1:4–9).

The maxim concerning household stewards supports Paul's example as a leader who is *pistos* (4:3–5; see Timothy as Paul's *pistos* "double" in 4:17 and Paul's continuing appeal in 7:25).[63] According to Paul's example, true leaders

self-test their work and "purposes of heart" so as to receive commendation before God (the master of the house) at the parousia (4:5; see 3:12–17), which
is the judgment that matters. They are aware of the instability of public censure or affirmation,[64] and they are particularly aware of their own capacity for
self-deception (4:4).

With his address of the entire community (*adelphoi* [brothers and sisters]) in
4:6, Paul brings the broader community to accountability. They attach themselves to leaders, thereby gaining derivative status and the opportunity to boast
in things that should be regarded as God's gifts. Paul's earlier maxims are still
in view in 4:7. The Corinthians misunderstand the source of their lives, which
precludes all boasting except in God (see 1:31),[65] and they do not understand
God's graciousness, which provides all things without distinction (see 3:21–
23).[66] These misunderstandings have resulted in divisions within the community
as members relate to one another outside a proscribed track of cooperation.[67]

Paul has begun to speak openly, fully abandoning his "covert allusion" (4:6).
What follows is a stinging indictment of the Corinthians' getting way out ahead
of themselves in terms of being filled with wisdom, being rich, and reigning (4:8).[68] This is in stark contrast to Paul's *peristasis* catalog which contrasts
the apostolic example of weakness with their striving after worldly wisdom,
strength, and honor (4:9–13). At least in Paul's opinion, they have collapsed the
"now" and "not yet" of the ages into one fully realized spiritual realm.[69] This
"spiritual elitism"[70] drives the Corinthians' continuing quest for spiritual status
markers, such as wise speech, freedom from worldly constraints, and speaking
in tongues or prophecy, which are encountered as issues throughout the letter.[71]

Paul rhetorically denies that he is shaming the Corinthians in 4:14. The previous *peristasis* catalog, of course, would have had a shaming effect along with its
further function of providing behavioral guidelines for unity and reconciliation
(renounce status seeking in 4:10–12a; bless, endure, conciliate in 4:12b–13).[72]
Paul, however, prefers to relate to the Corinthians as a father who admonishes
his children. In 4:15, Paul employs a maxim that not only asserts his position as
father but also emphasizes his privileged place as guide and model.

Paul has either fashioned his maxim in 4:15 from prevailing cultural wisdom
or co-opted a gnomic maxim for use in the symbolic universe of the believing community: "For though you might have ten thousand guardians in Christ,
you do not have many fathers."[73] In either case, the maxim is in the form of a
gnomic sentence sharpened to the specific occasion — the question of appropriate guidance in the community. The maxim is keenly constructed in a compact
form[74] with balanced overstatement on both sides: ten thousand (myriads of)
guardians; not many (=one) fathers. A supplement is attached to drive home
what should be an obvious point: "For I begot you in Christ Jesus through the
gospel" (my trans.).

Paul's maxim makes a strong appeal to character and authority. The maxim
functions by loose analogy in applying a self-evident truth from the larger
Greco-Roman culture to the social relationships between leader and followers

in the believing community. The Roman father holds pride of place in the guidance of his children by his counsel and example.[75] This position takes precedence over the guidance of *paidagōgoi* who are under the father's employ.[76] As their father in the faith, Paul is entitled to a serious hearing by the Corinthians, and he should be considered an appropriate model for imitation (4:17).[77] Because of Paul's continuing absence, Timothy will remind the Corinthians of Paul's "ways in Christ."

In 4:18–21, Paul makes a threefold response to some who appear arrogant through their use of speech (*logos*): (1) he promises to come to Corinth soon; (2) he challenges the importance of their speech through a moral *sententia* (4:20); and (3) he threatens to come with a rod of discipline if things do not change (a prerogative of the father).

In 4:20, Paul advances an antithetical maxim based on what he believes the Corinthians will accept as a self-evident moral *sententia:* "The kingdom of God is power!"[78] The antithetical maxim ("For the kingdom of God does not consist in talk but in power"; RSV)[79] supplies a corrective by contrasting an improper behavior pattern with what should be a self-evident truth. In his maxim Paul contrasts mere "talk" (*logos* as worldly counsel) with "power" (Christ's weakness as a pattern for living)[80] and invalidates the positions of the "arrogant."[81] Such reasoning by maxim formulation is commonplace with Paul. Compare Rom 14:17: "For the kingdom of God is not food and drink but righteousness and peace and joy in the Holy Spirit."[82]

Paul's concluding maxim neatly contrasts the point at issue — *dynamis* versus *logos*. Paul argues freedom in the power of weakness; the Corinthians argue freedom informed by and expressed in the wisdom of the world (*sophias logous*). Paul is not content in waiting to test and correct their conduct by visit. Rather, Paul argues in the rest of the letter for the Corinthians to amend their conduct based on Christ's pattern of weakness embodied in Paul's own example. Power in weakness is the freedom to "look not only to one's own interests, but also to the interests of others" (Phil 2:4; my trans. based on RSV); it is the freedom to refrain from the exercise of one's right (1 Corinthians 9); it is to act in love (1 Cor 16:14).

The Rhetorical Situation of 1 Corinthians 1–4

Paul makes significant use of maxims to structure his argumentation in 1 Corinthians 1–4. In 1:31 and 3:21–23 maxims support and frame the high points of Paul's argument. They counter divisions within the community by asserting religious and moral patterns of thought and behavior that will bring the people of God together in unity. The Corinthians are to boast in the God who has extended all things to them for their mutual upbuilding according to God's purposes. Their boast and their freedom should stem from a sense of gratefulness to this gracious God (1:27–30; 4:7).

Maxims in one's speech increase the *ēthos* of the speaker as one who is moral and worthy of granting counsel. Paul has demonstrated his ability to use maxims effectively in 1 Corinthians 1–3 alone. But in 1 Corinthians 4 he specifically appropriates maxims to ensure that his *ēthos* is understood and that his counsel is given a careful hearing. Paul asserts that as God's steward he is trustworthy (*pistos*). By virtue of natural processes (he birthed the community) and by his desire to care for his children, Paul asserts that as father to the community he should be imitated. With his stature reinforced, Paul is able to state his position over and against those who might disagree with him: "The kingdom of God does not consist in talk but power."

In 1 Corinthians 1–4, Paul shows a skillful usage of the various maxim types (gnomic maxim, gnomic sentence, and moral *sententia*) in combination with a rhetorical strategy featuring "covert allusion." In addition, in 1 Corinthians 1–4 Paul's maxim usage is carefully intertwined with his use of the rhetorical device of *paradigma*, or example: 1 Cor 1:31 is exemplified in Paul's preaching example (2:1–5); 1 Cor 4:2 is exemplified in Paul's self-testing before God (4:3–5); 1 Cor 4:15 supports Paul as a proper example for imitation (4:16–17). Paul's maxim usage functions not only to structure 1 Corinthians 1–4 as a unit but also to lay the foundation for the larger argument throughout the letter. Three maxims (1:31; 3:21–23; and 4:20) provide strategic concluding summaries during the flow of the argument. Each maxim, however, connects ahead to the larger argument: 1:31 to 3:21; 3:21–23 to 4:20, 6:12, and 10:23 (also, cf. 4:2 to 7:25).

Maxim Confrontation in 1 Corinthians 7

Some Corinthians have experienced spiritual power, knowledge, and wisdom, but they have also lost their connection to the cross of Christ (1:5–7, 30; 3:18). The death and resurrection of Jesus mark for Paul an apocalyptic structure of two ages or times that overlap in history. Believers walk between the times, having been empowered with an "advance" of the Spirit that will only become complete in the parousia. Believers, however, continue in the old time, living *within the world* that is characterized by suffering loss of worldly status and by service to others (4:9–13).[83] In Paul's view, some of the Corinthians do not comprehend the cross of Christ as a pattern for living life between the times, misinterpreting their new spiritual power as bringing a *fullness* in which they feel inclined to boast (4:8). Paul indicates that God is already destroying this disengaging "worldly wisdom" of the Corinthians (1:19; 2:6). As the argument moves through 1 Corinthians 5–6 into 1 Corinthians 7, these issues of boasting in detachment and freedom continue.

In 1 Corinthians 5–6, Paul clarifies group boundaries in the interest of unity.[84] These boundaries, the vice-lists previously delivered by Paul and representative of the general term *porneia* (immorality), are known by the Corinthians.[85] The community as a whole had been remiss about the enforcement of these vice-lists that mark the community as a unit and protect it against outside defilement.[86] Even worse, some (boastingly!) have encouraged vice-list transgressions through the advancement of their moral or status positions (5:2, 6; 6:12–20).[87]

The community has allowed itself to be defiled from within and without. One man lives with his father's wife. Other believers defraud[88] one another through the worldly and high-status-favoring ways of the law courts.[89] Reminiscent of his pivotal maxim in 1:31, Paul informs these Corinthians, in the first instance, that their boasting opens them up to a cancerous spread of *porneia* (5:6–7) instead of God's grace.[90] In the second instance, Paul sarcastically points to their seeming lack of wisdom to judge even the smallest interpersonal matters.[91] He counsels them to remove the offender from their midst and to make proper judgments among themselves.

Whether informed by oral report or written correspondence, Paul has heard a voice of individualistic dissent and echoes it in 6:12: "All things are permissible to me!"[92] Paul responds that such a claim or position should be made in terms of what is advantageous or beneficial (*sympherei*).[93] Again, reminiscent of his other pivotal maxim in 3:21–23, Paul answers his interlocutor in 6:12–20 by indicating what is both the individual's and the community's true status and advantage: as those who possess all things, they are set apart to God (holy and pure); they belong to Christ; and they are responsible for one another as Christ's (corporate) body. Without this framework, they have become enslaved once again (6:12).

Paul's determination to deal with precisely these issues in 1 Corinthians 5–6 sets a context for his moral counsel in 1 Corinthians 7. He is concerned to instruct the Corinthians in holiness, in how properly to relate to one another, and as individuals in how to reason toward what is advantageous in moral matters.

More Than an Opinion: Establishing Paul's Maxim in 1 Corinthians 7:25–26

Chapter 7 of 1 Corinthians functions as part of Paul's deliberative rhetoric in a larger section from 1 Cor 5:1 to 11:1.[94] It is Paul's response to the Corinthians' written queries about matters of marriage and sexuality.[95] The chapter divides into three sections: a discussion concerning the married (7:1–16), a pivotal digression on the call of God and social-status indifference (7:17–24), and a discussion concerning the unmarried (7:25–40).[96] A variety of groups are addressed, including, at least, believing married couples, married couples with one or the other spouse outside the faith, singles, engaged couples, and widows.

Paul's use of the Greek word *gnōmē* once again marks the starting point from which to examine his maxim argumentation. When Paul states in 1 Cor 7:25, "I give my *gnōmē*," the Greek word *gnōmē* is better translated "maxim" (as in Greco-Roman rhetorical maxim) than "opinion."[97] This way Paul is following other moralists and rhetoricians of his time; he cites or creates ethical maxims as a mode of moral counsel. In making this suggestion, I part with previous scholarship that has categorized Paul's role in 1 Cor 7:25 as that of one who simply states an opinion, who is a "supposed adviser," or who is a purveyor of behavioral guidelines based on some pattern of rabbinic or protorabbinic halakha.[98]

Granted, then, that in 1 Cor 7:25 *gnōmē* has the meaning (among others) of rhetorical maxim;[99] granted that standard Greco-Roman educational training made prevalent the knowledge and usage of such maxims;[100] the evidence on formal grounds is now presented for why *gnōmē* carries this connotation in 1 Cor 7:25 and why 1 Cor 7:26 is a Pauline maxim formed on the pattern of the rhetorical maxim.[101]

In 7:25–26, Paul states, "Now concerning the unmarried, I have no command of the Lord, but I give my *gnōmē* [RSV; NRSV, opinion] as one who by the Lord's mercy is trustworthy. I think that in view of the present distress *it is well for a person to remain as he [or she] is*" (RSV). To begin, what is at issue is this last statement, properly 7:26b: "it is well for a person to remain as he [or she] is." The statement is perceived by G. F. Snyder as a *Tobspruch* (or "better...than" saying), although an incomplete one; C. K. Barrett assigns it either slogan or "maxim" status.[102] Snyder is correct in pointing to *kalon esti* as an established formulaic maxim phrase from which a *gnōmē* may be constructed.[103] Can we be more specific about Paul's usage?

One feature that distinguishes a maxim from just any stated opinion is its compact linguistic formulation. Such a construction is evident in 7:26b. The elements are (1) *hoti* = quotation indicator; (2) *kalon* = predicate adjective; (3) implied *estin* = main verb; (4) *anthrōpō* = indirect object; and (5) *to houtōs einai* = articular infinitive with enclosed adverbial modifier (a verbal noun and subject). So a literal translation would be: "The being thus (= "as one is")[104] for a person (is) good." Can this be established as a formulation of Paul himself? Quite possibly, for note the almost exact construction in Rom 14:21: (1) there is no *hoti* — Paul does not preface the maxim with an indication that he is giving one;[105] (2) *kalon* = predicate adjective; (3) implied *estin* = main verb; (4) implied hearer such as "for you Romans" or "for a person" = direct object; and (5) *to mē phagein*...[106] = articular infinitive with enclosed adverbial modifier. The literal translation would be "The not eating meat, the not drinking wine, and [the not eating or drinking anything] by which your brother or sister stumbles (is) good."

If the analysis of this Pauline maxim "form" stands, then it is not surprising that *kalon* maxim material holds together a majority of the ethical counsel in 1 Corinthians 7: 1 Cor 7:1 — "*kalon anthrōpō gunaikos mē haptesthai*" ("It is well for a man not to touch a woman"); 1 Cor 7:8 — "*kalon autous ean meinōsin hōs kagō*" ("It is well for them to remain unmarried as I am"); 1 Cor 7:40 does not have *kalon*, but it contains a reflection on Paul's *gnōmē* cast in "beatitude" form — "*makariōtera de estin ean houtōs meinē*" ("But more blessed is she if she remains as she is" [my trans.]). Paul adds that this is "*kata tēn emēn gnōmēn*" (according to my maxim).[107]

"It Is Well for a Man Not to Touch a Woman": A Corinthian Maxim and Paul's Response

Verse 7:1b represents a Corinthian quotation.[108] On analogy with Paul's maxim in 7:26, this quotation represents a maxim formed with the *kalon* linguistic pattern as explicated above.[109] In 7:1–24, there are a number of significant issues, not the least of which are theological views of marriage[110] and Paul's knowledge of and interaction with early Jesus sayings.[111] The analysis here, however, is concerned with how Paul shapes his argumentation in response to the Corinthians' proposed maxim in 7:1b.

Some Corinthians' advancement of this "ascetic"[112] moral position is surely connected to their perceived status as those who are wise and free. Apparently some wished to be liberated from marital obligations that would take them away from a free pursuit of spiritual wisdom.[113] This might be especially pertinent for women who now have an authentic freedom of expression in spiritual matters within the community.[114] Regardless of the particulars, the Corinthian maxim in 7:1b has had divisive consequences for the interpersonal male-female relationships in the community,[115] and it is therefore a point of some disagreement.

How does Paul affirm the Corinthian maxim in 7:1, if he does at all? In 7:2–6, Paul indicates that continued sexual relations among married partners[116] provide protection against *porneia*.[117] Not supplying the conjugal needs of a partner opens them up to *porneia* and therefore threatens the holiness of the individual and community (see 1 Corinthians 5–6). Paul, however, is only able to affirm the Corinthian maxim by suggesting that marriage partners may abstain from sexual relations for a short, agreed-upon time based on their ability to exercise self-control.[118] If some in the community were advocating strict "spiritual marriages" or lengthy abstention among the married, Paul does not lend his support.

We can view 1 Cor 7:7–9 as a connected section within the argument.[119] The section, as a digression from the discussion of the married, highlights Paul's own example of remaining unmarried. Such a life of celibacy is found in the gift of self-control that controls passion. The section is proleptic to the entire discussion in 1 Cor 7:25–40: it upholds the unmarried state as a valid and advantageous way of living (vv. 32–35); it names the unmarried and widows (vv. 25, 39);[120] it introduces the key term *menō* (remain: vv. 20, 24, 26 [implicit], 40); and it acknowledges self-control and passion as the measuring sticks by which decisions to marry or remain unmarried are determined (vv. 36–37).

Why, however, is 1 Cor 7:7–9 rhetorically effective at this point in Paul's argument? Three reasons. First, after finding the Corinthians' maxim largely unrelated to his counsel on married folks in 7:1–6, Paul is now able to affirm their maxim directly — but only by relegating its applicability to the sphere of the unmarried. Second, Paul keeps contact with their counsel by advancing a *kalon* statement that affirms (like their maxim) abstinence: *"kalon autois ean meinōsin hōs kagō"* ("It is well for them to remain unmarried as I am"). Third, Paul's counsel in 7:7–9 foreshadows his stance on the unmarried for his audience, effectively setting up his own maxim and expanded counsel in 7:25–40.[121]

Once again when he returns to issues of marriage in 7:10–16, Paul is unable to affirm the Corinthian maxim. Divorce among believing couples for the sake of spiritual enhancement is discouraged based on an oral tradition and command of Jesus (vv. 10–11). The exception of remaining single is remarkable in light of Paul's position in 7:2–5;[122] reconciliation, not remarriage to a different partner, is counseled. Regarding the new situation of mixed marriages in the Gentile communities ("to the rest I say . . ." [vv. 12–16]), Paul indicates that the believer should not divorce an unbelieving spouse. If, however, the unbelieving spouse chooses to separate, the believer is free.

In 7:12–16, Paul grounds his counsel not from a word of the Lord (which he does not possess) but on a moral *sententia:* "It is in peace that God has called you."[123] With regard to situations involving covenanted social obligations (here, married people), Paul finds this maxim in 7:15 more applicable than the Corinthian maxim in 7:1b. The Corinthian position advocates the advantage to an individual for ceasing from the social obligation of marriage. Paul, however, takes seriously the believer's freedom and obligation to participate in redeeming social relationships where God's peace is allowed to operate.[124]

In 1 Cor 7:1–16, the grounds for argumentation employed in Paul's rhetoric as a response to the Corinthian maxim include: (1) a warning about *porneia* for the married; (2) a digression that affirms *with modification* the Corinthian maxim as applied to the unmarried (a discussion Paul chooses to defer); (3) instruction from the Lord about divorce; and (4) his own maxim on peace for mixed marriages. Each concrete situation includes an exception.

In 1 Cor 7:17–24, Paul advances an important digression based on imperative and illustration.[125] In all his churches Paul directs individuals to live out[126] their lives in the present age according to the social situation in which they existed at the time of their call (7:17; see 7:20; 24).[127] They need not seek change in social situations because status differentiations before God are *adiaphora* (indifferent),[128] as shown by the illustration of whether or not one is circumcised. Paul drives home the point of the illustration with a maxim: "Circumcision is nothing and uncircumcision is nothing, but [what is something] is doing the commandments of God" (my trans.).[129] What is important for the individual[130] is being free from worldly structures[131] and doing covenantal stipulations[132] ("doing the commandments of God") that Paul elsewhere defines as "faith working through love."[133]

Thus, by analogy, whether one lives out his or her life in a married or celibate state is *adiaphora*[134] — provided he or she maintains social obligations. In most instances, the keeping of social obligations precludes the dissolution of marriages, but the case of the unmarried remains open. Generally, Paul anticipates that "each [*hekastos*] should remain in the state in which he or she was called" (7:20; my trans. based on RSV).

Consideration of the slave expands the illustration[135] and therefore the foundation for Paul's moral counsel. Again, with the slave, status is relativized (7:22) and remains an *adiaphoron*. But within this structure of indifference to social situations, "preferreds"[136] still remain for an individual. A slave may choose freedom, if given the opportunity (7:21).[137] Freedom, however, does not change one's status before God. What remains important (for all, free and slave alike) is to remember God's initiative of grace and not to become enslaved to human values and ways of "walking" in the world (7:23). Once again, in most cases Paul believes that "in whatever state each was called, brothers or sisters, there let him or her remain with God" (7:24; my trans.).

Paul's response in 7:1–24 redirects the Corinthians' maxim in 7:1b to its proper place as one option *for unmarried persons* amid the larger sphere of social commitments in the community. With both marriage and celibacy as *adiaphora*, how might the unmarried person make decisions between them as preferreds? To that question and situation, Paul directs his own maxim in 7:26 and his continuing counsel on marriage and celibacy in 7:25–40.

Paul's Rhetorical Maxim and Counsel in 1 Corinthians 7:25–40

As noted above, 1 Cor 7:26b betrays a stylized form concerning its formal features. With the use of a common linguistic formulation of the time, it is evident that Paul has constructed in 7:26 a two-part (supplement plus maxim) gnomic sentence from which to launch his counsel concerning the unmarried. What, if anything, however, suggests that Paul employs his maxim in conventional Greco-Roman usage?

The Greco-Roman rhetorical handbooks counsel that successful maxim usage is dependent upon the positive reception of the rhetorician's *ēthos* (character position).[138] In addition, moralists as well as rhetoricians could continually enhance this *ēthos* by their ability to form wise, succinct, and sometimes witty instructions and summaries.[139] This counsel on *ēthos* informs Paul's strategy as he states, "I give my *gnōmē* as one who by the Lord's mercy is trustworthy" (7:25b). Paul's reminder of the strength of his trustworthy *ēthos* is a position argued for previously in 1 Corinthians 4: trustworthy "steward" accountable to God (4:1–5); rightful "father" in the faith to the Corinthian community (4:14–16).

It is fascinating that Paul feels compelled again to remind the Corinthians of his *ēthos*, his character and trustworthiness, before his *gnōmē* is given. This seems to betray a fragility in the relationship between Paul and at least some in the Corinthian community. Explicitly reminding the Corinthians of his character may suggest that Paul must persuade some who may not be easily convinced; it may suggest that Paul must appeal to those who should know him well but who have begun instead to lean toward the persuasion of those who disagree with Paul.

Paul's usage of a maxim in argumentation in 1 Cor 7:26 is according to the counsel of the rhetorical handbooks of the time. Unlike the Corinthians' very general statement in 7:1b, Paul specifically follows the handbook counsel about adding a reason or supplement to any maxim that might be disputable, paradoxical, or unclear. The meaning of any maxim, therefore, is determined by its contextual factors or rhetorical circumstances; appropriate application always shows a maxim's level of effectiveness.[140] Paul takes great care to be precise about the contextual factors of his maxim — it is applied to the unmarried; it works within the context of the "present distress"; it is linked with Paul's *ēthos* (not limited to, but specifically here as one who is himself unmarried [see see 7:8]).

The rhetorical handbooks note that a maxim may function in argumentation as thesis statement, premise, or conclusion.[141] As J. Paul Sampley states, "For Paul, maxims not only conclude arguments, they sometimes launch them. Maxims can be the touchstone from which one tests out options."[142] This is precisely how Paul casts his argument in 1 Cor 7:25–40. While an exegesis of this section is not possible here, it is appropriate to sketch briefly the pattern of Paul's argumentation.

In 1 Cor 7:1–24, Paul has discussed issues of marriage. In v. 25, he responds to the issue of the "unmarried" (*peri de tōn parthenōn*).[143] A maxim supported by a reason is stated by Paul: "I think that in view of the present distress, it is well for a person to remain as he [or she] is" (RSV). Next both the maxim and the reason are amplified and refined respectively. In v. 27, although Paul directs his counsel to the "unmarried," obviously he still has married people in mind ("Are you bound?" "Are you free?"); indeed, as we will see, Paul's own maxim is applicable to both groups. In vv. 29–31, a highly stylized rhetorical *progressio* with antithesis and polysyndeton[144] clarifies relationships and obligations during this "present distress" (cf. also anaphora and *epanalepsis*). Careful observation notes that v. 28 refines the maxim and reason only by "extension" — "marriage is not sin; but the married will have worldly troubles" anticipates points in the following discussion. In 7:25–31, the reason (*A*) with maxim (*B*) and their following elaborations (*B'*, *A'*) are cast in a chiastic frame around v. 28 (*C*) — *A, B, C, B', A'*.[145]

Because vv. 29–31 are an explication of the reason ("in view of the present distress") that grounds Paul's maxim, they deserve further comment here. Paul believes the unmarried individual[146] should do his or her moral reasoning based on the recognition that "the present form of this world is passing away." As a result of the Christ-event, believers have a new, apocalyptically informed perspective on a world already judged by God and whose standards and values are passing away (see Gal 6:14).[147] This is over and against the view of some Corinthians who advocate a model of ascetic distance from the world.[148] The believer should reckon *hōs mē* (as if not):[149] remaining in a world connected with distress but looking forward to a new time marked by the absence of distress and single-minded devotion to God.[150]

Paul wrote 1 Cor 7:32–35 in support of his maxim as *confirmatio*. Why should unmarried people remain as they are? The proof takes the form of a rhetorical syllogism of probability (an enthymeme): *implied major premise* — less anxiety about externals increases undivided devotion to God; *minor premise* — the unmarried person has less anxiety about externals; *conclusion* — the unmarried person has unhindered devotion to God.

Paul presents two specific applications of his maxim in 1 Cor 7:36–38 and 7:39–40. Each includes a refinement of his maxim now in terms of what is "well" and what is "better" ("more" in v. 40). Now, remarkably, *not* to "remain as you are" is "okay" and not a sin[151] for both the betrothed (in light of lack of self-control) and the widow (because of freedom), but to remain in the unmarried state is "better" (because of access to undivided devotion to God). All of this, Paul states, is *"kata tēn emēn gnōmēn"* (according to my maxim). Further, Paul claims, as may have those who advanced the position in 7:1b, that his maxim also is informed by the Spirit of God (7:40).

What accounts for this remarkable flexibility in Paul's application of his maxim? What explains the movement in Paul's thought between the truth of a maxim and its variety of applications to social life in Christian community? To be more specific, one must consider the larger rhetorical situation of 1 Corinthians 7, which calls forth both Paul's response to the Corinthians' maxim in 7:1b and Paul's advancement of his own maxim in 7:26.

The Rhetorical Situation of 1 Corinthians 7

If it is granted that Paul bases his counsel on a rhetorical maxim and, then, argues this maxim according to the handbooks and in standard Greco-Roman rhetorical style, then a possible rhetorical situation for 1 Corinthians 7 may be suggested. In writing to Paul about the question of sexual relations within the community, the Corinthians include their own *"kalon*-styled" maxim — "It is well for a man not to touch a woman." Whether the maxim is their own, borrowed from Paul, or misrepresenting a maxim taught them by Paul is hard to decide.[152] Paul does not simply dismiss the Corinthian maxim, for that is not how one disagrees with a maxim, for maxims are thought to be indisputable. The rhetorician, rather, disagrees with the appropriateness of a maxim to specific situations, refining the maxim usage with reasons and illustrations. A more suitable maxim may be proposed.[153] This is precisely the pattern of argumentation that Paul employs in 1 Corinthians 7 as a whole.

The discussion in 1 Corinthians 7 functions like a response in deliberative debate of a general thesis.[154] In this particular case, the deliberation has advanced beyond the topos of whether or not to get married: Are sexual relations appropriate in *any* relationship if freedom is to be attained and if holiness is to be maintained? Assuming the stance of a debate respondent, Paul takes up the task of *refutatio* (refutation).[155] He examines the Corinthian position with respect to situations with which he cannot agree and offers stronger arguments.[156] Where Paul can agree with the Corinthians (in regard to the unmarried), the issue under deliberation is related through Paul's own maxim to the individual's ability and preference.

Paul's argumentation is a matter of craft. Judging from Paul's extensive use of a variety of traditions to undergird his argumentation in 1 Corinthians 7 — oral Jesus tradition, custom, pre- or para-Pauline tradition based on Gal 3:28[157] —

Paul may have viewed the developing position of those in disagreement with him as formidable. Paul refines the Corinthians' maxim in 7:1b by thoughtfully drawing out each particular situation and by carefully (and sometimes in anticipatory fashion [see 7:7–9]) introducing points that will undergird the maxim he is to offer at 1 Cor 7:26. These points are giftedness as gauged by self-control (7:7), acceptance of one's station in life (7:17, 20), and opportunity to choose between the acceptable and the better (7:21).[158] By 7:25–26, Paul's maxim works to suggest guidelines not only for the unmarried but also for the married — thereby subsuming the Corinthian maxim in 7:1 to Paul's own counsel.

The careful usage and application of maxims fit Paul's ethical stance. Sampley correctly states:

> [I]n Paul's thinking a particular action might be appropriate for one believer and not for another, depending on the measure of faith and the impact of the action on others. The Pauline maxims do not prescribe specific actions that all believers must perform in lock step; rather, they tell believers how they ought to behave with one another.[159]

Paul, however, did not agree with the maxim usage and application of some of his Corinthian followers. Thus, maxim confrontation becomes necessary through refinement, reapplication, and challenge.

Paul's counsel in 1 Corinthians 7 is in stark contrast to both the unrestrained Corinthian freedom maxim in 6:12a ("All things are permissible to me") and the ascetic preference maxim in 7:1b ("it is good for a man not to touch a woman"). Throughout his careful consideration of a variety of situations, Paul advocates the maintenance of covenanted social obligations. When considering the choices available to the unmarried individual, Paul helps each one to establish a pattern of moral reasoning: (1) individuals should not place themselves in a position to be overcome by *porneia* (that is, in the vicinity of the borders of Paul's vice-lists); and (2) the individual should avail himself or herself of preferences based on the ability to maintain a firm stance in heart[160] without doubts or wavering.[161] The maxim, which must be applied to the particulars of every different situation, provides the ideal vehicle for Paul's counsel in 1 Corinthians 7.

The form and the function of Paul's counsel in 1 Cor 7:25–26 indicate it is a rhetorical maxim and not merely an opinion. The rhetorical maxim demonstrates Paul's argumentative craft, providing not only a key to understanding the shape and purpose of the argument in 1 Corinthians 7 but also a window on the give-and-take moral persuasion occurring between Paul and members of the Corinthian community. Careful attention to the rhetorical situation and the argumentative pattern in 1 Corinthians 7 should also provide insight into maxim usage in 1 Corinthians 8 ("we all have knowledge"; "there is no God but one") and 1 Corinthians 10 ("All things are permissible").

Paul and the Maxim Rhetoric of Refinement in 1 Corinthians 8–10

Paul grants that God has given freedom to the Corinthian Christians. When freedom is misguided, it has the capacity to contribute to divisions (1 Cor 6:12a). Properly understood, however, freedom may provide a source for the end of divisions in the community because individuals must not become slaves of human beings (and worldly ways) but must determine appropriate moral behavior according to the gospel (1 Cor 3:21–23). Paul's proclaimed gospel is cruciform in shape (1:18–31; 2:2); it provides power and understanding through the Spirit (2:6–13); and it calls forth a recognizably set-apart believing community within the present evil age (5:9–13). Believers are called upon to reckon how to live uncontaminated (*hōs mē* = "as if the world does not direct one's standards and perceptions" [7:29–31]) as life marches through this age toward the parousia.[162]

Freedom understood, as Paul would have it, in the context of the whole community is grounded in belonging to Christ and God (3:23); not harming oneself (6:12–20); honoring social obligations (7:19); accepting one's social location as an appropriate place to live out one's call (7:24); and with regard to "preferreds," measuring one's own giftedness and self-control accurately in light of making it safely through to the parousia (7:25–40). In Paul's thought-world, however, the good of the individual and the good of the community work in tandem: the growth of the individual is best served in the context of healthy community (and vice versa).[163] With their freedom lacking community consciousness, some Corinthians (see 1 Corinthians 8–10) fail to perceive the contamination of the community that occurs when an individual's moral reckoning leads to the corruption of other members.

In 1 Corinthians 8–10, Paul takes up the subject of meat sacrificed to idols (*peri de tōn eidōlothytōn*). Some Corinthians advocate a moral stance based on cognitive theological positions (knowledge) and most likely their own strong example.[164] Paul counters with a qualification of this "strong" position and with the Christ-event that forms the self-definition and worth of every believer called into the community. In chapter 9, Paul expands his own example from 8:13: he vigorously claims his right to obtain support from the community, but he freely chooses to leave his right unexercised that no hindrance might be placed in front of the gospel. In 10:23–11:1, following negative examples of disqualification, Paul applies the full discussion of 8:1–10:22 to the Corinthian freedom maxim that was first encountered in 6:12.

In what follows, I give attention to how maxim usage and argumentation form an integral part of Paul's overall reasoning throughout the section as a whole. Special consideration is given to 8:1–13; the use of maxims within the diatribal style in chapter 9; and 10:23–11:1. The broad direction of Paul's argument is demonstrated, but a full exegesis and commentary on 1 Corinthians 8–10 in all its particulars are not possible here.

1 Corinthians 8: Maxim Explanation of What Is Ambiguous, Unclear, or Misunderstood

In 1 Cor 8:1–13, the rhetoric of Paul's argument incorporates five maxims. Three of these maxims are presented with the formula *oidamen hoti* (we know that)[165] as self-evident truths that relate to the moral question of eating food offered to idols: "all of us possess knowledge" (8:1); "'no idol in the world really exists'" (8:4); and "'there is no God but one'" (8:4). All three maxims are commonly accepted as Paul's quotations of the position of some "strong" Corinthians.[166]

The function of the Corinthian quotations taken together with their form indicates they are moral *sententiae*.[167] The origin of these maxims remains obscure, though the substance or import may be grounded in Paul's previous teaching.[168] Through their use of maxims in 8:1 and 8:4, some strong Corinthians support their position of unrestrained freedom (cf. 6:12a) with intellectual truths that are divorced from interpersonal consequences. Unfortunately we do not possess a full record of the maxim argumentation advanced by the Corinthians to Paul in 1 Corinthians 8. Nor can we be sure that Paul is repeating the Corinthians' argumentation in the same way in which it was advanced.[169] What is apparent, however, is that as Paul presents these Corinthian maxims, they have the potential for being morally ambiguous or unclear; if the maxims can be tied closely to Paul's earlier teaching, then given Paul's qualification and correction (8:1b; 8:5–7), they appear to have been misunderstood or misappropriated.

The other two maxims (8:1b; 8:8) are Paul's, the first most certainly so. In 8:1, Paul quickly moves to qualify and correct the Corinthian position with his composed antithetical moral *sententia*: "Knowledge puffs up, but love builds up."[170] Finally, in 8:8, Paul employs an *adiaphoron* as a gnomic sentence: "Food will not commend us to God. We are no worse off if we do not eat, and no better off if we do."[171]

The section 8:1–13 divides into two parts,[172] with each part corresponding to one side of Paul's antithetical maxim stated in 8:1b. In 1 Cor 8:1–8, Paul elaborates, refines, and qualifies the possession of knowledge; 1 Cor 8:9–13 elaborates on how love functions (or its absence fails) to build up. Hence, Paul's maxim in 8:1b is integral to the structure of his argument throughout the chapter.[173] Paul's maxim argumentation throughout 8:1–13 is based on a pattern of elaboration[174] following each presented maxim. Sometimes the elaboration of each maxim follows immediately; sometimes it resurfaces to signal and shape larger units. Paul's elaboration techniques include restatement with qualification (8:1b–3, 5–6), objection with contrast (8:7), proof (the maxim in 8:8 directly supports 8:1b), warning (8:9), and contrasting illustrative examples (8:10–13).[175] I now consider each division (8:1–8; 8:9–13) in turn.

Within the first section (8:1–8), 8:1–6 stands out as a carefully marked double section (8:1–3; 8:4–6) indicated by (1) the phrases *tōn eidōlothytōn* and *oidamen hoti*, (2) Paul's acknowledgment of the Corinthian maxim(s), and

(3) Paul's rejoinder that qualifies the Corinthian position. At 8:7–8, Paul indicates the flexible nature of a maxim as moral counsel when "preferreds" are at issue.[176]

In 8:1–3, Paul uses the Corinthians' maxim in 8:1a to set the common ground[177] for deliberation about the freedom to eat meat sacrificed to idols. Paul begins his argument with the maxim, "We know that 'all of us possess knowledge'" — the truth of which is not disputed and is indeed "admitted by either party" (Quintilian *Institutio oratoria* 5.10.14).[178]

Paul counters the possible ambiguity[179] of this initial maxim with his antithetical maxim of ethical import: "'Knowledge' puffs up, but love builds up" (8:1b). Paul now follows with an elaboration pattern consisting of two statements; each statement further explains one side of the antithetical maxim, respectively. "Knowledge" has the ability to lead to self-deception and self-inflation (8:2). There is, however, no boast in our love for God, for we have not come initially to this love by knowledge. Rather, it is God who has "known" (recognized or elected)[180] us (8:3; see 1 Cor 13:12b).

Paul's maxim in 8:1b signals a mediating stance between the two affected parties (the weak and the strong). Paul accepts the cognitive position of the strong, but he critiques sharply their resulting behavior. For those who advocate the Corinthian maxim in 8:1a are to be identified with those whom Paul has censured in 1 Corinthians 1–4 as "puffed up" ("'Knowledge' puffs up" [8:1b; see 4:6, 18]), boasting, and living according to human status-seeking ways. In Paul's view, any cognitive position advanced by these Corinthians must find its basis in the love of God that is demonstrated in God's redeeming act in Christ in behalf of all (8:11).[181]

In 8:4–6, Paul's elaboration pattern now explicates the Corinthian maxim in 8:1a, enlarging the discussion by clarifying the theological content of "knowledge." The quotations of the second and third Corinthian maxims are presented again as points of ostensible common agreement: "no idol in the world really exists"; and "there is no God but one." Again, Paul's concern is that these Corinthian maxims be circumscribed so that there is no ambiguity, lack of clarity, or misunderstanding.[182] Paul follows with a further explanation of each maxim, respectively. First, knowledge frees one from "so-called gods in heaven or on earth," although Paul's apocalyptic worldview still encompasses active forces at work in the world (8:5b; 10:20; see Gal. 4:8).[183] Second, using hymnic material,[184] Paul explains that knowledge of "one God" in the believing context ("for us") implies a *dependence* ("for whom we exist") on "one God, the Father," and "one Lord, Jesus Christ" (8:6). Freedom from all human conventions and norms of value is not unbridled freedom (see 6:12) but freedom in believing community marked by one God as source and one Lord as exemplar of weakness leading to power.[185] This continues Paul's refinement of the Corinthian freedom position.

Paul now moves in 8:7 to a consideration of what his maxim in 8:1b implies: proper moral reasoning is based not only on cognitive or theological truths but also on care demonstrated for one another in human interaction.[186] This "knowledge" of the strong is not in some persons (8:7), and the consistency of their weak moral consciousness (*syneidēsis*)[187] is threatened. The recognition of the weak person's position and danger frames the discussion in 8:9–13.[188]

Paul's maxim in 8:8 is aimed at the deficiency of the strong Corinthians' moral reasoning.[189] Some base their moral reasoning on the individual's *exousia*,[190] or "right" (8:9), to act in freedom as an expression of their wise, spiritual power. Paul identifies the eating of food as an *adiaphoron*,[191] and eating or not eating are only "preferreds": "We are no worse off if we do not eat, and no better off if we do." However, freedom's goal, and that of moral reasoning in general, is not the indiscriminate exercising of one's rights but the eschatological "commendation"[192] of God. Given the indifference of food, Paul's statement, "Food will not commend us to God," is an invitation to reflect upon what will indeed commend one to God.[193]

According to the moralists, the exercise of preferreds should contribute to what truly matters, that is, moral virtue (*aretē*).[194] According to representative Pauline *adiaphora* maxims (1 Cor 7:19; 8:8; Gal 5:6; 6:15),[195] what matters for the believer is participation in community as a new person who considers one's faith capacity (limitations and gifts) and responds with works of love toward others. Such faithful living will surely find commendation at the parousia (see 1 Cor 1:5–9).[196]

The second section, 1 Cor 8:9–13, elaborates on the latter half of Paul's maxim in 8:1b: "...but love builds up." The elaboration is in the form of a negative hypothetical (but probable) example of love's absence contrasted with the hyperbolic[197] positive example of Paul. Verse 9 is a transitional warning statement that ties together the strong's knowledge leading to *exousia* with the dire consequences that occur when love is neglected.

Paul's contrasting examples in 8:10–13 guide the Corinthians in considering the implications of the maxim put forth in 8:8. The negative example of a "knowledgeable" believer eating meat sacrificed to idols within a temple precinct to the detriment of another fellow believer does not receive commendation from God.[198] In reality, this strong believer "builds up" (*oikodomēthēsetai*; 8:10) the brother or sister for destruction because that person's weak conscience is violated. This is a distinct contrast to the work of love (*hē agapēn oikodomei*; see 8:1b) extended by God through Jesus' death to every believing person regardless of distinction (8:11).[199] The strong must ask once again if they are walking *kata anthrōpon* (according to worldly standards; 3:3–4; see 3:21; 7:23) or in the true wisdom of the crucified one (according to love).[200] To walk in worldly ways is to be puffed up; not to extend love in the pattern of Jesus is to sin against Christ[201] and (implicitly) to risk losing one's commendation from God.

Thus, 1 Cor 8:9–13 is crucial in further identifying Paul's mediating stance toward *both* the weak and the strong.[202] Paul supports the care of the weak, but he does not refuse the strong their freedom. Rather, Paul offers the strong his maxims in 8:1b and 8:8 as more appropriate foundations from which to formulate their moral reasoning: Is the chosen pattern of behavior informed by love? Will such behavior bring commendation from God?

Paul's own contrasting example is clear. Paul identifies with the freedom of the strong, but he considers the position of the weak in regard to preferred matters of indifference. Concerning the eating of meat sacrificed to idols, Paul refrains from exercising his *exousia* in a situation where a weaker brother or sister is in danger; Paul acts in love. Paul's example in 1 Cor 8:13 is the basis for the entire discussion in 1 Corinthians 9.

In summary, Paul responds to the Corinthian position of freedom based on knowledge by offering his own maxim in 8:1b as qualified refutation: " 'Knowledge' puffs up, but love builds up." In the course of his argument, which advances by the elaboration and qualification of individual maxims (8:1, 4), Paul introduces an additional *adiaphora* maxim in 8:8. With regard to eating sacrificial meat, the position of both the strong and the weak is indifferent, but one's behavior toward others is not. When considering preferred actions, the Corinthians should reflect on the qualifiers stated in Paul's two maxims: whether the action builds up (8:1b) and whether the action will meet with commendation before God (8:8). The measure of each maxim is intrinsically tied together with the other: faith working itself out in love finds commendation with God.[203]

Paul's use of maxims, once again, supports his moral reasoning. Paul's pastoral style in 1 Corinthians involves encouraging members of the community, individually and corporately, to reason out appropriate behavior (7:37; 11:13). Victor Paul Furnish is correct in stating: "He [Paul] is not just being tactful when he declines to issue an 'order' (7:6), and one must take him at his word when he says that he does not want to 'put a noose' around the necks of the Corinthians with his ethical counsels (7:35)."[204]

Neither does Paul wish that love be from necessity or compulsion. Rather, he desires that it be from free will.[205] It is the nature of maxims to demand involvement but not to dictate specific actions. Maxims point behavior in a certain direction, while allowing each person a freedom for reflection, responsibility, and a choice of actions.

1 Corinthians 9: The Maxim's Role in Establishing Positions of Freedom and Self-Control

Paul's example, not his "defense," is the primary concern of 1 Corinthians 9.[206] In 1 Cor 9:3, Paul uses the term *apologia* to frame a mock consideration of his "right" or "liberty" to be supported by his churches.[207] He expects the results of such an investigation to be obvious and resoundingly clear: Paul remains free because he exercises freedom with self-control; he does not allow his rights to harm anyone. Paul's discussion throughout 1 Corinthians 9 is an elaboration of his personal example stated in 1 Cor 8:13.[208]

Paul never renounces his rights; he voluntarily leaves his rights unexercised. In this way, he imitates the Christ (11:1) who for love's sake became a slave and died that every believer might be brought whole before God (see Phil 2:5–

11). Paul's "enslavement to all" that some might be saved is in direct contrast to the example of some strong Corinthians whose freedom from all restrictions (6:12) has brought destruction to the weak (8:11). Paul counsels the Corinthians to voluntarily exercise or not exercise their rights with self-control. To exercise self-control (*egkrateuetai;* 9:25) is not to be equated with the Stoic/Cynic struggle to live according to nature, overcoming one's "sense impressions, passions and emotions, and the whims of fortune";[209] rather the believer's self-control is measured by a readiness to act in ways that promote and expand the community through the gospel (see 8:1b).[210]

Paul's example in 1 Corinthians 9 addresses more than the issue of eating food offered to idols. As a model of the truly free person,[211] Paul counsels the Corinthians to a pattern of living that counteracts striving after worldly recognition in all its manifestations. Glancing back, Paul surely intends to exemplify the gospel in its cruciform shape, not according to human ways of seeking status but according to God's wisdom that is Christ (1 Corinthians 1–4). Looking forward, Paul's example in 1 Corinthians 9 provides a foundation from which moral counsel can be broadened further in 1 Corinthians 11–14. Paul's concern for the good of a brother or sister not only includes not causing the weak to overstep their possibilities in the faith (8:10–11) but also includes not causing weaker members to undervalue their place and participation within the community (see 11:20–22; 12:14–26; 14:26). Walking in the ways of the world that devalue rather than protect other community members results in schisms and destroys unity.[212] The introduction of Paul's example in 1 Corinthians 9 is integral to the letter's argumentation as a whole.

Paul's argumentation proceeds in four steps: establishment of Paul's freedom (9:1–14); statement of Paul's unexercised rights in Corinth (9:15–18); presentation of Paul's self-enslavement in behalf of the gospel (9:19–23); and discussion of exercising one's freedom with self-control, which brings commendation (9:24–27). Paul's maxim usage occurs in his argumentation — styled on the diatribe — found in the first and last sections. Here, attention is given to the function of these maxims within Paul's argumentation as a whole.

In 1 Cor 9:1–14, the argumentation is in the diatribe style.[213] No objection is quoted outright. In 9:1a, however, there is a response to some objection to Paul's example in 8:13 such as: "If you are prevented from eating meat, then you cannot be free."[214] Paul makes a "sudden turn" to face his interlocutor with the question, "Am I not free?" (= "Do you say I am not free?").[215] A series of four rhetorical questions (vv. 1b–2) that support Paul's claim to be free because he is an apostle (their apostle! see 1 Cor 3:10 and 4:14–15) follows in a "didactic tone."[216] Paul argues from what he and the Corinthians know together. Thus the argumentation parallels that in 8:1–13: freedom and authority from what is known. The rhetorical questions imply a lack of perception on the part of the interlocutor,[217] and their proposed path of thought seeks to correct it: apostles are free (assumed); obviously Paul is an apostle (vv. 1b–2); therefore the implicit conclusion is that Paul is free.[218]

Verse 3 is best taken as a restatement of v. 1a: "This is my reply to those who examine my qualifications for freedom."[219] Apostles have rights (food, drink, and similar support for a spouse), and Paul and Barnabas share them. These rights are firmly established in Paul's argumentation through diatribal techniques for countering an objection.[220] He advances arguments based on (1) the example of other apostles as reinforced by gnomic maxims (9:4–7); (2) a quotation from the scriptures of Israel as reinforced with a gnomic maxim (9:8–11); and (3) the example of temple servants as reinforced by an unspecified commandment of the Lord (9:13–14).

In 9:4–6, Paul uses three rhetorical questions to further a claim, surely agreeable to the Corinthians, that he and Barnabas are not to be treated differently from other apostles in terms of rights to support.[221] Why would an exception be made with regard to Paul and Barnabas (a false conclusion)[222] when a comparison with conventional wisdom states otherwise? In 1 Cor 9:7, three gnomic maxims (in the form of questions) support this point:[223] "Who at any time pays the expenses for doing military service? Who plants a vineyard and does not eat any of its fruit? Who tends a flock and does not get any of its milk?"[224] Paul uses self-evident examples that are agreeable to his hearers. The persuasion is not from prior argumentation but rather from ideas that are common to repeated observation (see 9:8a): Every kind of laborer is entitled to subsistence.

In 1 Cor 9:8–11, Paul fortifies his right to support from the law of Moses. The quotation is from Deut 25:4.[225] A concern for the laboring ox is analogous to a concern for laboring apostles. Paul makes the hermeneutic explicit by answering his own rhetorical question (9:10a) with a gnomic maxim in 9:10b: "It ['You shall not muzzle an ox while it is treading out the grain'] was written for our sake, because [*hoti*] 'whoever plows should plow in hope and whoever threshes should thresh in hope of a share in the crop.' "[226] The analogy to the plowman allows Paul to restate his claim in terms of sowing and reaping among the Corinthians (see 1 Cor 3:5–9). Thus vv. 11–12a form a ring-device through their restatement of vv. 4–6.

Verse 12b is an interruption in the diatribe style. The statement by Paul is a clear summary[227] that anticipates the discussion in 9:15–18.[228] Thematically, v. 12b ties the present discussion to 1 Cor 8:9–12.[229] Paul had warned the strong not to allow their *exousia* (liberty in eating) to become a *proskomma* (stumbling block) to the weak (8:9); now Paul indicates that he does not use his own *exousia* (right to support) in a way that puts an *egkopēn* (obstacle) in the way of the gospel (9:12b).

The diatribe style is continued in 9:13–14 as indicated by the *ouk oidate* ("Do you not know...?"). Paul brings forth an example from temple cultic norms that is clear both to Jews and to Gentiles.[230] The rather lengthy list of foundations[231] for Paul's right to support is concluded with an allusion to a saying or command of Jesus that is presumably familiar to the community.[232] Most likely such a "command" of Jesus originated in the proverbial form, "The worker is worthy of his wages" (Luke 10:7; my trans.).[233]

In 1 Cor 9:1–14, Paul's maxim argumentation supports his claim to be a very free person. At significant places in Paul's response to the objection that he is not free, maxims are employed as counter-responses familiar to the diatribe style. These maxims work in conjunction with examples and quotations to mount an ever-increasing and forceful argument for Paul's "rightful claim" to support.

In 9:15–18, Paul states the example of his own practice in Corinth. Paul makes a distinction between his commission to preach the gospel and the moral obligation he has to live out the gospel in love (9:12, 15–18). The commission is of necessity (*anagkē*) and without choice.[234] The careful use and the voluntary nonuse of rights provide Paul with a proper boast: that is, in his walk he has loved well and advanced the gospel.[235] In Corinth, Paul's boast is that he makes the gospel free of charge; Paul does not exercise his right to material support, and he therefore leaves himself open to express love fully, without the worldly barriers of the patron-client relationship.[236]

How Paul lives out the gospel in love is determinative of his commendation before God at the judgment. With this in mind, 1 Cor 9:15 anticipates the following discussion in 1 Cor 9:24–27. Using a gnomic form in 9:15 (the *Tobspruch;* see the discussion of 1 Cor 7:25–26 above), Paul contrasts dying as better than (presumably) forfeiting his boast through the agency or example of another. The interpretation is difficult because Paul breaks off the gnomic form with an interjection:

> *Kalon gar moi mallon apothanein ē —*
> *to kauchēma mou oudeis kenōsei.*
>
> [For dying is good for me rather than —
> no person shall empty my boast!] [my trans.].

Because the Pauline boast is individuated,[237] Paul must have in mind here a loss of freedom, presumably along the lines of 1 Cor 7:23b (see 1:31; 3:21a), in which one becomes the slave of humans and their worldly strivings.

In 9:19–23, Paul illustrates the use of individual rights in community through the example of his missionary practices. He makes a number of points in v. 19 and then illustrates them in vv. 20–23. In v. 19, Paul reasserts that he is free from all persons. This is a stance of freedom that Paul expects from all the Corinthians (3:21–23). Paul does not become a slave of human beings and their ways (7:23b), but he voluntarily enslaves himself (*emauton edoulōsa*) for the purpose of making the gospel more effective.[238] The reiteration of this passage in 1 Cor 10:32–11:1 indicates that Paul believes his way of acting is worthy of example because it imitates Jesus.

Paul's enslavement is an accommodation to various groups such as Jews, those under the law, and those without law (9:20–21).[239] This accommodation is expressed in a highly stylized listing[240] in which the final specific group mentioned, before the broad generalization of "all people," is the weak (9:22).[241] The mention of the weak is a sure indication that Paul is tying his mission example to how community practices in Corinth should proceed.[242] There is a significant change in verbs from *kerdainō* (gain) to *sōzō* (save; see 10:33) that signals a re-thinking, once again, concerning actions that *destroy* a weaker member of the community (8:11). Paul concludes, "I do it all for the sake of the gospel, so that I may share in its blessings" (9:23).

Paul's voluntary enslavement of himself (9:19) is identical to his accommo-dation to the various groups mentioned and to all people (9:20–23). The *kai* beginning 9:20 is epexegetical; it indicates that "[t]he two actions, linked by the simple 'and' are parallel to each other."[243] Paul's qualifications ("though I myself am not under the law"; "though I am not free from God's law") are a signal to those (strong) who would follow Paul in his example of self-enslavement: their beliefs and liberty *are not renounced* by their accommodation of behav-ior through love. Viewed in this manner, 1 Cor 9:19–23 supports and expands Paul's specific conduct (refusal of support from the Corinthians) as set forth in 9:15–18. Believers maintain their freedom and are called upon by God to exercise it responsibly.

Paul resumes his maxim argumentation and diatribe style in 9:24–27 by explaining more precisely to the Corinthians his own example of freedom. Paul's explication runs in reverse order to the summary conclusion of 9:23. The maxim, "In a race the runners all compete, but only one receives the prize" (9:24a),[244] relates to the phrase, "that I may share in its blessings," of 9:23b.[245] The following exhortation, "Run in such a way that you may win it," highlights the firm focus of 9:23a: "I do all for the sake of the gospel."[246]

"Every athlete exercises self-control in all things" (RSV). Paul's maxim in 9:25a is central to this final section and ties together 1 Corinthians 8 and 9 as a whole.[247] Self-control with respect to one's *exousia* brings about the imperishable wreath (9:25b) or commendation from God, that is, what really matters (see 8:8). Believers must act accountably before the God who is responsible for all things and who provides all things to believers for proper use (1 Cor 3:21–23; 10:26). True freedom for the individual takes place in the believing community. At all times believers maintain their individual liberty, but they restrict its use when harm may result to a member of the community.

Exercising one's freedom with self-control brings commendation, not dis-qualification (9:27). Paul illustrates his maxim in 9:26–27 as a personal example. As a runner Paul takes aim; as a boxer he masters himself.[248] Likewise, through self-control, the strong can aim at love (see 14:1), preserve weak community members, advance the gospel, and receive commendation from God. Paul's maxim in 9:25 counsels *panta egkrateuetai* (freedom under control) in behalf of others, not *panta exestin* (freedom without restraint) in behalf of oneself (*moi;* 6:12).[249] Paul's freedom, his example, and his maxim counter the unrestrained freedom of some Corinthians.

To summarize, in 1 Corinthians 9 maxims function in Paul's argumentation as supporting proof in the diatribe style of Greco-Roman rhetoric. Paul's pat-tern is to use his maxims in conjunction with examples. Within the diatribe style, maxims provide support for (1) a direct example based on the conduct of other apostles (9:4–7); (2) an example drawn from Israel's scriptures (9:8–10); and (3) Paul's personal example (9:24–27). In one case, Paul begins a maxim in support of his personal example but breaks it off with an interjection (9:15b).

In the first and second instances, Paul uses his maxims to establish his unqualified freedom to be supported as an apostle. The gnomic maxims in 9:7 establish the point: every kind of laborer is entitled to subsistence. In reiterating this point through the scripture, Paul quotes a gnomic maxim (9:10b) from an unknown source. Yet Paul voluntarily leaves his right to support unexercised in order that no hindrance is placed before the gospel. Through his personal example (9:19–23), Paul indicates that in his freedom he can accommodate his behavior to engage all people without obstacles. In doing so, Paul's beliefs and liberty remain unchanged.

In the third instance, Paul uses his maxims (9:24a, 25) to develop further his personal example. In 9:24a, the maxim emphasizes the aim and resolve of the free individual before God: to obtain commendation. In 9:25, freedom under control (*panta egkrateuetai*) is contrasted to freedom without restraint (*panta exestin*); the Corinthians are invited to consider one another and the gospel as being as important as they consider themselves.

1 Corinthians 10: Paul's Pattern of Refinement and the Corinthian Freedom Maxim in 10:23–11:1

Paul grants the Corinthians the right to freedom with respect to the eating of meat sacrificed to idols. Freedom is not, however, exercised properly when it either harms one's faith and relationship to God or divides the community of believers through the harm of another member. With regard to the *adiaphoron*, eating or not eating food (8:8b), Paul offers his own personal example (8:13; 1 Corinthians 9). With respect to receiving the commendation of God (8:8a) and not suffering disqualification (9:27), Paul reinforces his personal example (1 Corinthians 9) in 1 Cor 10:1–22 with a negative example from Israel's history (10:1–13) and a more direct warning against participation in pagan cultic ceremonies (10:14–22). Paul's final section in 1 Cor 10:23–11:1 concludes the discussion on eating meat offered to idols.[250]

In 1 Cor 10:1–13, Paul patterns the experience of the wilderness community as analogous to the believing community in Corinth.[251] Both have received grace in full measure: marked as God's community, sustained by spiritual food and drink, provided with divine guidance and protection. Then in a rather jolting fashion, Paul reminds[252] the Corinthians that "God was not pleased with most of them [the wilderness community], and they were struck down in the wilderness" (10:5).

Paul finds in the Exodus community a pattern of inappropriate responses to God from which the Corinthians are to learn.[253] In 10:6–10, exhortation against four inappropriate responses is given under the general rubric of "desiring evil": do not be idolaters; do not indulge in immorality (*porneuō*); do not put the

Lord to the test; and do not grumble.[254] The ordering of this list bears some attention. Idolatry, first in position, is central to Paul's discussion at this point (see 8:1–13; 10:14) and is appropriately placed.[255] Immorality has been dealt with in 1 Corinthians 5–7 in response to the Corinthian assertion of freedom (6:12; see 10:23) and is closely tied to idolatry in that discussion. Putting the Lord to the test plays a key role in subsequent sections (10:22; 11:27–30), where the proper response should be, instead, to examine or test oneself (10:12, 31; 11:13, 28, 31; 13:4–7; 14:20). Likewise, grumbling is antithetical to the proper unity and order that Paul seeks to encourage both at the Lord's supper and in the larger context of community worship (1 Corinthians 11–14).[256]

Paul concludes 1 Cor 10:1–13 with a warning and promise in 10:12–13 for believers advancing toward the parousia (10:11; see 7:29–31).[257] The warning is to self-test properly and not to overestimate (v. 12).[258] This is surely related to the Corinthian freedom position (6:12; 8:9) and its contribution to immorality in 1 Corinthians 5–6 and the demise of community members in 1 Corinthians 8.[259] In addition, the warning in v. 12 serves as an appropriate transition to 10:14–22 and the need there to properly discern idolatry. In v. 13, a promise is made to those who stay within the proper bounds: God will provide strength and a way of escape, an exodus, for every external temptation or trial.[260]

Beginning in 10:14–22, Paul again asks the Corinthians to choose an appropriate course of action (v. 15) from what he and they know together (vv. 16–17; see 8:1–6). Common knowledge indicates that the cup and the bread of the Lord's supper are key identifying markers for the cultic community of believers who make up "one body" (10:17).[261] Analogous to this believing community is the cultic unity of the people of Israel as established in ritual sacrifices. The entire section, however, is prefaced with a strong exhortation: "Flee from the worship of idols" (v. 14). Paul, therefore, expects the Corinthians' sensibility to agree with his directive.[262]

What is the inference to be drawn from Paul's two examples of the believing community and Israel? What is it that is of weight? Paul is not speaking of the *adiaphoron* of eating meat sacrificed to the idols (10:19; see 8:8) or of the common knowledge that "no idol in the world really exists" (10:19; see 8:4, 8). Paul is concerned, rather, for the ritual connections (*koinōnia*)[263] between the worshipers and the one God. Paul explicates this ritual partnership by negative contrast in order to drive a deep wedge between the believers' supper and other pagan cultic ceremonies (10:20–21). Idolatry does not connect the believer to the one God or to other gods (who do not exist), but to demons.[264] The followers of the one God do not share space and participate with demons (10:21–22; see Deut 32:21–22). Paul's concluding rhetorical questions, "Are we provoking the Lord to jealousy? Are we stronger than he?" are a firm reminder of the wilderness community having been overthrown (10:5–10).

In 1 Cor 10:23–11:1, Paul's maxim argumentation is continued once again. Most scholars recognize this final section as the conclusion to Paul's argument in 1 Corinthians 8–10.[265] Paul's second quotation of the Corinthian freedom maxim ("All things are permissible" [10:23; cf. 6:12, which adds "for me"]) indicates that the question of the freedom to eat meat offered to idols extends to the larger context of what constitutes the personal freedom of believers (6:12–11:1). The faithful believer does not exercise personal freedom when an action would harm him- or herself, harm another, or negate the relational bond of belonging to Christ[266] and God.[267] This perspective informs the understanding of 1 Cor 10:23–11:1.

Paul uses two maxims in 10:23–11:1. The first (10:23a) is composed of a restatement of the Corinthian maxim in 6:12a ("All things are permissible for me"; Paul drops the "for me") with Paul's antithetical qualification ("but not all things are beneficial").[268] The Corinthian maxim with its "for me" (*moi*) represents an individualistic unrestrained freedom characteristic of Cynics and more strict Stoics.[269] In both 1 Cor 6:12a and 10:23a Paul places the Corinthian maxim within the deliberative context concerning what is most profitable (*sympherein*),[270] and his qualification resembles the position of Stoics who argue for responsible freedom.[271] The second maxim is 10:31: "So, whether you eat or drink, or whatever you do, do everything [*panta*] to the glory of God."[272] This maxim is a fit conclusion to Paul's discussion of eating meat offered to idols; it suggests that the principles applied to that situation have far-reaching implications for all behavior, as already evident in Paul's personal example.[273]

The structure and flow of 1 Cor 10:23–31 have been much discussed.[274] Four issues are central. What is the meaning in vv. 25 and 27 of the twice-repeated phrase *mēden anakrinontes dia tēn syneidēsin* (without raising any question on the ground of conscience)? Is 10:23–11:1 directed primarily to the strong, or to the weak, or to both? Are vv. 28–29a a parenthesis that interrupts the argumentation? If so, for what purpose? Finally, what should be made of the two rhetorical questions in vv. 29b–30 that are neither self-evident nor clearly answered in the text that follows?[275]

As of yet, 1 Cor 10:23–11:1 has not been analyzed as a pattern of maxim argumentation. Such an analysis illuminates both the flow of the argument and its interpretation. The elaboration of a maxim using the rhetorical technique of refining (*expolitio*) has been preserved in the Hellenistic rhetorical handbook *Ad Herennium*.[276] It is this technique of refining that undergirds the argumentation of Paul's maxim in 10:23a ("All things are permissible, but not all things are beneficial"). For our purposes, an analysis of Paul's use of refining in 10:23–11:1 is undertaken first; then interpretive comments engaging the central issues stated above follow.

In *Ad Herennium* 4.42.54–43.56, the technique of "refining" is described:

> Refining consists in dwelling on the same topic and yet seeming to say something ever new. It is accomplished in two ways: by merely repeating the same idea, or descanting upon it. We shall *not repeat the same thing precisely* — for that, to be sure, would weary the hearer and not refine the idea — *but with changes.* Our changes will be of three kinds: in the

words, in the delivery, and in the treatment. *Our changes will be verbal when, having expressed the idea once, we repeat it once again or oftener in other, equivalent terms.* (4.42.54; my emphasis)

The first step in "refining" is that of repetition or restatement with changes. This type of restatement is found in 1 Cor 10:23–24:

> "All things are permissible," but not all things are beneficial. (v. 23a)
> "All things are permissible," but not all things build up. (v. 23b)

Paul begins with the maxim core, "All things are permissible," and qualifies it antithetically. He then repeats the same maxim core and refines the antithesis by changing the words slightly from *sympherei* to *oikodomei* (following the counsel of *Ad Herennium* 4.42.54, above).[277]

Each of the first two antitheses recalls prior argumentation — "but not all things are beneficial" (1 Cor 6:12–20); and "but not all things build up" (1 Cor 8:1–13). Paul has dropped the phrase "for me" (1 Cor 6:12) from the maxim, perhaps hoping that he has persuaded the Corinthians to view relationships in proper individual *and* community terms. In doing so, Paul balances individual rights with sensitivity to others. In v. 24, Paul refines (that is, changes the wording) in both the maxim core and the antithesis based on the refinements made in 10:23a and 10:23b:

> Let no one seek his or her own [advantage][278] [only],[279] but [what builds up][280] the other. (v. 24; my trans.)

One has rights, but they cannot be narrowly focused on oneself to the exclusion of building up or seeking what is helpful for other community members.

Paul restates the truth of the maxim core again in v. 25 — now in the form of a practical application. Then v. 26 follows as the ground from which the proper behavior called for in v. 25 is deduced:

> Eat whatever is sold in the meat market without raising any question on the ground of conscience. (v. 25)

> For "the earth and its fullness are the Lord's."[281] (v. 26)

Both of these statements restate the "all things are permissible" side of the antithetical maxim in 10:23a. Verse 26, in particular, recalls Paul's argumentation for freedom in 3:21–23 and 8:6.

Verse 27 restates v. 25, making the practical application more vivid and more identifiable to the reader/hearer. The eating occasion, offered as one example, is a dinner at the house of an unbeliever:

> If an unbeliever invites you to a meal and you are disposed to go, eat whatever is set before you without raising any question on the ground of conscience. (v. 27)

Verses 28–29a introduce a very common rhetorical device used with refining. This device, "dialogue," is described in *Ad Herennium* 4.43.55:

> The third kind of change, accomplished in the treatment [of refining], will take place if we transfer the thought into the form of Dialogue. Dialogue . . . consists in putting in the mouth of some person language in keeping with his character.

Verses 28–29a, then, continue the vivid application of v. 27 with the use of "dialogue":

> But if someone says to you, *"This has been offered in sacrifice,"* then do not eat it, out of consideration for the one who informed you, and for the sake of conscience — I mean the other's conscience, not your own. (vv. 28–29a)

In this way, vv. 28–29a further refine the antithetical supplement to "all things are permissible" (namely, "do not eat it" = "not all things are beneficial"; "not all things build up"; and "let no one seek his or her own advantage only"). In vv. 27–29a, then, we have the fifth restatement of the maxim core and the third restatement of the antithesis.

Paul now states two questions that fit perfectly the next rhetorical move of "refining":

> Again, the idea is changed in the treatment [of refining] by means of a transfer to the form of Arousal, when not only *we ourselves seem to speak under emotion,* but *we also stir the hearer.* (*Ad Herennium* 4.43.55; my emphasis)

Note the rise of emotion as Paul places himself directly into the hypothetical situation:

> For why should my liberty be subject to the judgment of someone else's conscience? (v. 29b)

> If I partake with thankfulness, should I be denounced because of that for which I give thanks? (v. 30)[282]

Again both these questions affirm the maxim core: "All things are permissible."

Paul concludes his refinement of the maxim in 10:23a in two ways: the restatement of the maxim in a new form (10:31) and the appeal again to his personal example (10:32–11:1).[283] His maxim in 10:31 refines the position of eating and drinking to include all behavior ("whatever you do"). The directive of the maxim core now includes care for oneself and others as a balanced position (*panta eis doksan theou poieite* ["Do all things to the glory of God"]; see 1 Cor 6:20: "Glorify God in your body"). Paul's personal example embodies the restatement of the maxim in 10:24: he seeks not just his own advantage (*to symphoron*) but that of others ("the many") for the sake of the gospel. In his behavior Paul acts as the crucified one, and, once more, he invites the Corinthians to imitate him (11:1; see 4:16).[284]

Granted, then, that Paul is constructing his maxim argumentation according to a pattern of refining (*expolitio*), how does this analysis help to illuminate some of the interpretive issues within 1 Cor 10:23–11:1? First, Paul's maxim refinement is in service of the recapitulation of his argument.[285] Paul signals this summing up process immediately in 10:23ab by the restatement of his earlier qualifications in 6:12a ("but not all things are beneficial") and 8:1b ("but love builds up"). Paul's strategy is to incorporate key points from 1 Corinthians 6, 8, and 9 into his maxim refinement in 1 Corinthians 10.[286]

Hence, given that Paul is recounting his previous argumentation, it is appropriate to interpret "*mēden anakrinontes dia tēn syneidēsin*" ("without raising any question on the ground of conscience" [10:25, 27]) in light of Paul's discussion in 1 Cor 8:7–13. The eating of meat offered to idols remains *adiaphoron* (a matter of indifference). One can eat meat from the meat market, including eating socially in an unbeliever's home, without any questioning or investigation that may be prompted by worry over "possible bad feelings which may arise in the weak."[287] It is only when the conscience of a (presumably)[288] weak fellow believer (10:28–29a) puts the matter to an issue that one need abstain — not as loss of freedom (10:29b–30), but as care or love for the fellow believer. As an extended illustration, vv. 25–30[289] refine Paul's maxim in 10:23ab by recapitulating his argument in 1 Cor 8:7–13. The one who wishes to eat should be mindful of the weak, but not mindful of the meat.

Second, Paul's maxim refinement proceeds by restatement with a continuity of movement that appears to preclude the introduction of entirely new information or categories.[290] Within the pattern of *expolitio*, v. 27 (eating in an unbeliever's home) is a refinement of v. 25 (eating anything sold in the meat market), and it is, therefore, to be seen as *one* of a possible number of more specific applications. It is not legitimate to limit Paul's discussion of eating situations to a rigid three: at sacrificial feasts, at meals at which one is offered what is bought in the market, and at an unbeliever's home.[291] In 1 Corinthians 8–10, Paul is concerned with (1) eating at the *trapeza daimoniōn* (the pagan cultic ceremony represented as "the table of demons," which is forbidden by Paul) and (2) other eating situations that must be measured by care for the fellow believer.[292] Verses 28–29a, then, follow not as a parenthetical interruption but as the appropriate and applicable consideration for *any* eating situation (that is, care for the weak conscience of a fellow believer), here attached to v. 27 in order to round out the application.[293]

Given the continuity of restatement in the section, it also seems inconceivable to think that Paul has suddenly turned to addressing the weak in v. 25[294] or that the passage as a whole is made up of a back-and-forth movement of addresses to the strong and weak.[295] What is clear is that Paul is continuing to refine the position of some strong Corinthians about personal freedom (10:23a; "All things are permissible, but ... ").[296] Although the force of Paul's counsel focuses primarily on the strong (and his direct address is always to the strong),[297] it is by no means conclusive that he does not have the weak in mind as well.[298] As

Paul recapitulates his argument, he has, most likely, the "education"[299] of both the strong and weak in view.[300] Paul mediates between *both* the weak and the strong in hopes of restoring harmony to the community.

Third, the analysis of Paul's maxim refinement of 10:23a indicates that the emphasis in 10:23–11:1 lies on the side of the individual's rights. Verses 23–24 indicate a balance between individual rights and community sensitivity. Verses 25–30, however, indicate a stronger emphasis on the "all things are permissible" thesis (the antithesis is only mentioned once in the short phrase "do not eat it"). Given the movement of Paul's thought in the direction of individual rights, his two rhetorical questions in vv. 29b–30 appropriately complete the refining pattern and are understandable as restatement (and insistence!) of the maxim core that Paul is emphasizing throughout. Paul does not resolve the Corinthian problem concerning "freedom" by denouncing it in favor of community sensitivity. Rather, freedom is maintaining one's individuation in the context of community sensitivity or love.[301] The aim of Paul's rhetoric is to use careful "refining" as a means of encouraging his Corinthian hearers to this balanced position.

The Rhetorical Situation of 1 Corinthians 8–10

In 1 Corinthians 8–10, Paul pursues an ongoing engagement with the maxim positions advanced by some Corinthians. Paul's maxim argumentation is characterized by partial agreement, qualification, and correction of the Corinthian positions coupled with his own advancement of more appropriate maxims. Paul's approach in 1 Corinthians 8–10, then, is a more concentrated but structurally similar engagement with Corinthian maxim positions already characteristic of the argumentation in 1 Corinthians 1–4 (1:12 replaced by 1:31 and 3:21–23) and 1 Corinthians 7 (7:1 qualified by 7:25–26).

In 1 Corinthians 8, Paul responds to the Corinthian debate concerning when it is appropriate to eat meat sacrificed to idols. He responds directly to the maxim positions advanced by the strong (8:1, 4). These positions advanced by some strong Corinthians reflect an unrestrained personal freedom that leaves moral behavior unclear and ambiguous. Paul qualifies, refines, and corrects the Corinthian position to consider the need, protection, and care of weaker community members.

Paul's immediate response to the Corinthian maxim in 8:1a is his own somewhat confrontational maxim in 8:1b. These two maxims, taken together, represent a fine line of (seeming) agreement and correction that characterizes Paul's argumentation throughout the passage as a whole. In 1 Cor 8:8, Paul advances another maxim indicating that eating food is an *adiaphoron;* what truly matters is receiving the commendation of God. Paul counsels the example of the Christ and his own example of leaving liberty unexercised in instances where a fellow believer might suffer harm as the means for attaining commendation before God.

In 1 Corinthians 9, Paul considers how his example stated in 1 Cor 8:13 is related to his status as a free individual. Paul maintains that he is very free; his use of maxims in 1 Corinthians 9 is in support of demonstrating this freedom and its proper use. Paul emphatically states that leaving his *exousia* unexercised does not affect his freedom. Paul is in control of his freedom, and he uses it in service of the gospel. Paul freely enslaves himself to all, but he is the slave of no human being. To some Corinthians who advocate a maxim of unrestrained freedom (*panta moi exestin* ["All things are permissible for me"]) Paul offers his own maxim (*panta egkrateuetai* ["self-control in all things"]) and his personal example of a firm focus on the gospel and a resolve to receive commendation and not disqualification.

In 1 Corinthians 10, Paul presents a warning from Israel's history and makes quite clear that he does not want to confuse eating meat sacrificed to idols with idolatry itself. Having established this, Paul draws together his argument advanced not only concerning eating meat sacrificed to idols but concerning the issue of personal freedom as well. Paul uses the *expolitio* (refining) of a maxim to structure his recapitulation. This allows Paul to bring together threads of his argument from 1 Corinthians 6, 8, and 9 in a manner that sets a balance between individual rights and community sensitivity.

Indeed, after pushing hard on the side of community sensitivity in 1 Corinthians 8–9, Paul returns to emphasize the proper use and retention of individual rights in 10:23–11:1. Believers have individual rights that remain their own. Rights are not surrendered or given up; rights are granted by God to be exercised responsibly. The freedom of the individual must not be enslaved by the scruples of the weak.[302] Paul concludes by advancing (1) a maxim suited to all (*panta eis doksan theou poieite* ["Do all things to the glory of God"]) and (2) his personal example, which reflects the Christ. Here, yet again, Paul makes an appeal for Corinthian unity by advocating the same spoken expression (*gnōmē*) and the mind of Christ (cf. 1:10 with 2:16 and see the discussion of 1 Corinthians 1–4 as advanced above).[303]

Conclusions

Maxims in Paul's World

This study sets Paul and his relationship with the Corinthians in the context of Greco-Roman education and rhetoric. The young person who came through the Greco-Roman educational system was very knowledgeable and competent with respect to maxims and their usage. Primary education instilled a knowledge and stock of maxims in the memory through the teaching of letters. Secondary and rhetorical training furthered knowledge of maxim material through reading, discussion, and practice exercises that honed the students' abilities in speech composition and argumentation patterns. At all levels maxims were equated with esteemed moral counsel and viewed as a source of *paideia*.

Taken as a whole, our understanding of Greco-Roman education, in general, and the rhetorical and exercise handbook traditions, in particular, indicates that the effectiveness of maxim usage is relative to a number of factors: the perceived *ēthos* of the maxim's initiator; proper identification with one's audience; the clarity and form of the formulated wisdom and its applicability to particular situations; and finally the confirming, refuting, and embellishment of maxims through elaboration patterns. A rhetorician's attention to these factors constitutes maxim argumentation.

The forms of the maxim varied. On the one hand, there were gnomic maxims and gnomic sentences applied to matters of practical conduct as described by Aristotle and followed by others. On the other hand, moral *sententiae*, those brilliant, short, and sometimes witty statements of practical conduct or general observation, developed from the milieu of declamatory exercises and popular declamation exhibitions. Quintilian (*Institutio oratoria* 8.5.3–34) established the use and recognition of all three forms in the first century c.e.

Beyond the sphere of Greco-Roman education proper, rhetoric and its use of maxims moved out among a variety of social spheres. Debates, symposia, public speeches, private conversations, private meetings, and local assembly meetings were all arenas for the use and display of rhetoric in general and maxims in particular and were venues for the status approval connected with such displays. Maxims were integral to the social and moral thought-world of Paul and the Corinthian community.

Maxims in Corinth

This study has identified the forms of the maxim at the time of Paul. The history (both historical and social) of maxims has witnessed the genesis and continuation of at least three identifiable forms: the gnomic maxim, the gnomic sentence, and the moral *sententia*. General indicators for maxims were combined with the particular features of each maxim form in order to determine representative maxims in Paul's correspondence. In our examination of portions of 1 Corinthians, Paul has shown himself to be aware of all three maxim forms and even skillful concerning their use. In the undisputed Pauline corpus, excepting only Philemon, Paul's letters to his communities contain maxims.[1] The maxim is a Pauline didactic technique and a means of rhetorical expression.

As evidenced in 1 Corinthians, Paul's dealings with the Corinthians show a particular concern for the use of maxims. Some Corinthians, who appear enthusiastically motivated and self-importantly wise, make claims to knowledge and freedom through the advancement of moral and theological positions in maxim form (6:12a [cf. 10:23a]; 7:1; 8:1, 4). Their freedom gives them a certain latitude with regard to sexual immorality, a ground for the dissolution of full marriage commitments, and the liberty to eat meat sacrificed to idols.

These maxims advanced by some Corinthians in support of their positions are loosely contextualized or concluding *sententiae*. The use of the *sententia* form is indicative of a popular and persuasive rhetorical style within the first century c.e. Paul's critique of a status-seeking rhetoric in 1 Corinthians 1–4 may also include[2] an implicit criticism of the way some Corinthians were using maxims to support moral positions and advance directives in the community.

As noted in our analysis of the texts, Paul responds directly to the Corinthian maxim positions. In addition, as one moves through the argumentation from 1 Cor 6:12 to 1 Cor 11:1, there is a type of give-and-take maxim argumentation or maxim exchange occurring between some of the Corinthians and Paul.

The focus of our investigation has been on maxims in Paul's argumentation. A fluid but certain pattern emerges. Paul responds to a Corinthian maxim (or to a number of maxims) with (1) a statement of ostensible agreement followed by serious qualification;[3] (2) elaboration of his qualification; (3) a new maxim that he deems appropriate as proper moral counsel for the given situation; and (4) elaboration of the new maxim.[4] Only in 1 Cor 6:12–20 does Paul deviate slightly by advancing a direct exhortation rather than a new maxim.[5]

A second pattern in Paul's maxim argumentation emerges when the movement of 1 Corinthians 1–10 is observed as a whole. Paul anticipates the give-and-take maxim argumentation between himself and the Corinthians *before* his first direct response in 1 Cor 6:12–20. As our investigation has shown, Paul indicates in his theme statement (1:10) that he wants the Corinthians to be united in the same *gnōmē*. Then he offers two maxims in 1:31 and 3:21–23. The second maxim (3:21–23: "All things are yours") indicates that Paul is willing to speak with the Corinthians in terms of freedom. Paul, however, qualifies his freedom maxim (*panta hymōn estin*) in a way that takes aim at the Corinthian freedom maxim in 1 Cor 6:12 (*panta moi exestin*). He indicates that freedom's source is in Christ and God (3:22–23) and not in attachment to human guides, seeking worldly status or power, or the attainment of knowledge. Paul then continues throughout the letter either (1) to qualify the Corinthian freedom maxim (6:12a and b; 8:1, 8; 10:23a and b)[6] or (2) to advance what he considers more helpful and appropriate *panta* maxims (9:25; 10:31; 11:12; 14:26, 40; 16:14; see 12:6b; 13:7).[7]

Given the evidence from this second pattern, it seems fair to conclude that throughout this letter Paul's mind is never far away from calling the (individualistic-minded) Corinthians to use freedom properly in particular ways. Freedom used properly monitors one's relationship to Christ and God, one's concern for self, and the well-being of others. The Corinthian freedom maxim ("All things are permissible to me") does not necessarily stand as *the* central problem in the Corinthian community.[8] Their freedom maxim is, however, an individualistic position that has influenced decision making about sexual relations and eating questions throughout the section of 1 Cor 6:12–11:1. This Corinthian emphasis on the individual over the community, with its improper view of grace, may well have combined with additional worldly valuations and behaviors that then led (in Paul's opinion) to divisions in the community.

Finally, this study has shown that Paul's maxim argumentation has a firm basis in the Greco-Roman rhetorical traditions as evidenced in the handbooks. A crucial aspect of maxim usage is the *ēthos* of the speaker. As we have shown, both some of the Corinthians and Paul claim to provide moral counsel through their use of maxims. Paul's rhetoric throughout 1 Corinthians 1–10 significantly elevates his trustworthy and other-regarding *ēthos* (1:1; 2:6–7, 15–16; 3:10; 4:2, 15–16, 20; 7:25, 40; 9:1–12, 24–27; 10:31–11:1) while downplaying the more haughty and self-serving *ēthos* of those Corinthians with whom he disagrees (1:11; 3:1–4, 18; 4:6–8, 18–19; 6:12a; 8:1b; see 11:17–22). Paul gives special attention to the clarity of his maxims. He uses the standard techniques and devices to elaborate his positions when stated in maxim form. In addition to the use of illustrations, examples, enthymemes, objections, and contrast, Paul seems particularly fond of using personal example and restatement with his maxim argumentation. His knowledge and use of maxim "refinement" are evident in a loose form in 1 Cor 8:1–7 and in a more developed and structured form in 10:23–11:1. Paul's maxim argumentation benefits the larger sections of the overall argument. These inherent patterns of maxim argumentation remain Paul's own, creative in composition and arrangement.

Paul's Maxim Argumentation in 1 Corinthians 1–10

In 1 Corinthians 1–3, Paul's maxim argumentation redirects the Corinthians from boasting in human leaders and human ways to finding their identity in the grace of God as demonstrated in the cross of Christ and Christ's ensuing lordship (1:31; 3:21–23). The common identity of believers in Christ begins with a dependence on God that excludes the boasting in oneself or others. Believers are free because God has freely bestowed resources for new community apart from and against human status-seeking ways. Paul hopes the Corinthians will be united through his maxims and the example of cooperation and concord portrayed in his relationship with Apollos.

Paul knows that some Corinthian "leaders" have led other members to engage in worldly ways within the community. In 1 Corinthians 4, Paul discloses his "covert allusion" and exposes his displeasure with the practices of these individuals (4:8, 18). At the same time, through his maxim argumentation, Paul undergirds his *ēthos*, thus protecting his leadership integrity and his rightful claim to be heard. Paul is a faithful steward (4:2); he is a father to the community (4:15); he, as a weak person, has demonstrated power in the community (4:20). Paul's maxim argumentation supports his personal example, and Paul calls "leaders" and the community at large to imitate him.

With 1 Cor 6:12–20 as an introduction, Paul responds to the Corinthian maxim in 7:1. Unable to agree with this maxim in many respects, Paul provides a key illustration in 1 Cor 7:17–24, suggesting that individuals can fully serve God in the station of life in which they find themselves. Paul's maxim argumentation is advanced through his own *gnōmē* in 7:25–26. His maxim forms a foundation for expanding ethical counsel concerning the unmarried and widows (7:27–40). Paul counsels that given the close proximity of the parousia and the distractions inherent in worldly obligations, "it is good for a person to remain as he or she is" (7:26b).

Yet as long as social obligations remain fulfilled, each individual does remain free in Christ ("not to put any restraint upon you" [7:35]; "she is free" [7:39]). Thus Paul's maxim is elaborated in such a way that each individual must determine what is advantageous (6:12a) and what does not compromise her or his freedom (6:12b). There can be a determination between what is good and what is better. Paul's argumentation counsels the Corinthians in making proper individual moral decisions: "[I]f someone stands firm in his resolve, being under no necessity but having his own desire under control, and has determined in his own mind . . ." (7:37).

In 1 Corinthians 8, Paul's maxim argumentation is in direct and immediate response to the Corinthian maxim: "All of us possess knowledge." Some Corinthians have argued a position for eating meat offered to idols (1) based on knowledge about the one God and the nonexistence of idols and (2) in conjunction with the unrestrained freedom represented by the maxim in 6:12a ("All things are permissible for me"). Paul counters with his own maxim, which qualifies knowledge with love (8:1b); his more appropriate maxim is based on what truly matters — love leading to the commendation of God (8:8) and his personal example of leaving liberty unexercised when it might cause harm to a fellow believer for whom Christ died (8:13).

In 8:13, Paul anticipates that his personal example might call into question his status as a free individual. Using the diatribe style, Paul asserts that his rights remain under his control and that he voluntarily uses or leaves unexercised these rights in accord with his gospel. He refuses to put any obstacle in the way of the acceptance and advancement of the gospel. This stance allows him to do what is in the best interests of all parties, of whom the weak are specifically noted. Paul refuses support from the Corinthians because this is to their benefit and (most likely) ensures Paul's freedom. Paul uses a series of self-evident gnomic maxims (9:7) to maintain his right to support from the Corinthians. He concludes the chapter with a maxim that bolsters the aim and focus evident in his own personal example: "Every athlete exercises self-control in all things" (9:25).

Paul makes it quite clear that he does not endorse idolatry. He does, however, employ maxim argumentation in 1 Cor 10:23–11:1 to recapitulate points made in chapters 6, 8, and 9 that support the freedom to eat meat offered to idols. Paul employs the rhetorical technique of *expolitio* to refine the Corinthian freedom maxim to a balance between individual rights and community sensitivity through love (building up of the other). The rhetorical weight in this section is on the retention of the individual's rights over and against a loss of freedom due to the scruples of the weak. Rather than making hard and fast rules for particular situations, Paul provides a moral pattern for reckoning one's behavior in all situations, encapsulated in his concluding maxim: "So whether you eat or drink, or whatever you do, do all things to the glory of God" (10:31).

Maxims and Paul's Moral Reasoning

Paul, like other early Christian writers, was involved in creating moral communities.[9] Wayne Meeks has described this process:

> By far the most common thing that we see happening in Paul's letters is his attempt to form moral communities: to instruct, admonish, cajole, remind, rebuke, reform, and argue the new converts to this strange new cult into behaving in ways "worthy," as he puts it, "of the God who called you." We may say, then, that the letters of Paul were preeminently instruments of resocialization and evidence of a larger process of resocialization. That process (Paul's word for it is *oikodomē*) was forming and reforming moral intuitions; its aim was to create moral confidence — the confidence that obtains when worldview and ethos match.[10]

Paul's argumentation in 1 Corinthians 1–10 demonstrates a particular type of moral reasoning. Knowing full well that he is in disagreement with some, Paul deliberates with the entire Corinthian community about certain moral behavior that has led to divisions. Paul addresses the community as free moral agents who have the ability to determine their actions according to the gospel in which they have been called. Remarkably, Paul refuses to lay down a set of hard and fast rules;[11] rather, he reminds the community of the gospel message and offers paradigms for proper decision making (as demonstrated in Paul's discussion of marriage relations in 1 Corinthians 7 and of eating meat sacrificed to idols in 1 Corinthians 8–10). Paul lays claim to be their exemplar, not their rule-giver (see 4:16; 11:1).

Maxims are appropriate to Paul's moral reasoning. They provide paradigms and general direction from which a variety of appropriate behaviors can be determined. When Paul declares that "knowledge puffs up, but love builds up" (1 Cor 8:1), one is forced to reckon both what is the proper use of knowledge and what forms love will take when put into action. When Paul states his *gnōmē* in 1 Cor 7:26, "I think that in view of the present distress, it is good for a person to remain as he or she is," he intends the Corinthians to work out marriage decisions based on a variety of marital statuses and each individual's giftedness and firmness of heart. The issue becomes one of what is good and what might be better.

Rather than setting down rules and regulations, maxims participate in and promote the process of moral reasoning. They suit Paul's purposes for developing moral confidence among the members of his communities because *each member* must measure the truth and guidance of the maxim to his or her measure of faith and giftedness.[12]

Within the context of Paul's moral reasoning, it has been possible to speak of the function of maxims in Paul's argumentation in 1 Corinthians. Paul uses maxims to support his *ēthos* as the founder of the community (1 Corinthians 4), as a free individual (1 Corinthians 9), and in general as a moralist who composes and applies maxims for edification. Paul, as apostle and father, makes use of maxims for correction in the community; members are prompted to rethink the implications of the gospel (1 Corinthians 1–3; 8–10). Closely akin to the function of correction is that of exhortation. Paul's maxims set guidelines for and stimulate the development of individual freedom within the context of community formation (1 Cor 8:8; 9:25; 10:23b, 31). Paul concludes his exhortation to the Corinthians with a maxim stack that paints a picture of what he thinks true believing community looks like: "Be watchful, stand firm in your faith, be courageous, be strong. Let all things you do be done in love" (1 Cor 16:13–14).

There is a certain complexity both to maxims and to their usage. A maxim may summarize a position of truth without a full explanation of the larger moral thought-world from which that maxim originates. This is why Paul is able ostensibly to agree with the Corinthian freedom maxim ("All things are permissible") while he also attempts to rearrange the contours of the Corinthians' thought-world according to the message of the cross. If the content and form of the Corinthian freedom maxim originated with Paul,[13] then some Corinthians have reduced the maxim's capacity to promote the gospel by allowing their thought-world to be guided in human fashion (*kata anthrōpon*).

Further, 1 Corinthians provides a glimpse of the limitations and problems inherent in Paul's use of maxims. As a Pauline didactic technique, maxims have both a great potential for producing insight and, at least in the case of the Corinthians, a potential downside as teachings that can be minimized and

misunderstood. Reducing theological truth and ethical directions to short con-
densed statements like maxims diminishes some of the complexity — opening
up such teachings to misunderstanding and misapplication. Therefore, quite
possibly Paul's own example of moral counsel through maxims has led some
Corinthians to seize upon this common Greco-Roman rhetorical convention as
a means of legitimating their own ethical behavior apart from the gospel and,
in doing so, to persuade others to follow them.

What is truly remarkable, and telling of the conviction that Paul has for how
moral reasoning should be carried out, is that Paul does not abandon the maxim
approach in Corinth, but he creates new maxims or constructs antithetical maxims from the Corinthians' misguided statements. Maxims find an essential place
in Paul's moral pattern of "reasoning from what is known."[14] In this sense, maxims and maxim argumentation provide ready access and keen insight into the
bedrock of Paul's thought-world. Paul feels confident, even in Corinth, that
when the cruciform gospel is in place, both his and the Corinthians' maxim argumentation will contribute significantly to growth, love, and harmony within
the community. Paul continues in his stance as both rhetorician and moralist,
using maxims, among other things, to contribute to the process of bringing
believers to maturity and instilling within them a sense of moral accountability.

Maxims, Freedom, and Rights

In encouraging the formation of moral community at Corinth, Paul advocates
the use of individual rights with a freedom constrained by love. Paul's maxim
argumentation is structured to promote a proper freedom among the believers
in Corinth in contradistinction to the unrestrained freedom position of some
Corinthians. The strong advance their position with maxims, and Paul responds
(in behalf of the weak) with refinement, correction, and refutation. Paul's personal example in 1 Corinthians 9 is crucial for understanding Paul's counsel to
both strong and weak believers in Corinth. Believers have individual rights that
remain their own. Rights are not surrendered or given up; rights are granted by
God to be exercised responsibly. To act responsibly means not harming one's
relationship to God, one's care of self, or one's love for a fellow believer.

In Paul's thought-world, believers move along a path to maturity. As faith
increases, the believer's options in freedom increase. The determination of acting responsibly with respect to one's rights, of becoming a capable moral agent,
should not be abdicated by the individual to any other person. Such a move
would constitute slavery and not freedom. Within the Corinthian community
abdication of rights occurs when some members boast in human leaders as
a means of obtaining worldly status and power, not realizing that true status
before God and access to all things are already theirs (1 Cor 3:21–23; 7:23).

When Paul lends his voice to the weak over the strong in 1 Corinthians 8–
10, he does it not at the expense of *any* believer's individual rights. To do so
would lead to the slavery of both weak and strong. Indeed, Paul's concern in

1 Cor 10:23–31 is to affirm the use of individual rights when an understanding of community sensitivity is firmly in place. In his exclamation, "For why should my liberty be subject to the judgment of someone else's conscience? If I partake with thankfulness, should I be denounced...?" (10:29–30), Paul speaks for the preservation of the strong's rights amid proper accommodation out of love (10:28). The freedom of the individual must not be enslaved by the scruples of the weak because the very identity of believers is as those who, having been freed in Christ's death, are now graced by God with all things to be used for God's glory (10:31). The choice must remain with the strong to exercise or not exercise their rights responsibly.

When Paul advocates the full expression of individual rights wherever the advantage of the community can be enhanced and not impeded, he sets the stage for his counsel in 1 Corinthians 11–14. In these four chapters the issues center on the exercise of individual rights and the opportunity for participation in the context of community worship (how meals are conducted prior to the celebration of the Lord's supper; prayer and prophecy among women; the expression of spiritual gifts in common worship). In such a context, the expression of individual rights is as important for the weak as it is for the strong. For without the retention and encouragement of rights, the weak would never have the space to develop their own voice, their own sense of self-esteem, and the power to say no to following after leaders who seek to lead the community on the basis of worldly ways rather than the cruciform gospel characterized by love and service.

If the strong can exercise their rights in the power of the gospel (that is, with love and care) and the weak can find courage to exercise their gifts according to their own proper measure of faith, then Paul has done his part to encourage concord within the Corinthian community. Essential to his rhetorical strategy is the use of maxims that confront and challenge both weak and strong in Corinth to rethink and explore options for doing moral reasoning and for responding in behavioral patterns that conform to the gospel. "All things are permissible, but not all things are helpful" (10:23a); "Exercise self-control in all things" (9:25a); "Let all that you do be done in love" (16:14); "So, whether you eat or drink, or whatever you do, do all to the glory of God" (10:31). Paul's maxims point the entire community in a direction from which they may work out a unity amid all things — all things gracefully provided by God for their freedom.

Paul's Moral Reasoning and Communities Today

Do ancient writers have any counsel to offer to communities today? Is there value in considering lessons and strategies from the past? To these questions we can answer in the affirmative. The counsel of earlier thinkers such as Paul deserves our attention for at least two reasons.

First, ancient thinkers placed a high premium on healthy, functioning community. The backbone of community was the moral stance and confidence of its individual members. Within such a perspective, these thinkers gave due weight to the relationship between the individual and the community; and they never trivialized the resulting tensions apparent in this relationship. Ancient thinkers gave hard, deliberate, and focused thought to how the individual and the community could thrive together.[15]

Second, the problems and tensions encountered by individuals and communities in the Hellenistic world were remarkably similar to those experienced by modern persons and groups.[16] As in our own day, the Hellenistic individual, trying to make it in community, labored amid rapid social-political and intellectual expansion.[17] Characterized as a whole, the Hellenistic world saw a fragmentation of local communities that, in turn, set individuals afloat into the murky waters of fate, devoid of the capacity to control their own lives and destinies.[18] The search for significance and the longing for freedom were real.

Like their counterparts in Hellenistic culture, many modern people are socialized away from true human community, which once found its basis in common, localized, and time-honored traditions. Based on this study of 1 Corinthians 1–10, the apostle Paul's words and example still speak, at least in part, to the fractured community whose foundation has pulled away from its mooring, whose direction is uncertain, and whose members have lost a common sense of connectedness.

In the process of restoring a community to wholeness, Paul *never* compromises any individual's freedom.[19] Paul acknowledges the complexities of human interaction, with all its contingencies and multiple options for response. In his concern for *equal and full* participation for all, Paul refuses to silence the rights of those who may and should rightfully claim them. Indeed, he offers his own voice to bolster the weak and underrepresented.

At the same time, Paul believes that the healthy functioning and proper maintenance of a community is due to *unity among the individual members.* And herein the potential for tension and division becomes apparent: for there are moments when the individuals' rights (freedom) and the community's[20] sensibilities appear to be or will be at odds. How does one establish both the freedom of the individual and a unity around the common good in such situations?

Paul's answer to the tension between individual rights and community sensibility is to stress commonly held elements of unity, without requiring full uniformity of thought and behavior among individuals. As a religious individual and thinker, Paul considers the foundational basis or charter of a community's unity to be located *outside the group itself.* For Paul this charter is the character of God as revealed to the covenant people in the Jewish scriptures and in the death, burial, and resurrection of Jesus.

Paul does not believe in a strict moralism as a means to unity but rather in a community charter built on the exemplary model of the character of God as demonstrated in Jesus. Hence a true community must exercise a pattern of moral reasoning that consistently applies its charter to the variegated affairs of life, among which there will be diversity (lack of uniformity) and (apparently) some disagreement.

Participating in the moral reasoning process is what has the potential for keeping members free and unified. Unity is found among members in their common faithfulness to the charter. Freedom is found among individuals in their responsibility and obligation to reason morally from the charter to specific situations. Paul believes that this is only possible in a religious context: members are ultimately accountable to God for both faithfulness and morally reasoned actions.[21] Hence, individuals have no right to judge one another with respect to faithfulness.[22] When the charter is respected, tolerance in diversity and disagreement should follow.

Finally, Paul, like others who knew and understood maxims well, insists that *individual community members* must carefully evaluate the "sound bites" of potential leaders based on the charter. Otherwise individual members may become enslaved to human beings (and not the charter), and such a stance threatens the unity of the group. Paul insists that all those who advance "sound bites" must show them to be well argued, applicable to the situation addressed, and faithful to the charter. Paul understands well both the power of maxims for providing moral direction and their potential for misuse and misappropriation.

In the end, how we appreciate or even appropriate Paul's counsel most likely varies according to the perceived congruence between Paul's own thought-world and our modern conceptions of reality. Paul, for his part, meant his counsel for a religious audience, and he truly thought that believers were directed by Jesus from heaven through God's Spirit. Hence, the legislating of unity or morals by or through the political powers of the time would be quite unacceptable to Paul. Community, for Paul, is an achievable human enterprise when aided by divine help. He finds the direction and focus for such an enterprise in the maxim: "Let all things be done in love."

Appendix A

Maxim Investigation in Pauline Studies

Interest in Paul's use of maxims has been scarce until recently.[1] Past New Testament scholarship has devoted much more time and attention to the wisdom sayings of Jesus. Rudolf Bultmann most closely analyzed Jesus' sayings within the formal genre of the apothegm or pronouncement story. As his background for the analysis and identification of Jesus' sayings, Bultmann used the comparative studies of oral tradition previously applied to Hebrew Bible studies.[2] Bultmann knew the Greco-Roman rhetorical traditions from his work on Paul,[3] but his usage of these rhetorical traditions remained somewhat divorced from his consideration of these sayings of Jesus.

By incorporating insights from the field of literary studies, modern biblical scholars have pursued an understanding of Jesus' sayings as proverbs, maxims, or aphorisms. The early studies of William Beardslee on "proverb"[4] and the extensive work, both in contribution and editing, by John Dominic Crossan on "aphorism"[5] have been the most influential. These enterprises, however, seem to have been fundamentally misguided. Rather than finding definitional criteria for aphorisms in the literature of the time, these works interpreted the aphorism in the much later literary tradition of Francis Bacon and others from the sixteenth century forward. Aphorism became predominantly defined as a literary device for "world-reversal" or "world-shattering" rather than tradition-affirming and world-ordering.[6] The insight that a maxim or proverb can be provocative and challenge the imagination is an important contribution from literary studies. This insight, however, can be demonstrated more appropriately from rhetorical and literary counsel of the first century. By and large, then, most of the early literary studies are tangential, at best, to our consideration of maxims in Paul.

Charles E. Carlston's article "Proverbs, Maxims, and the Historical Jesus" is a notable exception to the direction of Beardslee and Crossan. Through the examination of ancient sources and with some awareness of rhetorical handbook counsel, Carlston ascertained that "the whole point of proverbial wisdom is the communication of the generally accepted, the universal, the tried and true, not the striking or innovative."[7] A. P. Winton's recent work, with its critique and correction of both Beardslee and Crossan, is also a valuable addition to and turning point in the field. Winton's examination of the sayings of Jesus from the perspective of folklore studies and performance rhetoric emphasized careful consideration of contextual factors and the determination of the "force" of a saying. Winton, however, drew his rhetorical insights from a theory of socio-linguistics ("speech-acts") rather than from classical rhetoric.[8]

Scholars have now begun to analyze Jesus' sayings within the context of Greco-Roman rhetorical patterns. The wisdom saying forms an integral part of the rhetorical pattern of the elaboration called the *chreia* (memorable saying of a well-known authority) and may take the technical term "maxim."[9] In his programmatic *Rhetoric and the New Testament*, Burton Mack carefully sketches out the various parts of a speech and the argumentative pattern for proof at the time of the New Testament. In doing so, he elaborates on Pauline argumentative patterns that could well have included the maxim.[10]

As with the early investigation of Jesus' sayings, the consideration of Paul's use of maxims began as a discussion outside the context of rhetoric proper. John C. Hurd investigated what had been observed by numerous scholars before him — 1 Corinthians contained identifiable quotations. The question then was, To whom did the quotations belong? From whom did the quotations originate? Because these quotations appeared to be Paul's restatement of the Corinthians' understanding and communication (to him) back to them, Hurd (and others before him) referred to these quotations as "slogans."[11] Presumably, a "slogan" is appropriated by a group as a means of identification, resulting, of course, in some kind of differentiation from others.[12] Hurd, however, went on to posit that these quotations had originated with Paul as capsule teachings, but due to the Apostolic Council, Paul had reneged on them. The Corinthians challenged Paul with his own statements, and Paul's reply in 1 Corinthians is an attempt simultaneously to own and refine his teaching.[13] It is fair to say that a number of studies, including commentaries, have followed Hurd in considering Paul's use of or response to a slogan, maxim, or rule.[14]

Another source of "maxim" identification in Paul, again outside rhetoric proper, has come from important and useful studies that compare historical parallels. These sometimes note a common "Stoic maxim," "political slogan phrase," "gnomic exhortation," or some other means of designating a "traditional saying."[15] For example, Hans Conzelmann notes traditional sayings in 1 Corinthians on the basis of formal features and ancient parallels.[16] The identification of traditional material is helpful, but Conzelmann's terminology (maxim, principle, proverb, slogan, aphorism, "wisdom style") is undifferentiated and therefore somewhat imprecise. In addition, he shows little concern to illuminate Paul's choice and use of this material.

Therefore, whether studies follow Hurd or they focus on establishing historical parallels, descriptive terms such as proverb, maxim, aphorism, rule, epigram, and slogan make up a somewhat undifferentiated categorization. These terms nuance neither what identifying features warrant which particular description (for example, aphorism vs. epigram) nor, granting for the moment that these descriptions represent functioning literary devices, why Paul selects such a device to support his argumentation. By and large, the enterprise has been more descriptive ("an aphoristic expression," "surely a Corinthian slogan," "following a common Stoic maxim," "employing a proverb") than analytic.

With regard to ancient rhetoric, some significant study has been done on maxims in Paul's letters. Hans Dieter Betz has accomplished important work in 2 Corinthians and Galatians.[17] He points, on the one hand, to Paul the rhetorician who uses individual *sententiae* to support his argumentation according to the counsel of the rhetorical handbooks (2 Cor 8:10–12, 9:6; Gal 4:12–20). He refers, on the other hand, to Paul's skill in using *sententiae* as a gnomic poet (Gal 5:25–6:10). Significant in both contexts is Betz's consideration of possible Pauline composition behind the maxims used.[18] In conjunction with his investigation of Plutarch's *Moralia*, Betz notes the likely borrowing or imitations of the Delphic maxim by Paul in 1 Cor 3:18; 11:28a, 31; 2 Cor 13:5; Gal 6:3, 4. At various points in his works, Betz describes the functions of *gnōmai* or *sententiae:* it is the nature of maxims to present several possible understandings; they are built on common-sense; they are sometimes used as an opening thesis in a *probatio* (proof); and they are often used as a concluding point in argumentation.

Walter T. Wilson has illuminated Paul's maxim usage as a gnomic poet.[19] Wilson, however, concentrates solely on a Hellenistic-Jewish *gnomologia* paradigm that he convincingly demonstrates to be the background of Paul's construction in Rom 12:9–21. Wilson makes a significant contribution to the discussion by analyzing ancient terms such as apothegm (terse saying), epigram, *aphorismos* (aphorism), and *paroimia* (proverb) that maintain resemblances to *gnōmē*. He distinguishes between these related terms and the maxim by drawing attention to each particular term's literary and social function.[20] While making observations about the historical development of the *gnōmē* in general, Wilson notes a number of functions: "(1) maxims may be 'personalized';[21] (2) they may be supported by reasons or epilogues; (3) they may be supplemented with examples or illustrations; (4) they may be employed as evidence or proof; (5) they may operate at the beginning or conclusion of a distinct section of text."[22]

Abraham J. Malherbe's treatment of Paul as one of many eclectic moralists gives valuable background for maxim usage as a combination of moral philosophy and rhetoric.[23] In addition, Malherbe discusses Paul's use of "sententious statements" in relation to diatribe style. Stanley K. Stowers has placed the diatribe within a philosophical teaching context, noting the maxim's place as a response to the objection or false conclusion.[24] Overall, "maxims were compatible with the simple, terse sentences and sharp, pointed style characteristic of many diatribes."[25]

J. Paul Sampley approaches Paul as both moral philosopher and rhetorician in his discussion of maxim usage within moral reasoning.[26] Sampley notes that maxims often are created by rhetoricians to recapitulate their teachings; maxims tend to bring authority and *ēthos* (stature) to those who use them; while applications may vary, maxims are usually thought to be indisputable; the general nature of maxims allows the maxim to be used in different situations; maxims may emphasize a conclusion, or they may be a "touchstone" from which argumentation begins or toward which the reasoning leads.[27] Sampley's suggestions call for more extensive analysis.

Appendix B

Reading the Rhetorical Handbooks

Because the rhetorical handbooks provide a remarkable amount of the extant counsel on any particular aspect of Greco-Roman rhetoric, their use and value should not be underestimated.[1] Interpreters are, however, in danger of overestimation and restricted investigation if they do not regard these handbooks as part of a larger whole. At least three considerations should be borne in mind.

First, the rhetorical handbooks functioned within the larger context of the Greco-Roman educational system. They presupposed a complex and thorough primary and secondary training whether they were used within the curriculum at the rhetorical-training level or they were used for self-education with minimal instruction. Students came to rhetorical training extremely well equipped with a knowledge of memorized or recognizable maxims from the great poets or wise men. They were also familiar with argumentative patterns that elaborated, confirmed, or refuted maxims to be used or encountered.[2] By centering my investigation on maxim usage in the entire Greco-Roman educational system, I provide the background presupposed by the rhetorical handbooks and remind the reader that the goal was not simply excellence in court cases,[3] but the preparation for productive social life.[4]

Second, the rhetorical handbook tradition was only one of two modes of conveying the art of rhetoric. The handbooks began as a practical means of transmitting technical rhetoric for specific occasions.[5] Soon after, rhetoric began to be perceived as more useful in a variety of settings, and the imitative tradition became influential in establishing rhetoric as the goal of *paideia*.[6] The extant rhetorical handbooks come down to us as technical rhetoric with glimpses of imitation theory mixed in. By Greco-Roman times, rhetoric was taught through a combination of technical instruction, imitation, and the use of practical exercises.[7] It is appropriate, therefore, to follow the handbooks in supplementing technical counsel with an understanding of imitation procedures and practical exercises current in Greco-Roman society.

Third, rhetorical handbooks should be used as the handbooks themselves suggest. Quintilian's counsel is very applicable to this point:

> For the present I will only say that I do not want young men to think their education complete when they have mastered one of the small textbooks of which so many are in circulation, or to ascribe a talismanic value to the arbitrary decrees of theorists. The art of speaking can only be at-

tained by hard work and assiduity of study, by a variety of exercises and repeated trial, the highest prudence and unfailing quickness of judgement. But rules are helpful all the same so long as they indicate the direct road and do not restrict us absolutely to the ruts made by others.... The orator's task covers a large ground, is extremely varied and develops some new aspect almost every day, so that the last word on the subject will never have been said. I shall however try to set forth the traditional rules and to point out their best features, mentioning the changes, additions, and subtractions which seem desirable. (*Institutio oratoria* 2.13.15–17)

Rhetorical handbook theory gives techniques and sometimes examples that must be selected according to the exigencies of the case, the situation at hand, or some aspect of social life in question. Rhetoric has a flexible nature because it operates in the realm of social life, which is itself changing, shifting, and transforming.[8] Attention to the precise rhetorical situation may indicate how maxim usage is effective and what other rhetorical counsel might be expected to accompany or combine with it.[9]

In method, this study begins with cultural particulars before it moves to cross-cultural universals.[10] Therefore, priority is given to a Greco-Roman approach rather than a cross-cultural approach.[11] The reflection that the Greco-Roman cultural tradition had on its own use and development of rhetoric (and particularly the maxim's place within rhetoric) is studied in its various social situations. Then, Paul's appropriation of Greco-Roman rhetorical maxim usage is analyzed within the context of his interactions with the community at Corinth. Wherever possible the terms from Greco-Roman usage are maintained.[12] When I do supplement my understanding with cross-cultural information, it is clearly indicated.

An ethnographical description (that is, one that focuses on "cultural particulars") of a noncontemporary culture can be exceedingly difficult. There are gaps in information, questions left unanswered, and assumptions to be made. The study of the maxim in the social spheres of Greco-Roman education is remarkably informative given the great length of time that separates us from the sources. We have a wide variety of information concerning the maxim's usage in antiquity, including the prominent role the maxim had in all three training levels of Greco-Roman education. Yet for all the information available, we are still left with lacunae. Therefore, some probable inferences must be made, based on what information is available. Some initial presuppositions follow.

First, some scholars presume that our best extant handbooks for the first century c.e., although being Latin (*Ad Herennium*, Quintilian's *Institutio oratoria*), reflect to a large degree their contemporary Hellenistic counterparts.[13] As such, they still provide a background for Greek writers outside of Rome proper, such as the Hellenistic-Jewish apostle Paul. Second, the level and sophistication of rhetorical technique displayed by Paul's writings lead one to believe that Paul had formal rhetorical training of some type.[14] Finally, both the level of Paul's rhetoric used in 1 Corinthians and the direct references to rhetoric in 1 Corinthians 1–4 (1:17; 2:1, 4) lead some to believe that at least a portion of the Corinthian audience may have been rhetorically trained or competent.[15]

I have proposed (1) examining maxim usage in the rhetorical handbooks within their larger primary context of Greco-Roman education and social life and (2) keeping the historical lines of maxim inquiry within the Greek and Roman traditions (ethnographical investigation). It remains now briefly to describe what kind of conceptual model is most appropriate for organizing and explaining the descriptive results of an investigation of maxims in Greco-Roman culture.

A dynamic conceptual model is to be preferred over a synthetic model. Standard reference works like Heinrich Lausberg's *Handbuch der literarischen Rhetorik* and Josef Martin's *Antike Rhetorik: Technik und Methode*[16] are helpful for providing the broad range of rhetorical texts that apply to a specific aspect of rhetoric and for noting broad generalizations. They may, however, tempt the interpreter to form a synthetic rather than a dynamic conceptual model for interpretation and have, therefore, certain drawbacks, as pointed out by F. Delarue:

> We have to adopt a very clear methodological position. Some works like those of Lausberg, which currently are very much in favor, could give an improper idea of ancient rhetoric: they seem to consider the latter [rhetoric] as a unified and coherent whole, mentioning all authors on the same plane, from Aristotle to Isidore de Séville — without personal reelaboration.[17]

A synthetic model for studying the maxim has a universalizing tendency that draws information from a variety of sources in the Greco-Roman tradition into a generalized prototype.[18] A dynamic model, however, follows maxim definition, use, and development through time, noting changes, transformations, and variations in different historical periods. By using a dynamic model, I can place Paul at the appropriate place in these developments and note the options for maxim usage called forth by the social and historical circumstances of Paul's time. The present study makes clear that by this period the maxim had a variety of forms and usages as it continued in a period of transformation.[19]

In sum, the rhetorical handbooks provide a wide variety of understanding, but not a complete knowledge for the comprehension of maxims. Other aspects of Greco-Roman education and social life need to be considered carefully in order to understand the subject more fully. The subject is best served if our understanding of maxims is (1) formed from an ethnographical approach to the Greco-Roman tradition and, then, (2) constructed into a dynamic model from which we can identify Paul's options for usage in the first century. These observations inform the investigation of Greco-Roman maxims in chapter 1 above.

Notes

Introduction

1. A good introduction that examines a wide range of texts and includes additional bibliography is Burton L. Mack, *Rhetoric and the New Testament* (Minneapolis: Fortress, 1990). Also see George A. Kennedy, *New Testament Interpretation through Rhetorical Criticism* (Chapel Hill: University of North Carolina Press, 1984). For the influence of language and rhetoric in the oral period, see Werner H. Kelber, *The Oral and the Written Gospel: The Hermeneutics of Speaking and Writing in the Synoptic Tradition, Mark, Paul, and Q* (Philadelphia: Fortress, 1983).

2. Recent studies are numerous. In addition to those cited in this study, see Duane F. Watson, "The New Testament and Greco-Roman Rhetoric: A Bibliography," *Journal of the Evangelical Theological Society* 31 (1988): 465–72; and idem, "The New Testament and Greco-Roman Rhetoric: A Bibliographic Update," *Journal of the Evangelical Theological Society* 33 (1990): 513–24.

3. Early influential and ground-breaking works were provided by Hans Dieter Betz, *Galatians: A Commentary on Paul's Letter to the Churches in Galatia*, Hermeneia (Philadelphia: Fortress, 1979); and Wilhelm Wuellner, "Greek Rhetoric and Pauline Argumentation," in *Early Christian Literature and the Classical Intellectual Tradition*, ed. William Schoedel and Robert L. Wilken, Théologie Historique 53 (Paris: Beauchesne, 1979), 177–88. Again, numerous recent studies are listed in the bibliography to the present work and in the bibliographies of Watson (see n. 2 above). For a provocative and at times problematic work on audience response to Paul's rhetoric, see Antoinette Clark Wire, *The Corinthian Women Prophets: A Reconstruction through Paul's Rhetoric* (Minneapolis: Fortress, 1990).

4. Of the few, some notable and important studies would be George Lyons, *Pauline Autobiography: Toward a New Understanding*, SBL Dissertation Series 73 (Atlanta: Scholars Press, 1985); Benjamin Fiore, *The Function of Personal Example in the Socratic and Pastoral Epistles*, Analecta Biblica 105 (Rome: Biblical Institute, 1986); Karl A. Plank, *Paul and the Irony of Affliction* (Atlanta: Scholars Press, 1987); Walter T. Wilson, *Love without Pretense: Romans 12.9–21 and Hellenistic-Jewish Wisdom Literature*, Wissenschaftliche Untersuchungen zum Neuen Testament 46 (Tübingen: Mohr, 1991); Stanley N. Olson, "Pauline Expressions of Confidence in His Addressees," *Catholic Biblical Quarterly* 47 (1985): 282–95; A. H. Snyman, "Style and the Rhetorical Situation in Romans 8.31–39," *New Testament Studies* 34 (1988): 218–31; Duane F. Watson, "1 Corinthians 10:23–11:1 in Light of Greco-Roman Rhetoric: The Role of Rhetorical Questions," *Journal of Biblical Literature* 108 (1989): 301–18. Most intriguing for its examination of a rhetorical device as support for Paul's argumentation in promotion of his gospel is Wilhelm Wuellner, "Paul as Pastor: The Function of Rhetorical Questions in First Corinthians," in *L'Apôtre Paul: Personnalité, style et conception du ministère,*

ed. A. Vanhoye, Bibliotheca ephemeridum theologicarum lovaniensium 73 (Louvain: Louvain University Press, 1986), 49–77.

5. See *The Oxford Classical Dictionary,* 2d ed. (Oxford: Clarendon, 1970), s.v. "Gnome" and "Sententia."

6. *Webster's New World Dictionary* gives the definition of "maxim" as "a concisely expressed principle or rule of conduct; a statement of general truth." In this sense, usage of the word "maxim" indicates moral counsel (*Webster's New World Dictionary of the American Language,* 2d ed. [1970], s.v. "maxim"). Cf. *Oxford English Dictionary,* 2d ed. (1989), s.v. "maxim": "A rule or principle of conduct; also, a precept of morality or prudence expressed in sententious form."

7. Betz, *Galatians,* 291–311; idem, "De laude ipsius (Moralia 539A–547F)," in *Plutarch's Ethical Writings and Early Christian Literature,* ed. idem, Studia ad corpus hellenisticum novi testamenti 4 (Leiden: Brill, 1978), 379–93; idem, *2 Corinthians 8 and 9: A Commentary on Two Administrative Letters of the Apostle Paul,* Hermeneia (Philadelphia: Fortress, 1985), 64–67, 77, 102–9, 113.

8. Betz, *Galatians,* 291 n. 5. Betz, of course, has a specific investigation in mind — the examination of maxims in the context of ancient rhetoric — an investigation left behind after the much earlier work of Johannes Weiss, Rudolf Bultmann, and Norbert Schneider. Given that caveat, it is useful to note maxim investigation in a slightly broader context. John C. Hurd identified quotations of the Corinthians as slogans or maxims that originated with Paul. His list included 1 Cor 6:12, 13; 7:1; 8:1, 4, 5, 6, 8; 10:23; and 11:2 (John C. Hurd, *The Origin of 1 Corinthians* [New York: Seabury, 1965], 67–68). Hans Conzelmann notes and comments on proverbs, maxims, and principles without attempting a comprehensive investigation of their choice, function, or rhetorical background. His list includes 1:25; 3:22b; 4:20; 5:6; 6:7, 12, 13; 7:1; 8:1; 9:10; 10:12, 23, 24 (cf. Rom 14:19; 15:2; Phil 2:4); 15:21 (Hans Conzelmann, *1 Corinthians: A Commentary on the First Epistle to the Corinthians,* trans. James W. Leitch, Hermeneia [Philadelphia: Fortress, 1975]). Two more recent works have considered maxims in Paul's letters with examples: Abraham J. Malherbe, *Moral Exhortation: A Greco-Roman Sourcebook,* Library of Early Christianity (Philadelphia: Westminster, 1986), writes both of the use and background of maxims in general (19, 21, 105, 109, 111, 115–20, 125, 126–28, 138, 144) and of "sententious statements" (Rom 14:7; 1 Cor 5:6) and "quotations from the poets" (1 Cor 15:33) used in Paul's diatribe style (130). J. Paul Sampley, *Walking between the Times: Paul's Moral Reasoning* (Minneapolis: Fortress, 1991), 78, 94–98, lists and comments on Rom 12:9–21; 1 Cor 6:12; 7:19; 8:4; 10:23; 14:33; 2 Cor 10:18; 13:11–13; Gal 3:19–20, 28; 5:6, 6:15; 1 Thess 5:12–22. And 1 Cor 14:40 and Phil 4:4–9 are added by J. Paul Sampley, "From Text to Thought World: The Route to Paul's Ways," in *Pauline Theology,* ed. Jouette Bassler (Minneapolis: Fortress, 1991), 1:14. Other Pauline studies occasionally discuss a maxim, proverb, rule, axiom, and so on. These are noted further in Appendix A.

9. *Gnomologia* are collections or anthologies of gnomic sayings written in succession. Walter T. Wilson argues convincingly that a Hellenistic-Jewish pattern of *gnomologia* usage was present in Paul's time, and Paul used it (Wilson, *Love without Pretense,* 91–148, esp. 68–81).

10. I use the terms "isolated embedded maxims" to denote those maxims that stand independently (not part of a collection or *gnomologium*) in a written text as an important part of the argumentation. Wilson's list includes Rom 12:3, 9–21; 13:7; 14:7, 22b; 1 Cor

1:25; 3:18b, 19a; 8:1b, 2; 13:13; 16:13–14; 2 Cor 6:14b; 8:12; 9:6; 10:14b, 18; 13:5a; Gal 4:18a; 5:9; 5:25–6:10; Phil 2:4, 14; 3:16; 4:5a; 1 Thess 5:13b–22. For further consideration he lists Rom 1:22; 2:11; 3:4a, 8b; 5:3–4; 13:8; 1 Cor 1:29; 14:38; 15:32–33; 2 Cor 8:21; 9:7; 12:9b; Gal 4:12; Phil 2:1–3; 4:8 (*Love without Pretense,* 4 n. 6).

11. I limit my discussion to what current scholarship has designated the seven "indisputable" writings of Paul: Romans, 1 and 2 Corinthians, Galatians, Philippians, 1 Thessalonians, and Philemon.

12. This is carefully presented in Howard Clark Kee, *Knowing the Truth: A Sociological Approach to New Testament Interpretation* (Minneapolis: Fortress, 1989), 7–64.

13. My analysis of maxims in Paul has run concurrent with Wilson's study. I identify "maxim stacks" or *gnomologia* constructions in Paul's letters as Rom 12:9–18; 1 Cor 16:13–14; 2 Cor 13:11b; Gal 6:1b–6; 1 Thess 5:16–22. Wilson listing (see note 10) is very similar with the exception of 2 Cor 13:11b.

14. Roger D. Abrahams, "The Complex Relation of Simple Forms," *Genre* 2 (1969): 104–6; idem, "Introductory Remarks to a Rhetorical Theory of Folklore," *Journal of American Folklore* 81 (1968): 143–58. See also Paul D. Goodwin and Joseph W. Wenzel, "Proverbs and Practical Reasoning: A Study in Socio-Logic," in *The Wisdom of Many: Essays on the Proverb,* ed. Wolfgang Mieder and Alan Dundes (New York: Garland, 1981), 140–160; Peter Seitel, "Proverbs: A Social Use of Metaphor," in *The Wisdom of Many,* ed. Mieder and Dundes, 122–39; E. Ojo Arewa and Alan Dundes, "Proverbs and the Ethnography of Speaking Folklore," *American Anthropologist* 66 (1964): 71. And the biblical studies noted in Appendix A, n. 8.

Chapter 1: Maxims in Paul's World

1. A perspective solidified in the Hellenistic expansion and continued with appropriate additions and adaptations in combined Greco-Roman culture. See the important discussion in H. I. Marrou, *Education in Antiquity,* trans. George Lamb, 3d ed. (Madison: University of Wisconsin Press, 1982), 95–101. On *paideia* in the Greco-Roman educational system, see Stanley F. Bonner, *Education in Rome: From the Elder Cato to the Younger Pliny* (Los Angeles: University of California Press, 1977), 212–49.

2. In many cases, but by no means all, the path of study was a progression from rhetoric into philosophy. Roman influence later made the study of law the crowning achievement in imperial times. See Marrou, *Education in Antiquity,* 284–91, and Bonner, *Education in Rome,* 288–327.

3. This perspective was formulated by Isocrates: "As for his actual teaching, Isocrates always remained vitally concerned with practical effectiveness.... [T]he best pupils in our literature classes are chosen and brought up to be teachers themselves — or expert debaters — *agōnistai:* or else — and these were his particular province — men of culture, people with a good sense of judgment, able to take part quite naturally in any sort of discussion: as will be seen, he was chiefly concerned with the average cultivated Athenian" (Marrou, *Education in Antiquity,* 81). See Donald Lemen Clark, *Rhetoric in Greco-Roman Education* (New York: Columbia University Press, 1957), 64–65; and Werner Jaeger, "The Rhetoric of Isocrates and Its Cultural Ideal," in *The Province of Rhetoric,* ed. Joseph Schwartz and John A. Rycenga (New York: Ronald, 1965), 84–111. Isocrates' form of rhetoric won out as rhetorical training developed further in the schools. His influence is traceable through Cicero to Quintilian and beyond. See Brian R. Vickers, *In Defense of Rhetoric* (Oxford: Clarendon, 1988), 8–12.

4. While Greek or Roman rule may have decreased the opportunity for deliberative and judicial oratory, it certainly did not eliminate it. Local autonomy and governance were dependent upon community leaders' ability to keep at least the appearance of peace. See deliberation, debate, and the need for order in Ephesus as recorded in Acts 19.

5. It becomes necessary, therefore, to consider what presuppositions and what interpretive framework one brings to a reading of the rhetorical handbooks through time. My reading utilizes a dynamic social and historical approach that is set forth in Appendix B.

6. It is beyond the scope of this study to rehearse in full detail the pattern of Greco-Roman education. A brief synopsis is given here, and the reader should consider the works of Marrou, *Education in Antiquity,* and Bonner, *Education in Rome,* for full details.

Greco-Roman education was divided into three levels: primary education (ages seven to eleven or twelve), secondary education (ages twelve to fifteen), and advanced education in rhetoric (or, in fewer cases, philosophy; ages sixteen to twenty plus). At the primary level, students were trained in the letters (writing, reading, and reciting) by the grammatist (*grammatistēs*). At the secondary level, the grammarian (*grammatikos*) taught knowledge of the classics and poets; reading, recitation, and explanation of texts; grammar; and composition exercises (*progymnasmata*). In advanced training under the guidance of the rhetor (*rhētōr, sophistēs*), students were taught techniques of persuasion embodied in the full composition and delivery of speeches. Girls were trained in the earlier levels but, with exceptions, were tracked into household management (*oikia*) instead of advanced study.

Early education was carried out in several different contexts. A child might be trained at home by a relative or family member, by a privately hired grammatist, or in some cases by an educated slave. Finally, through sponsorship or pooled resources, a grammatist could be hired for schooling in a group setting. See Bonner, *Education in Rome,* 165. On the spread of Greek and Roman schools and the issues of public and private financing, see Marrou, *Education in Antiquity,* 102–15, 142–49, 242–54. Cf. Bonner, *Education in Rome,* 146–62.

7. The method of teaching letters consisted of imitation, repetition, and advancement by graduated difficulty — typically, the writing and sounding of letters, then syllables, words, short sentences, and finally longer passages. For a full consideration of the process of teaching letters, see the literature cited in note 8 below. For the role of imitation as a key factor in Greco-Roman education from its beginning and throughout every succeeding level, see Clark, *Greco-Roman Education,* 144–76. Cf. James J. Murphy, "Roman Writing Instruction as Described by Quintilian," in *A Short History of Writing Instruction: From Ancient Greece to Twentieth-Century America,* ed. idem (Davis, Calif.: Hermagoras, 1990), 44–53.

8. For the best description and a very detailed analysis of these various exercises, see Bonner, *Education in Rome,* 165–80. Our most complete source for primary education is Quintilian's *Institutio oratoria,* book 1. Bonner considers Quintilian, and I think rightly so, an appropriate representation of Greco-Roman education as a whole. As Marrou states, "There was not a Hellenistic civilization on one side and a Latin civilization on the other, but ... a *hellenistich-römische Kultur.* It is only legitimate to speak of Latin culture in a secondary sense, as a particular variety of this single civilization. In education, for example, the distinctive contributions made by Roman sensibility, the Roman character and the Roman tradition, only appear as slight alterations of detail, or as trends that sometimes tended to favour and sometimes tended to inhibit certain aspects of the

Greek attitude towards education" (Marrou, *Education in Antiquity*, 242). Bonner's extensive reliance on Quintilian is balanced with a wide use of relevant archeological and epigraphical materials.

9. Bonner, *Education in Rome*, 174; "These maxims had also to be learned by heart, and it is not surprising that pupils acquired a very considerable stock of them, and that authors in later life sometimes recalled a *sententia* which took them back to the lessons of the primary schools" (with reference to Seneca the Younger and Phaedrus).

10. See n. 1 above.

11. Bonner, *Education in Rome*, 172–75; Marrou, *Education in Antiquity*, 95–101; 217–26. Maxims are from Menander as quoted in Bonner (174).

12. Bonner, *Education in Rome*, 17.

13. Plutarch, "How the Young Man Should Study Poetry," *Moralia* 36E.

14. The relationship between child and pedagogue was strong in some cases, perhaps even being solidified from the child's birth. In the Roman household, the Greek pedagogue was particularly popular because of his ability to provide bilingual education. See Bonner, *Education in Rome*, 41.

15. Ibid.

16. Ibid., 42. In agreement is Marrou's lengthier assessment: "The schoolmaster was only responsible for one small section of children's education — the mental side. He did not really educate his pupils. Education means, essentially, moral training, character-training, a whole way of life. The 'master' was only expected to teach them to read — which is a much less important matter.... If anyone other than the parents was ever given the job, it was the pedagogue, who was only a slave, no doubt, but who was at least one of the family. Through his daily contact with the child, and his example — whenever possible — and at any rate *by his precepts* and the careful watch he kept over him, he made a far greater contribution to his education, especially his moral education, than the purely technical lessons provided by the schoolmaster" (Marrou, *Education in Antiquity*, 147; emphasis added). The influential and thorough New Testament study by Norman H. Young ("Paidagogos: The Social Setting of a Pauline Metaphor," *Novum Testamentum* 29 [1984]: 150–76) provides a wealth of texts describing the role of the pedagogue, including a large number that depict the pedagogue as an important moral guide (159–65, 167–68).

17. See Young ("Paidagogos," 164–65) for the pedagogue's accompaniment of his charge in social settings besides to and from school. "The pedagogue went everywhere with the boy in his care" (164).

18. See n. 6 above.

19. The grammarian directed the student through an elaborate process of establishing a critical text, reading it correctly, explaining it (literally), and finally drawing out its implications. This latter step often employed an allegorical interpretation to input a moral aspect (Marrou, *Education in Antiquity*, 165–70). Bonner disputes whether establishing a critical text was true for the average school (Bonner, *Education in Rome*, 249).

20. Bonner, *Education in Rome*, 227–49; see especially his illustration through the simile (235–36). "Just as the primary teacher had given his boys single-line maxims from the poets to write out and memorize, so the *grammaticus* drew attention to them as they arose in context" (248). I am not attempting to attribute the rhetor's jurisdiction to the grammarian. The stance of the grammarian with respect to these devices (tropes

and figures) is recognition and clarification on the literary level. A large part of the task was simply pointing out devices and providing background material for the text so that appreciation of technique could be illuminated. The stance of the rhetor is to show how literary devices can function rhetorically, that is, how they can be used as models and applied persuasively to speech situations. While rhetoricians continued to find the poets useful, rhetorical training preferred the examination of the works of historians like Herodotus or Thucydides and the written speeches of figures like Demosthenes and Cicero.

21. This broad-based introduction of traditional works, along with a critical apprehension of their function, importance, and counsel, provided the student with a stock of material from which rhetorical persuasion would be constructed and reinforced. See Marrou, *Education in Antiquity,* 165–70; and Bonner, *Education in Rome,* 227–49. The first two stages of rhetoric, *inventio* (selection) and *dispositio* (arrangement), were dependent on this secondary training (Bonner, *Education in Rome,* 244–46).

22. Bonner, *Education in Rome,* 247–48. As recognized and acknowledged by Quintilian in *Institutio oratoria* 10.1.50, 52, 60, 68.

23. "[R]eady-made collections, drawn, for instance, from such writers as Hesiod, Theognis, Epicharmus, and, most particularly, Euripides and Menander, were in circulation in Hellenistic times." In addition to verse, "sayings of famous men" had been collected into prose anthologies (Bonner, *Education in Rome,* 173–76 with discussion; cf. Marrou, *Education in Antiquity,* 153, 156). For a more detailed discussion of *gnomologia,* see John S. Kloppenborg, *The Formation of Q: Trajectories in Ancient Wisdom Collections* (Philadelphia: Fortress, 1987), 289–306.

24. Clearly by the turn of the eras early rhetorical exercises were available at the secondary level. Whether the grammarian resented the extra responsibility of teaching early rhetoric or whether the rhetor despised the teaching of rhetoric at the secondary level need not detain us here (see Bonner, *Education in Rome,* 252–53). These *progymnasmata* (preliminary exercises) were probably relegated to the secondary level as rhetorical instruction began to concentrate on training in declamation (Quintilian *Institutio oratoria* 2.1.1–9). Marrou (*Education in Antiquity,* 172) attributes the shift to the increase in technical aspects of rhetoric that forced preliminary work to the secondary stage. Whatever the reasons, these preliminary exercises formed a bridge between the acquisition of cultural knowledge and its selection, elaboration, and use in argumentation.

25. These *progymnasmata,* then, marked the initial training in invention. The standard order of exercises, recently supported by a closer investigation of Quintilian, runs: fable, narrative, *chreia,* maxim, confirmation/refutation, commonplaces, encomium/censure, comparison, speech in character, thesis, and the proposal of a law. See Ian H. Henderson, "Quintilian and the *Progymnasmata,*" *Antike und Abendland* 37 (1991): 82–99; and cf. Marrou, *Education in Antiquity,* 173. From the first century B.C.E. forward, the *gnōmē* or maxim occupied an early position among the *progymnasmata;* this probably reflects its ease of learning, familiarity, and usefulness in support of the later exercises. The *progymnasmata,* as a whole, provided a step-by-step progression toward composition and rhetorical speech forms.

26. I am using the description "rhetorical exercise handbook" to distinguish those manuals designed to guide the grammarian or rhetor in instructing students in the preliminary exercises or *progymnasmata.* I use the description "rhetorical handbook" to refer to treatises that present a more or less ordered discourse on the five parts of rhetorical

speech. See notes 27 and 44 below for lists of the extant rhetorical exercise handbooks and the rhetorical handbooks, respectively.

27. Knowledge of the *progymnasmata* is preserved in the extant rhetorical exercise handbooks by Aelius Theon of Alexandria (ca. 50–100 C.E.), Hermogenes of Tarsus (ca. 180 C.E.), Aphthonius of Antioch (ca. 391 C.E.), and Nicolaus of Myra (ca. 450 C.E.). Aphthonius follows Hermogenes closely in design, but with much fuller examples. Largely, though, Aphthonius offers little, if any, advancement; more negatively, in Aphthonius we have the imprecision of moving four centuries beyond our period of study. Much the same can be said for Nicolaus of Myra. For introductory matters and dating see the essays in Ronald F. Hock and Edward N. O'Neil, *The Chreia in Ancient Rhetoric*, vol. 1, *The Progymnasmata* (Atlanta: Scholars Press, 1986). Full English translations are available for the three earliest handbooks. See James R. Butts, "The 'Progymnasmata' of Theon: A New Text with Translation and Commentary" (Ph.D. diss., Claremont Graduate School, 1987); Charles S. Baldwin, *Medieval Rhetoric and Poetic* (New York: Macmillan, 1928), 23–38 (Hermogenes); and Ray Nadeau, "The Progymnasmata of Aphthonius in Translation," *Speech Monographs* 19 (1952): 264–85.

In addition, some indication of the preliminary exercises is recorded by Quintilian (*Institutio oratoria* 1.9.1–6). Quintilian explains briefly some of these exercises as *progymnasmata* in 1.9 before explaining them (and others) more fully as rhetorical devices and techniques under the guidance of the rhetor. See James J. Murphy, *Quintilian on the Teaching of Speaking and Writing: Translations from Books One, Two, and Ten of the "Institutio oratoria"* (Carbondale: Southern Illinois University Press, 1987), xxii–xxiii, xxxiii.

28. "[E]very concise maxim, if it is attributed to a character, produces a chreia.... The maxim, however, differs from the chreia in these four ways: (1) The chreia is always attributed to a character, whereas the maxim never is. (2) The chreia sometimes makes a general statement, sometimes a specific one, whereas the maxim, makes only a general one. Furthermore, (3) the chreia is witty, sometimes containing times [*sic;* "matters"?] having nothing useful for living, whereas the maxim is always concerned with matters useful in life. And (4) the chreia is an action or saying, whereas the maxim is only a saying" (in Butts, "'Progymnasmata' of Theon," 187–89).

29. "A proverb [*gnōmē*] is a summary saying, in a statement of general application, dissuading from something or persuading toward something, or showing what is the nature of each: dissuading, as in the line 'a counsellor should not sleep all night'; persuading, as in the lines 'he who flees poverty, Cynus, must cast himself upon the monster-haunted deep and down steep crags.' Or it does neither of these, but makes a declaration concerning the nature of the thing: 'Faring well undeservedly is for the unintelligent the beginning of thinking'" (Baldwin, *Medieval Rhetoric*, 27). Baldwin's translation is inaccurate. The Greek word for proverb is *paroimia*. *Gnōmē* should be read as "maxim."

30. Such evaluation can be helpful in training a hearer or reader to be attentive to the linguistic or structural features that signal proverbial or maxim usage. The broad understanding of universal features for traditional sayings has been a concern for modern scholars, especially within the field of folklore.

31. *Progymnasmata* taught at the secondary level were probably more limited, with expansion, usage, and placement given further instruction later by the rhetor (see the evaluation of Marrou, *Education in Antiquity*, 172–73). Also note how the earlier rhetor-

ical handbook, *Ad Herennium*, carefully instructs in the elaboration of the maxim (see *Ad Herennium* 4.42.54–44.58 and our discussion on pp. 19–20). This two-stage transmission is found in Quintilian *Institutio oratoria* 1.9 and 2.4, as pointed out in Henderson, "Quintilian," 88–91. Quintilian concedes the teaching of the most basic *progymnasmata* to the grammarian (1.9) but reserves the more advanced exercises with fuller instruction for the rhetor (2.4). The maxim (*sententia*) is introduced as a *progymnasma* in 1.9 but is elaborated by the rhetor in 8.5. At any rate, the time and attention devoted to developing maxims in the secondary level *progymnasma* are noteworthy.

32. Butts, "'Progymnasmata' of Theon," 205; with examples, 205–21. Throughout this section Theon's counsel for the development of *chreiai* and maxims is fused. This is most notably expressed in his remarks concerning refutation and confirmation: "The same commonplace arguments could also be used for refuting and confirming maxims" (221). The first two exercises, recitation and inflection, reinforce previous grammatical training rather than developing elaboration and argumentation.

33. Baldwin, *Medieval Rhetoric*, 27. The counsel of Hermogenes shows the direction in which technical rhetoric continued into the late empire. The distinctions and patterns are surely based on earlier tenets, but they have probably reached a more set form than at the time of Paul. Considering this, we should expect more flexibility in the construction of Paul's maxim argumentation than the more static outlines presented by Hermogenes.

34. Among the rhetorical handbooks, Aristotle *Rhetorica* 2.21.13–14 provides the only extant counsel on maxim refutation.

35. For a useful summary on the appeal to advantage in deliberative oratory, see Margaret M. Mitchell, *Paul and the Rhetoric of Reconciliation: An Exegetical Investigation of the Language and Composition of 1 Corinthians*, Hermeneutische Untersuchungen zur Theologie (Tübingen: Mohr/Siebeck, 1991), 25–32. The appeal to advantage consists of a number of different "heads" (for example, the just, the necessary, the natural). Refutation in deliberative rhetoric (and with maxims) argues that the course of action proposed is marked by the opposite of that which is advantageous or true (ibid., see esp. 26 n. 20). The counsel of Theon presents a very complete and useful number of heads for deliberative refutation.

36. On Theon's treatment of the *chreia* and maxim together, see n. 32 above.

37. Butts, "'Progymnasmata' of Theon," 217; with examples, 217–21.

38. Hermogenes lacks specific counsel like Theon's for the refutation and confirmation of maxims. Refutation and confirmation (advanced along similar lines as Theon's counsel) become their own *progymnasma* following the *chreia* and the maxim. The overlap between the *progymnasmata* proper and the makeup of their ancillary exercises indicates that they must have been interactive to some extent in instruction.

39. Butts, "'Progymnasmata' of Theon," 515.

40. The use of the maxim as an actual thesis statement has been demonstrated by Wilson from a variety of gnomic texts in antiquity (see Wilson, *Love without Pretense*, 48–49).

41. Such a perspective fits the relationship of rhetoric and *paideia* as set out in Marrou, *Education in Antiquity*, 95–101, 194–96.

42. See n. 6 above.

43. Using the categories of Marrou, *Education in Antiquity*, 197–203. This sequence is clearly reflected in Clark, *Greco-Roman Education*, 65–261, and in principle by Bonner, *Education in Rome*. Bonner, however, does not have as clear a differentiation between the

three stages, and this probably, and rightly I think, shows a closer integration of the three methods at the time of the empire.

44. The earliest rhetorical handbooks provided technical rhetoric with examples. Using these handbooks and collecting a fee, rhetors trained one to prepare for specific, limited situations — usually judicial speeches, but possibly deliberative oratory as well. As the art of rhetoric developed from the fifth century B.C.E. into the imperial period, the rhetorical handbooks reflected a combination of technical, imitative, and practical elements. This development and its procedures are carefully laid out in George A. Kennedy, "The Earliest Rhetorical Handbooks," *American Journal of Philology* 80 (1959): 169–78; cf. idem, *Classical Rhetoric and Its Christian and Secular Tradition from Ancient to Modern Times* (Chapel Hill: University of North Carolina Press, 1980), 18–24.

The rhetorical handbooks most germane to this study are Aristotle's *Ars rhetorica* (fourth century B.C.E.), Anaximenes' *Rhetorica ad Alexandrum* (fourth century B.C.E.), *Rhetorica ad Herennium* (first century B.C.E.), Seneca the Elder's *Controversiae* and *Suasoriae* (first century C.E.), Demetrius's *On Style* (third or first century B.C.E.), and Quintilian's *Institutio oratoria* (first century C.E.). I use the term "rhetorical handbook" broadly, realizing, for instance, that Aristotle's work is based on still incomplete lecture notes and Demetrius's piece is most certainly first a work on literary criticism. Seneca's work contains a series of prefaces to the individual books that provide didactic counsel, criticism of technique and style, and background to historical declaimers based on Seneca's memory. Hence, his work is, in a sense, a rhetorical handbook built on the *imitatio* rather than the technical tradition. Citations and translations will be from the editions of the Loeb Classical Library unless otherwise noted. For a full discussion of date and authorship issues as well as content, see the entries in Kennedy, *Classical Rhetoric*.

45. Quintilian discusses *sententiae* at length, and his counsel represents the current thinking, issues, and problems of the first century C.E. Consideration of the *sententiae* appears in three places in the *Institutio oratoria:* 1.9; 8.5; and 12.10.48. The section in 1.9 gives instruction on the use of *sententiae* in secondary *progymnasmata* (see n. 31 above). The section 12.10.48 is a recapitulation of a caveat against the abuse of *sententiae* already considered in Quintilian's longest and most thorough section on the *sententiae*, 8.5.

46. In book 8 of the *Institutio,* Quintilian treats the excessive use and abuse of *sententiae;* the section is held together with an introduction of these issues at 8.5.2 and a more detailed critique closing the section in 8.5.25–34. Quintilian knows of declamation abuse (see Stanley F. Bonner, *Roman Declamation in the Late Republic and Early Empire* [Berkeley: University of California Press, 1949], 81–82), and it appears that the overuse and abuse of *sententiae* resulted from problems connected with the continual rise in declamation practices. While treating the negative issues, Quintilian, nevertheless, gives due attention to the history of gnomic statements and to what he believes is "the possibility of appropriate and effective uses" (see Henderson, "Quintilian," 83). Unlike the Aristotelian tradition, but in the pattern of *Ad Herennium,* Quintilian relegates the discussion of *sententiae* to ornamentation rather than proof. Despite the misuse of the *sententia,* a persuasive quality still remains in a variety of areas: "Does it not help our case, or move the judge, or commend the speaker to his audience?" (8.5.32).

47. See D. M. Kriel, "The Forms of the Sententia in Quintilian VIII.v.3–24," *Acta Classica* 4 (1961): 80–89; and F. Delarue, "La sententia chez Quintilien," *Formes brèves: De la gnōmē à la pointe: Métamorphoses de la sententia = La Licorne* 3 (1979): 97–99.

48. The works of Kriel and Delarue have clarified the classes and types of *sententiae* discussed in book 8. Much confusion seems to have prevailed between what Quintilian has designated particular types of *sententiae* and what should be considered subclasses. Kriel's division into *gnōmē* (gnomic), *enthymema ex contrariis, noema, clausula,* and *magis nova sententiarum genera* has been persuasive. This amounts to two classes: the *gnōmē* (8.5.3–8) and the *sententia* (8.5.9–34). Delarue has confirmed this division and has added helpful explication. See Kriel, "Forms of the Sententia," 89, and Delarue, "La sententia chez Quintilien," 106–23.

Quintilian knows of and uses the Greek word *gnōmē* as a category that he calls in Latin *"antiquissimae [sententiae]"* (8.5.3). The "new" Latin *sententia* (according to Delarue, "post-Ciceronian") known to Quintilian is marked by *"magis nova sententiarum"* (8.5.15). This implies that the *enthymema ex contrariis,* the *noema,* and the *clausula* types fit the new category as well. See the discussion in Kriel, "Forms of the Sententia," 80–85, and Delarue, "La sententia chez Quintilien," 98–106, 116–17.

49. These categories are based on the work of J. P. Levet, *"RHĒTŌR et GNŌMĒ:* Présentation sémantique et recherches isocratiques," *La Licorne* 3 (1979): 34–38, and Delarue, "La sententia chez Quintilien," 98. I have adjusted Delarue's *"sententia*-trait" to what is more specific to our purposes, the moral *sententia.* Clarification for this description will be given below.

50. See Lewis A. Sussman's comments on the *sententiae* as discussed in light of their development from the *gnōmē* (*The Elder Seneca* [Leiden: Brill, 1978], 37).

51. "The term [*gnōmē*], however, is of wide application (indeed, such reflexions may be deserving of praise even when they have no reference to any special context), and is used in various ways" (8.5.3).

52. For example, "Complaisance wins us friends, truth enmity," and "Death is not bitter, but the approach to death" (8.5.4–5). The majority of examples for the *gnōmē* type take the form of the gnomic sentence, probably reflecting Quintilian's choice of Ciceronian and other contemporary Latin texts for examples.

53. In 1.9, Quintilian had referenced the gnomic maxim as a *progymnasma.* Further, in book 10 he advises accomplished rhetors constantly to take note of gnomic maxims through their attention to the poets. And see the discussion on the maxim's role in primary and secondary education on pp. 5–8 above.

54. J. Villemonteix, "Remarques sur les sentences homériques," *La Licorne* 3 (1979): 85–96. This study is particularly valuable for its stylistic analysis of Homeric maxims.

55. Ibid., 91–92. *Odyssey* 17.347: "Modesty, for a man in need, is not a good quality" (trans. in Richard Lattimore, *The Odyssey of Homer* [New York: Harper and Row, 1965], 262). *Iliad* 1.80, "For a king when he is angry with a man beneath him is too strong" (Richard Lattimore, *The Iliad of Homer* [Chicago: University of Chicago Press, 1951], 61). As rhetoric moved forward, especially in the Hellenistic school system, it cast its eyes back to the poets of old or their heroes and placed such evaluations as the "individual wise sage" upon them. Odysseus finds wide recognition as a wise man, and, of course, the most notable example is Homer now become the father of rhetoric itself! Indeed, as we have seen in our study of the maxim in primary and secondary levels, the Greco-Roman educational system encouraged this perspective in its perpetuation of *paideia.* Villemonteix notes that the lack of comparative material from Homeric times makes it impossible to decide whether any part of the "stylistic" form of the maxims can be

attributed to individual characters (but he finds the idea unlikely). See Villemonteix, "Les sentences homériques," 85–96, esp. 96.

56. Peter Karavites has surveyed the early Greek literature from its beginning to the fifth century B.C.E.: the gnomic and lyrical poets Theognis, Pindar, Baccylides; the tragedians Aeschylus, Sophocles, Euripides, Aristophanes; and the prose writers Hippocrates, Herodotus, Thucydides. See Peter Karavites, *"Gnōmē*'s Nuances: From Its Beginning to the End of the Fifth Century," *Classical Bulletin* 66 (1990): 9–34, esp. 10. His study is particularly valuable for its enumeration of idiomatic expressions that occur with the word *gnōmē* and for its judicious attempt to understand the nuances of the *gnōmē* in light of changing political, cultural, social, and economic factors.

Levet's independent investigation is in close agreement with Karavites' study regarding the nonuse of *gnōmē* as designation for maxim. Karavites (*"Gnōmē*'s Nuances," 10) lists one instance of "saying" in the mid-sixth-century text of *Theognis* 717. Levet (*"RHĒTŌR et GNŌMĒ,"* 34) lists only Euripides frag. 362.

57. Perceptions of intellectual faculty can be reified; thus *gnōmē* can be interpreted as "intent, plan, or purpose." A further extension provides a usage of "motion or proposal" or "decree or verdict" in the assembly. See Karavites, *"Gnōmē*'s Nuances," 14–15, 19.

58. Evident throughout, but most effectually presented in the consideration of Theognis, in ibid., 9–34. Levet makes a stronger case, again leaning heavily on the evidence from Theognis as one of our best examples, concluding: "The faculty of *gnōmē* enables, then, a person to conduct his reflections with rigor, and it offers to him a means of discerning his duty.... [I]t [the study] shows a particular aspect of the *gnōmē*, to know it as a sign which allows one to distinguish the good from the bad" (Levet, *"RHĒTŌR et GNŌMĒ,"* 35, 36).

59. "He is no lover who does not love always" (*Rhetorica* 2.21.2) and "A mortal should have mortal, not immortal thoughts" (*Rhetorica* 2.21.6) respectively.

60. "The best of omens is to defend one's country," and "The chances of war are the same for both" (*Rhetorica* 2.21.11).

61. Anaximenes' definition is more pointed—an "expression of an individual [direction]" (*Ad Alexandrum* 1430b.1–2). See n. 79 below. His primary interest is in "making a supply of maxims" (1430b.9–10). Certainly his examples do not resemble the gnomic maxim. Most likely Anaximenes presumes the student's knowledge of the gnomic maxim and is taking up a more current trend at the advanced level.

62. Sussman, *Elder Seneca*, 38. This preference is inherent in *Ad Herennium*'s definition of the maxim: "A Maxim is a saying drawn from life, which shows concisely either what happens or ought to happen in life" (4.17.24).

63. This seems to be a problem when one's methodology is formulated by generalizing from reference works like Lausberg, *Handbuch*, or Martin, *Antike Rhetorik*, or when generalizations are constructed from an examination of the extant rhetorical handbooks without consideration of historical, social, and rhetorical developments through time. See Appendix B above.

64. The usage of *gnōmē* as "saying" is largely unattested in the fifth century B.C.E. or before, but it is widely attested from the fourth century onward. See Levet, *RHĒTŌR et GNŌMĒ,"* 34–40, and n. 56 above.

65. Villemonteix, "Les sentences homériques," 87, in agreement with the hypothesis of Taillardat.

66. The terms *rhētōr* and *gnōmē* are closely linked in the evolution of rhetoric. The

early rhetor was a public servant who regularly brought issues or proposals before the developing democratic assemblies. With the rise of rhetoric and its movement to the populace through sophistic teaching, the ability to put forward a proposal, and then to formulate the wise saying or sentence in counsel, was extended to all. See Levet, "*RHĒTŌR et GNŌMĒ*," 12–17. For a full discussion of the role of the rhetor in the classical period, see Mogens Herman Hansen, *The Athenian Assembly: In the Age of Demosthenes* (Oxford: Blackwell, 1987), 49–93.

67. See Levet, "*RHĒTŌR et GNŌMĒ*," 32–40. For a detailed examination of the worldview, methods, and teachings of the Sophists, see Kennedy, *Classical Rhetoric,* 25–40.

68. Levet has pointed to *Oration to Nicocles* 44 as evidence that Isocrates knew of this new usage of the gnomic sentence:

> And, again, if one were to make a selection from the leading poets of their maxims, as we call them [*tas kaloumenas gnōmas*], into which they have put their best thought, men would show a similar attitude toward them also; for they would lend a readier ear to the cheapest comedy than to the creations of such finished art. (Isocrates, *Isocrates I,* trans. George Norlin, Loeb Classical Library [New York: Putnam's, 1928], 65)

> If this text, and precisely the participle *kaloumenas,* prove that the use, in the fourth century, had established behind *gnōmē,* the sense of "sentence," and even of "maxim built with craftsmanship," then it also shows that Isocrates disputes this appellation because it does not correspond exactly to reality.... [T]he well comprised *gnōmē* is truly a moral judgment that has been suggested by others, and which one recognizes for oneself in a given moment. (Levet, "*RHĒTŌR et GNŌMĒ,*" 39)

69. Levet ("*RHĒTŌR et GNŌMĒ*," 34) notes the negative spin (*coloration péjorative*) placed on the use of *gnōmai* by Aristophanes (*The Clouds*) as another indicator of negative reaction to some type of erroneous Sophistic practice.

70. "*Anthrōpinē doksa*" (human opinion) (Levet, "*RHĒTŌR et GNŌMĒ*," 39).

71. "In opposition to *doksa*-opinion as mere apprehension of reality, *gnōmē* is accordingly [ethically] restrained opinion" (ibid., 38). Note our discussion of the distinction made between the *gnōmē* and the rhetor's *doksa* (opinion) in the work of *Rhetorica ad Alexandrum* in n. 77 below.

72. Levet, "*RHĒTŌR et GNŌMĒ,*" 38.

73. Ibid., 39–40.

74. Ibid., 39.

75. See n. 81 below.

76. This is evident throughout Aristotle *Rhetorica* 2.21.2–16. Maxims are considered in regard to the rhetor's *ēthos,* the audience perception, and the logical clarity of the proposal.

77. Indeed, they are mainly concerned with the gnomic sentence rather than the gnomic maxim, as recognized for Aristotle by Delarue, "La sententia chez Quintilien," 100. This is true for *Ad Alexandrum* by virtue of its definition of the maxim: "A maxim may be summarily defined as the expression of an individual opinion [*dēlōsis,* "pointing out"; "direction"(!); not *doksa,* "opinion"] about general matters of conduct" (1430b.1–2).

Rackham's translation of *dēlōsis* as "opinion" is regrettable. Liddel and Scott list "pointing out; explaining," "direction; order," "Urim (LXX Lev. 8:8)," and "interpretation (LXX Dan. 2:27)." According to Anaximenes: "Of proofs there are two modes: some proofs are drawn from words and actions and persons themselves, others are supplementary to what the persons say and do. Probabilities, examples, tokens, enthymemes, maxims, signs and refutations are proofs drawn from actual words and persons and actions; the opinion of the speaker, the evidence of witnesses, evidence given under torture, oaths are supplementary" (*Ad Alexandrum* 1428a.16–23). The use of maxims and the use of the opinion of the speaker (*doksa tou legontos*) are part of two different categories ("modes") and have entirely separate sections in Anaximenes' treatise (*Ad Alexandrum* 1430b.1–25, 1431b.9–15, respectively). Neither the words *dēlōsis* and *doksa* nor these two separate sections of counsel should be confused.

78. In *Institutio oratoria* 8.5.6–7, the maxims restated from more simplistic expressions are clearly gnomic sentences according to the definition advanced here. Also see the additional evidence from Quintilian in the discussion that follows.

79. The fourth-century rhetorical handbooks of Aristotle and Anaximenes show considerable interest in the rhetor's creation of gnomic sentences. This is due most likely to their chronological proximity and connection to the Sophists as the gnomic sentence developed. Anaximenes, in particular, shows concern to instruct the student in the "making of a supply of maxims" (*Ad Alexandrum* 1430b.7–29). He suggests constructing a supply "from the particular nature of the case or by using hyperbole or by drawing a parallel." "It is characteristic of sensible people to use the examples of their predecessors and to endeavour so to escape the errors arising out of imprudence" (nature of the case). "I think that thieves commit worse outrages than highwaymen, because the former rob us of our property by stealth, the latter openly" (hyperbole). "I think that those who cheat people out of money act exactly like those who betray their country, because both of them after being trusted rob those who have trusted them" (parallel). Aristotle's counsel on maxims, while being admittedly more indirect, nevertheless presumes the rhetor's shaping of the maxim material through attached reasons (*Rhetorica* 2.21.2–7) and counterargument (*Rhetorica* 2.21.13–14). Aristotle can also speak of "country folk who strike maxims" (*Hoi agroikoi gnōmotupoi* [*Rhetorica* 2.21.9], as trans. George A. Kennedy, *Aristotle on Rhetoric: A Theory of Civic Discourse* [New York: Oxford University Press, 1991], 184). Cf. Quintilian *Institutio oratoria* 8.5.3–7.

80. *Ad Alexandrum* 1430b.17 introduces the maxim with a first-person (indirect) formulation: *moi dokousin* ("I think that" [Loeb Classical Library] or "[subject] seems to me" [literal]). This construction is used four times in the passage. See full citations in n. 79 above. Also see Aristotle *Rhetorica* 2.21.7 for *phēmi* as a maxim formulation in the first-person.

81. In *Institutio oratoria* 8.5.5–7, Quintilian notes what makes *gnōmai* striking (*notabile*). He discusses opposition, direct statement, change of figure, and transference of the general to the particular and personal. This last attribute is notable for our point here. According to Henderson ("Quintilian," 85), this is the first time the general to the particular and personal (*a communi ad proprium; ad personam* in 8.5.6–7) is stated explicitly in the rhetorical literature. I am inclined to see the *a communi ad proprium* already in Anaximenes with the *ad personam* only implied. *Ad Alexandrum* counsels that created maxims "should be related to the matters at hand" (1430b.7–8). It is profitable to construct maxims from "the particular nature of the case" (1430b.9–11). This

point is implicitly behind Aristotle's counsel to attach a reason or supplement to maxims that might otherwise stand alone (*Rhetorica* 2.21.2) as well as his suggestion that "the speaker should endeavour to guess how his hearers formed their preconceived opinions and what they are, and then express himself in general terms in regard to them" (*Rhetorica* 2.21.15–16).

82. Aristotle *Rhetorica* 2.21.9; Quintilian *Institutio oratoria* 8.5.7–8.

83. Aristotle *Rhetorica* 2.21.3–8; *Ad Herennium* 4.17.24; Quintilian *Institutio oratoria* 8.5.4. Succinctly put in *Ad Alexandrum* 1430b.5–7: "[B]ut when what you say is paradoxical, you must specify the reasons briefly, so as to avoid prolixity and not arouse incredulity."

84. Aristotle *Rhetorica* 2.21.13–14. Aristotle believes that advancing a good counter-maxim will greatly enhance one's moral character as well. *Ad Alexandrum* (1430b.1–3) indicates the possibility of maxim dispute but does not address the subject directly. Of course, both maxim confirmation and refutation were familiar from the *progymnasmata* exercises, as we have shown.

85. The *suasoriae* developed from the Greek *logos protreptikos* and *logos apotreptikos*, a discussion of which is found in Aristotle's *Rhetorica*, book 1. The *suasoria*, as deliberative argumentation, developed naturally from the "thesis." The best available building blocks were common philosophic theses (for example, "What is the difference between a king and a tyrant?") or citations of (quasi-) historical examples (for example, "Should Agamemnon sacrifice Iphegenia?") (see Bonner, *Roman Declamation*, 2–11). Deliberative oratory such as that of the *suasoria* was firm ground for moralizing. During the Greco-Roman period "[m]oralizing is most concise when presented in the form of a maxim (*sententia*), as, for instance, when Alexander is advised that 'the sign of a great spirit is moderation in success'" (Bonner, *Education in Rome*, 284).

The *controversia* as a speech on judicial issues was given a more definite shape through Hermogoras's second-century B.C.E. "status" theory. Determining where the issue lay — whether question of fact, definition, or intent — more easily set the lines of argumentation. See Bonner, *Roman Declamation*, 12–13.

The standard order for a declamation speech was introduction (*exordium*), narration (*narratio*), proof (*argumenta*), and conclusion (*peroratio*). See Bonner, *Education in Rome*, 288–308, with a detailed development of each section. Deliberative oratory, and hence the *suasoria*, might differ in makeup by not including a *narratio*.

86. Clark, *Greco-Roman Education*, 215; Bonner, *Roman Declamation*, 49. Declamation exercises have a long history in Greek education apparently reaching back, in the case of the *controversia*, to Demetrius of Phalerum (ca. 350–ca. 280 B.C.E.), according to the evidence of Quintilian *Institutio oratoria* 2.4.22–23, as noted in Bonner, *Roman Declamation*, 12. In agreement is D. A. Russell, who establishes sources roughly contemporaneous to this date and provides detailed information on Greek origins (D. A. Russell, *Greek Declamation* [Cambridge: Cambridge University Press, 1983], 1–20).

Greco-Roman education took over the use of declamation exercises at various chronological stages. According to Seneca the Elder (*Controversiae* 1.pf.12), the standard general thesis (Gr. *thesis*) was practiced first (before the time of Cicero), followed by the *causae* or particularized thesis (Gr. *hypothesis;* during Cicero's time), and, then, the declamation proper, of which the *controversia* form became the most important (after Seneca's own birth). For comments on this important passage with further citations in Cicero and *Ad Herennium*, see Bonner, *Roman Declamation*, 7, 27–50, and Sussman, *The*

Elder Seneca, 6–10. According to Cicero, Hermogoras (ca. 150 B.C.E.) was the first to make the division between thesis and hypothesis. The word "declamation" for practice speeches occurs late. It was used for quite some time to designate exercises in pronunciation and delivery (*pronuntiatio*, from the sphere of the stage or theater) and then developed the connotation of practice speech at a time after Cicero. See Bonner, *Roman Declamation*, 20–22.

87. The movement of declamation into wider Greco-Roman society must be reconstructed, and Bonner's views are generally accepted. The following is Sussman's summary of Bonner's work on this point:

> In the late Republic adults declaimed primarily in private gatherings of close friends, as in the case of Cicero. From this beginning, Bonner envisions the following developments:
>
> (1) Professors declaim in schools for the benefit of pupils (3 pr. 16; 7 pr. 1); and orators at home among friends (4 pr. 2; 10 pr. 3, 4).
>
> (2) Professors invite the public to their schools on special occasions (3 pr. 1); some kept an open school (3 pr. 16). But the conservative orators viewed this with contempt (10 pr. 4), though some admitted the public (4 pr. 7). The professors invited parents to hear their sons (Persius 3.45; Quint. 2.7.1; 10.5.21).
>
> (3) The presence of other professors encouraged the introduction of meetings for friendly competition which became popular social occasions, often elsewhere than in the schools. Even those who did not declaim publicly came to listen and joined in the critical discussion, many of whom were famous people.

Sussman, *Elder Seneca*, 15; cf. Bonner, *Roman Declamation*, 39–41, and M. L. Clarke, *Rhetoric at Rome: A Historical Study* (London: Cohen and West, 1953), 85–86.

88. Sussman, *Elder Seneca*, 12, and Bonner, *Roman Declamation*, 38–39.

89. On the rhetoricians' social position, see Marrou, *Education in Antiquity*, 284–85, and Bonner, *Education in Rome*, 117–25. See also Clarke, *Rhetoric at Rome*, 86. Political factors had contributed to preparing a large base of potential declamation participants. "After the fall of the Republic, the men who by experience, background, talent, wealth, and ambition would have been drawn to active political careers were discouraged from participation because of their distaste for the new regime, or the dangers and uncertainties inherent in close association with court politics.... A large number of talented men, the product of an educational system whose overriding concern was with rhetoric, were now set adrift in a period when their oratorical training could no longer be employed for gaining wealth and political power. It occasions little surprise that they redirected their energies and talents to the safer yet more sterile arena of declamation" (Sussman, *Elder Seneca*, 14, 13).

90. Themes suggestive of this aspect in Seneca the Elder are: "The Tyrannicide Who Cuckolded the Tyrant"; "The Hero without Hands"; "The Foreign Merchant." Concerning this entertainment value, Clarke notes, "The world of the declamations was a fantastic and melodramatic one, and for that reason perhaps popular in a humdrum age. Augustus brought peace and security to the world; the declaimers revelled in violence, in fire and shipwreck, poison, and hanging" (Clarke, *Rhetoric at Rome*, 91).

91. Sussman, *Elder Seneca,* 13–17.

92. The demands of the exercises, the structure of the sessions, and the audience expectations increased the use of imagination and promoted a motive of winning approval for oneself in addition to (or at the expense of) the case. Needless to say, at times improvisation gave way to abuse — the goal being to excite the crowd, draw applause, and demonstrate techniques as opposed to careful and convincing argumentation.

Declamation abuse is carefully examined and critiqued in Bonner, *Roman Declamation,* 71–83. The works of Bonner (*Roman Declamation,* 71–83; *Education in Rome,* 277–327) and Clark (*Greco-Roman Education,* 213–61), while knowledgeable of the tendency for abuse, regard declamation as a necessary development and effective when pursued correctly. This is in contradistinction to earlier critiques (Harry Caplan, "The Decay of Eloquence at Rome in the First Century," in *On Eloquence: Studies in Ancient and Modern Rhetoric* [Ithaca, N.Y.: Cornell University Press, 1970], 160–95; and Clarke, *Rhetoric at Rome,* 85–99) that tended to be more negative about the whole enterprise.

93. Seneca the Elder *Controversiae* 9.pr.2; and Quintilian *Institutio oratoria* 10.5.14. See Bonner, *Roman Declamation,* 70–73, 80–82; and Clark, *Greco-Roman Education,* 250–57.

94. Seneca's work and ideas reflect the transformation and adaptation of rhetorical technique and style appropriate to his changing times at the turn of the eras. As such, his work fills an important gap between Cicero's and Quintilian's counsel. See Sussman, *Elder Seneca,* 95; 104–7; and n. 44 above.

95. Sussman, *Elder Seneca,* 44. "Division was the manner in which a declaimer planned and outlined the argumentation of his case, and is not related to the similar term meaning the disposition of the various parts of speech." "Colors are subtle, unusual, and clever twists of circumstance and argumentation by which the declaimers tried to alter the interpretation of the facts in a case" (ibid., 38, 41).

96. Ibid., 58.

97. Ibid.

98. "A typical example of the universal type is: *omnis instabilis et incerta felicitas est,* 'All happiness is unstable and uncertain' (1.1.3). An example of the more specific type is in the words of Alexander's advisor as the king deliberates whether or not to sail across the ocean: *Non quaerimus orbem, sed amittimus,* 'We are not in search of a world — we are losing one' (*Suasoriae* 1.2)" (Sussman, *Elder Seneca,* 35 and n. 4). See Bonner, *Roman Declamation,* 54–55, for further examples of both kinds. Sussman notes appropriately that this second usage differs from the explicit counsel of *Ad Herennium,* where it is precisely the general over the specific that is emphasized. Hence, the effect and stance of both the gnomic maxim and the gnomic sentence constitute a background for the moral *sententia.* See Sussman, *Elder Seneca,* 35.

99. "No good fortune is secure" (*Controversiae* 2.1.9). "Madness cannot be diagnosed from a single fault. No-one is faultless: Cato lacked moderation, Cicero firmness, Sulla clemency" (*Controversiae* 2.4.4).

100. Bonner, *Roman Declamation,* 54.

101. Sussman, *Elder Seneca,* 38 and n. 11, 43, 114 and n. 80.

102. Ibid., 37–38.

103. Ibid., 107.

104. Ibid, 38.

105. Ibid.

106. Further evidence for Latro having *sententiae* commonplaces is provided in the preceding section, *Controversiae* 1.pr.22. Here, in an anecdote, Latro spontaneously provides all the necessary *sententiae* in support of the arguments of one Marullus, who, as a rather dry man (speaker), has left them out!

107. Quintilian can use the term *enthymema* in a variety of ways. In his discussion of the *sententia* as *gnōmē* in *Institutio oratoria* 8.5.4, he employs *enthymema* "as a *sententia cum ratione* (where the term *sententia* is non-technical: 'proposition or thought')." Here in *Institutio oratoria* 8.5.9-10, the term is employed as a "*mente conceptum*, that is, anything conceived in the mind of the speaker," but with the further specificity of employing *ex contrariis* (see Kriel, "Forms of the Sententia," 84-85).

108. "Caesar, shall the language of those whom it is your glory to have spared goad you to imitate their own cruelty?" (*Institutio oratoria* 8.5.10). Citing Cicero, Quintilian somewhat entangles himself in the various categories. Overlap between categories is evident with the type of *sententia* referred to as *clausula* (conclusion). In addition, some relationship with the *epiphonema* (final exclamation) is implied, though Quintilian stops short of identifying the *epiphonema* as a classification of *sententiae*. Demetrius (*On Style* 2.106-11) explicitly denies that a *gnōmē* can be an *epiphonema*, though he allows that a *gnōmē* may take the same final position. See Kriel's analysis of the difficulties in Quintilian's presentation at this point in "Forms of the Sententia," 85-86.

109. The use of the *noema* is attributed to the "modern rhetoricians," and its example comes not from Cicero but from a declamation exercise. A sister had cut off her brother's thumb in his sleep to release him from gladiator school. He demands similar infliction for her. She cries out, "You deserved to have all your fingers," meaning, "You deserved to be a gladiator all your days" (most likely intending "unto the death" [following Kriel, "Forms of Sententia," 86]). See *Institutio oratoria* 8.5.12. It is to be noted that from here to the end of Quintilian's discussion, many of the examples come from declamation exercises.

110. The term "period" has various shades of meaning, and I have in mind here Richard A. Lanham's general definition: "a complete thought expressed self-sufficiently" (see Richard A. Lanham, *A Handlist of Rhetorical Terms*, 2d ed. [Berkeley: University of California Press, 1991], 112-13). The *clausula* refers more to a place or position than to a type of *sententia* itself. See Kriel, "Forms of the Sententia," 87; cf. Delarue, "La sententia chez Quintilien," 113-14. Quintilian's selection of *clausula* as a separate classification appears to be influenced by the misuse of *sententiae* as *clausula* in his own day: "Our rhetoricians want every passage, every sentence to strike the ear by an impressive close . . . [resulting in] a number of tiny epigrams, affected, irrelevant and disjointed" (*Institutio oratoria* 8.5.13-14).

111. Kriel, "Forms of the Sententia," 89. "When the 29 examples of *sententiae* which are given in pars. 3-24 are subjected to a critical analysis, it appears that they fall into two main categories, namely those that contain a universal truth (maxims) and those that do not. The nine examples of gnomic *sententiae* all contain or imply general truths, whereas not one of the other examples (that is of *enthymema ex contrariis*, *noema*, *clausula* and the *magis nova genera*) [is] of universal application; it would therefore be incorrect to translate the term *sententia* in any of these latter cases as 'maxim' or 'general reflection'; at most they are pithy expressions (*pointes*)" (ibid.).

112. These classifications follow Delarue, "La sententia chez Quintilien," 115-24.

113. Ibid., 106-14.

114. "Consequently you will often find that such persons will produce a *division* or *argument* as if it were an epigram [*sententia*]" (*Institutio oratoria* 8.5.30).

115. Such as a division, commonplace, exemplum, color, stylistic ornament, or comparison. For the evidence from Seneca the Elder, see pp. 13–14 above.

116. Bonner, *Education in Rome,* 284.

117. Kriel states that it is "incorrect to translate the term *sententia* in any of these latter [modern or newer] cases as 'maxim' or 'general reflection'" (see n. 111 above for full quotation). But then in a note on the same analysis, he states, "A very few may perhaps be understood to imply a general truth, for example those in pars. 10, 13 and 19" (see Kriel, "Forms of the Sententia," 89 and n. 52). According to Sussman, Bonner's extensive analysis of *sententiae* in Seneca the Elder finds segments that are "gnomic, proverbial, universal in application." "A typical example of the universal type is: *omnis instabilis et incerta felicitas est,* 'All happiness is unstable and uncertain' (1.1.3)" (see Sussman, *Elder Seneca,* 35 and n. 4). See Bonner (*Roman Declamation,* 54–55) for full analysis and a listing of seventeen "gnomic" *sententiae* from Seneca's *Controversiae* and *Suasoria* as a few examples. This appears to be a case not of either/or but of both.

118. Roberts's translation seems particularly apt here. See Aristotle, *Rhetoric,* trans. W. Rhys Roberts, Modern Library (New York: Random House, 1954). A fuller citation of Aristotle's definition from the Loeb Classical Library: "Now, a maxim is a statement, not however concerning particulars, as, for instance, what sort of man Iphicrates was, but *general;* it does not even deal with all general things, as for instance that the straight is the opposite of the crooked, but with *the objects of human actions,* and with what should be chosen or avoided with reference to them" (*Rhetorica* 2.21.2; emphasis added). Agreement is evidenced in *Ad Alexandrum* 1430b.1–3; *Ad Herennium* 4.17.24–25 (by virtue of the examples offered); Quintilian *Institutio oratoria* 8.5.3–8 (by examples offered and description as "precepts").

119. This becomes a limitation for the study and recognizes the possibility of studying the *sententiae* in Paul's writings from a fuller perspective. Here, however, we are only concerned with those *sententiae* that fit the category of maxims.

120. It is proper to consider evidence in some of the moralists when speaking of maxim effectiveness and usage. Many of the moralists had rhetorical training, having followed the general pattern for education.

Seneca the Younger (4 B.C.E. — 65 C.E.), in particular, is important as a moralist who illustrates some of the points brought up in this study. While Seneca knows the word "maxim" (*Epistulae Morales* 33.5), he prefers the use of the words *praeceptum* (precept) and *sententia,* apparently used interchangeably. For in "On the Value of Advice," the conversation advances on the subject of "precepts," but specific examples from Cato and Marcus Agrippa are labeled as *sententiae* (*Epistulae Morales* 94.27, 46–47). Seneca speaks of the philosopher introducing "verses among his wholesome precepts" (*Epistulae Morales* 108.8–10), by which he is referencing the quotation of the poets. When prose precepts of general application are used, they have a particularizing activity in application to moral counsel (*Epistulae Morales* 94.32–33, 35–36).

121. Note 118.

122. See the section in chap. 1 above entitled "The Gnomic Sentence."

123. Aristotle *Rhetorica* 2.21.9; Quintilian *Institutio oratoria* 8.5.8. Maxims are inappropriate for those who lack experience, who come from the country, who are of low birth, who are youthful, or who lack education.

124. Quintilian *Institutio oratoria* 8.5.32, "Does it [the use of *sententiae*] not... commend the speaker to his audience?" *Ad Herennium* 4.17.25: "Furthermore, the hearer, when he perceives that an indisputable principle drawn from practical life is being applied to a cause, must give it his tacit approval." Cf. Aristotle *Rhetorica* 2.21.15. Among the moralists, Seneca indicates that stature is gained through the creation of one's maxims: "For a man, however, whose progress is definite, to chase after choice extracts and to prop his weakness by the best known and the briefest sayings and to depend upon his memory [of the work of others], is disgraceful; it is time for him to lean on himself. He should make such maxims and not memorize them. For it is disgraceful even for an old man, or one who has sighted old age, to have a note-book knowledge.... But what is your own opinion? How long shall you march under another man's orders? Take command, and utter some word which posterity will remember. Put forth something from your own stock" (*Epistulae Morales* 33.5–9).

125. Aristotle *Rhetorica* 2.21.16.

126. Ibid., 2.21.13–14. Given as an example is, "And one's character would appear better, if one were to say that it is not right, as men say, to love as if one were bound to hate, but rather to hate as if one were bound to love."

127. Quintilian *Institutio oratoria* 8.5.7.

128. *Ad Herennium* 4.17.25.

129. Quintilian *Institutio oratoria* 8.5.14. Here, as a criticism of using *sententiae* to close off every period in succession.

130. The role of maxims in the social construction of knowledge is explicitly pointed out in Peter L. Berger and Thomas Luckmann, *The Social Construction of Reality: A Treatise in the Sociology of Knowledge* (New York: Doubleday, 1966), 94, and Gerd Theissen, "The Sociological Interpretation of Religious Traditions: Its Methodological Problems as Exemplified in Early Christianity," in *The Social Setting of Pauline Christianity: Essays on Corinth*, trans. John H. Schütz (Philadelphia: Fortress, 1982), 182–86.

131. Aristotle *Rhetorica* 2.21.11.

132. Ibid., 2.21.15.

133. Ibid., 2.21.5. Also *Ad Alexandrum* 1430b.3–4; Seneca *Epistulae Morales* 94.10, 27, 44.

134. Aristotle *Rhetorica* 2.21.3–7. Also *Ad Alexandrum* 1430b.3–7; *Ad Herennium* 4.17.24; Seneca *Epistulae Morales* 94.10, 27, 44.

135. Aristotle *Rhetorica* 2.21.2. As an enthymeme (syllogism) of practical conduct designed to demonstrate "probability." Cf. Quintilian *Institutio oratoria* 8.5.4.

136. "There is no man who is really free, for he is the slave of either wealth or fortune" (Aristotle *Rhetorica* 2.21.2).

137. "A mortal should have mortal, not immortal thoughts" (Aristotle *Rhetorica* 2.21.6).

138. For example, Aristotle *Rhetorica* 2.21.13–14, "Nor do I approve the maxim 'Nothing in excess,' for one cannot hate the wicked too much," and Quintilian *Institutio oratoria* 8.5.7, "Caesar, the splendour of your present fortune confers on you nothing greater than the power and nothing better than the will to save as many of your fellow-citizens as possible."

139. Aristotle *Rhetorica* 2.21.14.

140. See p. 8 and n. 40 above.

141. It is closely connected with the *clausula* (conclusion). See our discussion on pp. 14–15 above with nn. 108 and 110.

142. See pp. 15–16 above.

143. See our discussion of the gnomic maxim and Homer's stylistic influence on the tradition on pp. 9–10 above.

144. Rhetoricians show a propensity for classification and attention to stylistic instruction. Anaximenes suggests hyperbole and parallel (*Ad Alexandrum* 1430b.10–11). *Ad Herennium* 4.17.24–25 notes single and double forms. Hermogenes proposes categorizing maxims into true, plausible; simple, compound, or hyperbolic (see p. 15 above). Finally, Quintilian sums up classification of stylistic techniques in his time, "There are some even who classify them under ten heads. . . . [T]hey class them as based on interrogation, comparison, denial, similarity, admiration, and the like, for they can be treated under every kind of figure." Quintilian then goes on to list some of his own favorites: opposition, simple statement, transference of the statement from the general to the particular, and giving the general statement a personal turn (*Institutio oratoria* 8.5.5–8).

145. To recap: Theon recommends comment, objection, expansion and condensation, and refutation and confirmation. Hermogenes proposes brief encomium of the one making the saying, direct exposition, proof, contrast, enthymeme, illustration, example, and authority. See pp. 7–8 above.

146. The later rhetorical exercise handbooks like those of Hermogenes and Aphthonius give little explanation. They are satisfied with presenting descriptions that are followed by examples to be analyzed. Of course the rhetorical handbooks have a great deal of counsel on individual rhetorical devices or strategies in general (for example, illustrations, examples, refutation).

147. See p. 9 above.

148. The examples in this passage clearly indicate that both proverbs and maxims are here in mind.

149. "It would be an instance of the latter if a man in a rage were to say, 'It is not true that a man should know himself; at any rate, such a man as this, if he had known himself, would never have claimed the chief command.' And one's character would appear better, if one were to say that it is not right, as men say, to love as if one were bound to hate, but rather to hate as if one were bound to love" (*Rhetorica* 2.21.14).

150. "... [B]y saying 'that it is right to love, not as men say, but as if one were going to love for ever, for the other kind of love would imply treachery'" (*Rhetorica* 2.21.14).

151. Actually, Aristotle has refuted this same maxim twice already. See nn. 149 and 150 above. He also refutes "Know thyself" and "Nothing in excess."

152. Cf. "Nor do I approve it" with reference to the following refutation of "Nothing in excess" (*Rhetorica* 2.21.14).

153. Presumably the maxim disagreed with is, "It is necessary to love as if one is bound to hate." Aristotle reformulates the necessity of the called-for action in terms of love's relationship to true friendship, not hatred's relationship to enmity.

154. Bonner is surely correct to point out that the example for this elaboration (*expolitio*) is a *sententia* and not a *chreia* (contra H. Caplan, *Ad Herennium*, Loeb Classical Library, 365)! "No peril is so great that a wise man would think it ought to be avoided when the safety of the fatherland is at stake" (4.42.54). See Bonner, *Education in Rome*, 259 n. 66.

155. For an application of the analysis of refining in this form to a Pauline text, see our discussion of 1 Cor 10:23–31 in chap. 3.

156. Following the breakdown of H. Caplan, *Ad Herennium*, Loeb Classical Library, lviii.

157. See Seneca the Elder *Controversiae* 1.pr.24 and our discussion on p. 14 above.

Chapter 2: Identifying Paul's Maxims and Reading Them within a Rhetorical Context

1. What gives force to a maxim and makes it work is the recognition of shared perceptions of a common world between the speaker/writer and the hearer/reader. From the perspective of the sociology of knowledge, maxims work within a shared symbolic universe. Persons within the same culture share in varying ways in a "social stock of knowledge" and thereby form a shared "symbolic universe" that regulates structures of reality expectations and role definitions (see Berger and Luckmann, *Social Construction of Reality*, 41–46; 92–104).

This social stock of knowledge or symbolic universe containing social practices, moral values, and ethical outlooks does not remain for us as a written and verifiable script. Scholars try to reconstruct this unwritten social script through careful social and historical investigation. With an understanding of the Greco-Roman social world, the goal is to be attentive to the wider symbolic universe of Paul and his Corinthian community, listening for echoes of traditional wisdom in the correspondence in general and the maxims in particular. The identification of echoes is tricky business — applauded by some and seriously questioned by others. See Hays, *Echoes of Scripture*, esp. 1–33, and the critiques of Hays's work and the rejoinder by Hays in Craig A. Evans and James A. Sanders, eds., *Paul and the Scriptures of Israel*, JSOT Supplement Series 83 (Sheffield, England: JSOT, 1993), 13–96.

2. Pauline believers view their world on two levels. One level is the continuity of history as it progresses along in the present symbol system of the larger Greco-Roman world. Economic, political, and social structures along with other various patterns of thought are common knowledge between Paul and his audience at Corinth. The other level is the reality (a parallel symbolic universe) in the present of living in a believing community that is the now/not yet of the fullness of God's rule to come. Paul is able to express this latter reality in short phrases such as "in Christ" or "the kingdom of God."

3. For an illustration of Paul's combining general wisdom from the larger culture with the in-group perspective of a new believing community, see our discussion of 1 Cor 4:15 in chap. 3 above.

4. The Corinthian position, however, may be based on previous counsel given by Paul that has now been expanded, changed, or misappropriated in some way.

5. Paul has learned of these positions by either letter or oral report. This is fully discussed in Hurd, *Origin of 1 Corinthians*, 61–94, and appropriately updated in Roger L. Omanson, "Acknowledging Paul's Quotations," *The Bible Translator* 43 (1992): 201–13.

In assessing the viability of any proposed quotation, standard criteria for establishing the presence of formal material in a continuous text are used. Criteria can be broken down into three areas. First, there is the detection of explicit introductory formulas such as the particle *hoti* after verbs of saying, less frequently *de* and *gar*, and Paul's use of phrases like "each of you says" (*ekastos hymōn legei*; 1 Cor 1:12) or "they say" (*phēsin*; 2 Cor 10:10), as pointed out by Omanson, "Acknowledging Paul's Quotations," 202.

Second, linguistic differences are important. The use of *hapax legomena* or the identification of grammatical incongruities or syntactical disturbance may support an argument for a quotation. Finally, the coherence of Paul's theological or argumentative position is important. For instance, coherence appears broken when Paul states, "All of us possess knowledge" (1 Cor 8:1), and then later disputes the position by stating, "It is not everyone, however, who has this knowledge" (1 Cor 8:7).

Works that are helpful for determining quotation criteria are Omanson, "Acknowledging Paul's Quotations," 201–13; W. Hulitt Gloer, "Homologies and Hymns in the New Testament: Form, Content and Criteria for Identification," *Perspectives in Religious Studies* 11 (1984): 115–32; Conzelmann, *1 Corinthians*, 108, 109, 140 (as noted in Omanson); Hurd, *Origin of 1 Corinthians*, 61–94; Christopher D. Stanley, *Paul and the Language of Scripture: Citation Technique in the Pauline Epistles and Contemporary Literature* (Cambridge: Cambridge University Press, 1992), 31–80.

6. See the discussion of 1 Corinthians 7 in chap. 3 above.

7. It should be noted that 1 Corinthians is part of a series of at least five different written messages from Paul to the Corinthians: a previous letter now lost (1 Cor 5:9), unless as some have argued it is to be identified with 2 Cor 6:14–7:1; 1 Corinthians; a "painful letter" (2 Cor 2:4) now lost, unless as some have argued it is to be identified with 2 Cor 2:14–6:13 and 7:2–4; 2 Corinthians 1–9; and 2 Corinthians 10–13. Further partitioning of 2 Corinthians has been proposed, especially chapters 8 and 9 as separate letter fragments. For full discussion of 1 Corinthians as part of an ongoing correspondence between Paul and the Corinthians, see Victor Paul Furnish, *II Corinthians*, Anchor Bible (New York: Doubleday, 1984), 32A:29–55. I assume the unity of 1 Corinthians. On this point, see Conzelmann, *1 Corinthians*, 2–4. This study concerns the earlier relationship between Paul and the Corinthian community. I do not attempt to understand 1 Corinthians by extrapolating back from later developments to be found in 2 Corinthians.

8. See Aristotle *Rhetorica* 2.21.2, 11–13, 15–16; *Ad Herennium* 4.17.24; Butts, "'Progymnasmata' of Theon," 187–89; Quintilian, *Institutio oratoria* 8.5.5; and the discussion in chap. 2 above.

The choice of figures (for example, antithesis, simile, *epanaphora*, interrogation, etc.) was unlimited (see Quintilian, *Institutio oratoria* 8.5.5). The maxim is distinguished from everyday speech by the inclusion of figures (see Snyman, "On Studying Figures," 100).

9. A stronger evaluation for commonly available and easily recognizable traditional wisdom adds credence. Here some of Hays's criteria for establishing plausible echoes of Israel's scriptures in Paul's letters can be applied profitably to detecting the reverberation of Greco-Roman traditional wisdom as well. For any proposed echo, what is its availability to Paul and his readers, its strength of volume determined by emphasis and rhetorical stress, its recurrence in Paul's larger corpus, its thematic coherence in argumentation, its historical plausibility with respect to Paul's intention and his readers' comprehension, and its previous history of interpretation? (see Hays, *Echoes of Scripture*, 29–32).

10. Paul views his relationship with the Corinthian community as one built on mutual and ongoing deliberation (see Mitchell, *Rhetoric of Reconciliation*, 33–39). With respect to authority, Paul believes that his counsel is to be given the most serious consideration based on his call from God and his position as the founder and nurturer of the community (1 Cor 4:1–21). Paul fully believes that nonnegotiable standards are established by societal norms (1 Cor 5:1; 11:14–15), the pattern of God's people in the past

(5:11; 6:9–10; 10:1–13), and developing community traditions (7:17; 11:16). In these cases, Paul often offers strong warnings. In many respects, though, Paul sees a rather broad area of living in the world that is to be worked out in his communities through the deliberation of its members. Cf. the discussion of maxims and Paul's ethical stance toward the Galatian communities in Betz, *Galatians*, 291–93.

11. For instance, Aristotle, whose examples are all relatively brief, has maxims from two to thirteen Greek words (*Rhetorica* 2.21.1–21). *Ad Alexandrum* offers examples averaging around seventeen Greek words each until Anaximenes concludes the section with a maxim of fifty-one words (1430b.1–29). *Ad Herennium*'s examples range from four to thirty-seven Latin words (4.17.24–25). Quintilian's longest maxim is nineteen Latin words (*Institutio oratoria* 8.5.7).

12. See n. 19 below.

13. Seneca *Controversiae* 7.pr.2 with respect to the style of Albucius. Cf. Demetrius *On Style* 4.203–208 and [Longinus] *On the Sublime* 17.1.

14. A rhetor's style was a live issue at the turn of the eras. Questions of style led to several important debates such as that between the Atticists (promoters of simple, plain, lucid style) and the Asianists (promoters of ornate, figurative, rhythmic, emotional style).

On the issue of Asianism and Atticism with reference to Cicero's perception and role during the first century B.C.E., see George A. Kennedy, *The Art of Rhetoric in the Roman World* (Princeton, N.J.: Princeton University Press, 1972), 239–59. On the development and spread of Asianism, see Cecil Wooten, "Le développement du style asiatique pendent l'époque helléistique," *Revue des études grecques* 88 (1975): 94–104. Cf. Clark, *Greco-Roman Education*, 156.

15. The NRSV will be quoted for all scriptural texts unless otherwise noted.

16. On the fluidity and variety of both the textual and oral traditions connected with Israel's scriptures, see Stanley, *Paul and the Language of Scripture*, 31–80.

17. This is a maxim usage underlined by recurrence (see below), as evidenced by 2 Cor 10:17.

18. Snyman, "On Studying Figures," 97. Snyman follows the semantic theory in E. A. Nida et al., *Style and Discourse: With Special Reference to the Text of the Greek New Testament* (Cape Town: Bible Society of South Africa, 1983), 11–18. "The macrolevel deals primarily with the units of the text which are normally related semantically, while the rhetorical features on the microlevel serve to relate parts on the macrolevel or to signify other important relations" (Snyman, "Rhetorical Situation of Romans 8.31–39," 220–23).

19. Rhetors have a penchant for categorizing the figurative forms that maxims can take. Aristotle speaks of the self-evident maxim or the one with attached reason. *Ad Alexandrum* counsels creation of maxims through hyperbole or parallel. *Ad Herennium* discusses the simple and the double forms. Hermogenes catalogs those that are true or plausible; those that are simple, compound, or hyperbolic. Quintilian knows of formations built on interrogation, comparison, denial, similarity, admiration, and any other figure. See the discussion and references in chap. 1.

Modern scholars classify traditional sayings (proverbs, maxims) in the biblical material according to the structural analysis advanced by Alan Dundes, "On the Structure of the Proverb," in *The Wisdom of Many: Essays on the Proverb*, ed. Wolfgang Mieder and Alan Dundes (New York: Garland, 1981), 43–64. Cf. Carol R. Fontaine, *Traditional Sayings in the Old Testament: A Contextual Study* (Sheffield, England: Almond, 1982),

34–36; A. P. Winton, *The Proverbs of Jesus: Issues of History and Rhetoric,* JSNT Supplement Series 35 (Sheffield, England: JSOT, 1991), 36–44; Wilson, *Love without Pretense,* 24–39. The advantage of this structural classification is that it simplifies analysis to a binary system in which propositions compare and/or contrast. Identification is made easier for nonnative speakers who may not pick up necessary cues from intonation, grammar, syntax, style, or rhythm (see Fontaine, *Traditional Sayings,* 36, and Wilson, *Love without Pretense,* 38–39). The drawback to a structural analysis is that all cross-cultural material is evaluated together, forming a supercultural model that tends to obscure the ethnographical distinctions of a single culture's usage and development. For a full discussion of this issue, see Ben-Amos, "Analytical Categories," 286, and the discussion of method in Appendix B. This study has advanced with ethnographical particularism, isolating not only the Greco-Roman maxim but its variety of forms.

What is needed in the study of Greco-Roman maxims is not only the classification of maxim patterns based on certain common figures but also an account of the typical Greek word combinations and syntax patterns that accompany these figures. A study along these lines is Graydon F. Snyder, "The 'Tobspruch' in the New Testament," *New Testament Studies* 23 (1976): 117–20. I have not found others. Cf., however, the analysis of maxims in Latin speeches in H. V. Canter, "Rhetorical Elements in Livy's Direct Speeches," *American Journal of Philology* 38 (1917): 130–34.

20. Detailed under the discussion of the gnomic sentence in chap. 1 above.

21. Addressed in chap. 3 above under the discussion of 1 Corinthians 7.

22. See p. 23 and n. 11 above. Consistent brevity is found when examining the *sententiae* section (8.5.12–35) of Quintilian's discussion in *Institutio oratoria* 8.5. Further, brevity is also characteristic according to Quintilian's own testimony in 12.10.48, "For they [*sententiae*] strike the mind and often produce a decisive effect by one single blow, while their very brevity makes them cling to the memory, and the pleasure which they produce has the force of persuasion."

23. Detailed under the discussion of the moral *sententia* in chap. 1 above. Also see p. 23 and n. 13 above.

24. For *lumina* as a description of the *sententiae,* see Quintilian *Institutio oratoria* 8.5.28–30; 12.10.49.

25. Maxims are consistent with Snyman's definition (following Perelman) of a figure as that which has "a discernible form and a use that is different from the normal." "The concepts of the milieu, the audience and the point in a discourse are all important factors in identifying a figure" (see Snyman, "On Studying Figures," 100). Terence Y. Mullins ("Visit Talk in New Testament Letters," *Catholic Biblical Quarterly* 35 [1973]: 357) distinguishes "among three different ways to study the New Testament material — analysis by theme, by form, and by words." Only in the broadest (but still important!) category of "moral counsel" does the sum group of maxims constitute a theme. For the most part, we judge the identification of maxims as a form. For studies applying identification criteria to thematic material, see Mullins, "Visit Talk"; and Stanley N. Olson, "Epistolary Uses of Expressions of Self-Confidence," *Journal of Biblical Literature* 103 (1984): 585–97; and idem, "Pauline Expressions," 282–95.

26. Snyman agrees with Perelman against the study of figures as purely formal speech or as the description of effect apart from its role in argumentation. According to Perelman, the goal of studying figures is "to show how and in what respects the use of particular figures is explained by the requirements of argumentation." Snyman

properly criticizes Perelman for downplaying how the aesthetic effect of figures (that which "can provoke admiration or cause a rise and fall of attention") plays a supporting role in argumentation. This is particularly important with respect to maxim usage and the *ēthos* of the rhetor. See Snyman, "On Studying Figures," 101–2; cf. Ch. Perelman and L. Olbrechts-Tyteca, *The New Rhetoric: A Treatise on Argumentation*, trans. John Wilkinson and Purcell Weaver (Notre Dame, Ind.: University of Notre Dame Press, 1969), 171.

27. According to Seneca's discussion of Latro's preparation examined above in chap. 1, 14.

28. Maxims came to be connected to certain topoi (places) or commonly discussed moral topics in the ancient world. See Betz, *Galatians*, 220–37, for a discussion of a number of maxims connected to the friendship topos. See Abraham J. Malherbe, "Hellenistic Moralists and the New Testament," in *Aufstieg und Niedergang der römischen Welt* 2:26/1, eds. H. Temporini and W. Haase (Berlin and New York: Walter de Gruyter, 1992), 320–25, for a discussion of the topoi in general and the presence of maxims within them.

29. A moral *sententia* created from the symbolic universe of the believing community in which peace forms a central idea. See, among other places, Rom 5:1; 14:7; and Phil 4:7, 9. I am assuming that 1 Cor 7:15 is the core of the *sententia;* 14:33 is shaped for the argumentation that is pertinent to the discussion under way there.

30. See the recent assessment of the situation in Pogoloff, *Logos and Sophia*, 7–35, 71–95; also the important discussion in Wilhelm Wuellner, "Where Is Rhetorical Criticism Taking Us?" *Catholic Biblical Quarterly* 49 (1987): 448–63, and the more reserved evaluation of Mitchell, *Rhetoric of Reconciliation*, 1–19.

31. Kennedy, *New Testament Interpretation*, 3–12; Pogoloff, *Logos and Sophia*, 10–26. See also Appendix B, notes 13 and 14 below.

32. Mack, *Rhetoric and the New Testament*, 24, 93–102.

33. The study is argued according to the generally accepted principles of investigation and evidence, and its resulting inferences are to be presented in a way that invites verification and dialogue. See Edgar Krentz, *The Historical-Critical Method* (Philadelphia: Fortress, 1975). The social construction of reality is also important, and the role of maxims in the social construction of knowledge is explicitly pointed out in Berger and Luckmann, *Social Construction of Reality*, 94, and Theissen, "Sociological Interpretation," 182–86.

34. These issues are clearly set out in Terence J. Keegan, *Interpreting the Bible: A Popular Introduction to Biblical Hermeneutics* (New York: Paulist, 1985), 24–39. A poignant critique of ahistorical literary theory can be found in Terry Eagleton, *Literary Theory: An Introduction* (Minneapolis: University of Minnesota Press, 1983), 194–217. Cf. Pogoloff, *Logos and Sophia*, 79–91.

35. Kennedy, *New Testament Interpretation*, 3–4.

36. The rhetorical situation or exigence was explicated by Lloyd Bitzer, "The Rhetorical Situation," *Philosophy and Rhetoric* 1 (1968): 1–14. According to Pogoloff (*Logos and Sophia*, 78): "Bitzer analyzes those constituents of a situation which both prompt and constrain the rhetoric of a speaker or writer. He defines rhetorical discourse as that which 'functions ultimately to produce action or change. [Such a] discourse comes into existence because of some specific condition which invites utterance.' The situation is constituted by an exigence ('an imperfection marked by urgency'), an audience, and con-

straints inherent in the situation. The speaker or writer 'finds himself obliged to speak at a given moment...to respond appropriately to the situation.'" Cf. Arthur B. Miller, "Rhetorical Exigence," *Philosophy and Rhetoric* 5 (1972): 111–18.

37. "[T]he three species are judicial, which seeks to bring about a judgment about events of the past; deliberative, which aims at effecting a decision about future action, often in the very immediate future; and epideictic, which celebrates or condemns someone or something, not seeking an immediate judgment or action, but increasing or undermining assent to some value" (Kennedy, *New Testament Interpretation*, 36).

38. These stages are taken from the initial methodology of Kennedy in ibid., 33–38. A discussion of Kennedy's method is undertaken in detail by Wuellner, "Rhetorical Criticism," 455–60. Kennedy's method has been further discussed and expanded in Duane F. Watson, *Invention, Arrangement, and Style: Rhetorical Criticism of Jude and 2 Peter*, SBL Dissertation Series 104 (Atlanta: Scholars Press, 1988), 1–28. Cf. the emphasis on the "patterns of argumentation" in Mack, *Rhetoric and the New Testament*, 31–48.

39. Kennedy, *New Testament Interpretation*, 33.

40. Mitchell, *Rhetoric of Reconciliation*, 20. As deliberative oratory, 1 Corinthians argues for the advantageousness, the necessity, the expediency, and the moral good of concord in the community.

41. The thesis statement of 1 Cor 1:10 is restated in a more developed form in 16:13–14 as a ring-device. See Wuellner, "Pauline Argumentation," 182–83.

42. This has been amply demonstrated by Mitchell, *Rhetoric of Reconciliation*, 20–64.

43. The critique of Mitchell on this point is penetrating. A number of studies force these categories on the material and become less than convincing. "[The] function of each part is determined by the compositional whole and cannot be correctly determined apart from it" (ibid., 15–16, and esp. n. 52).

44. On the mixing of the three genres as normative, see Brian R. Vickers, *In Defense of Rhetoric* (Oxford: Clarendon, 1988), 58, and the discussion in Pogoloff, *Logos and Sophia*, 91–95.

45. See 1 Corinthians 1–4, "Is it appropriate to attach oneself to human leaders?"; 1 Corinthians 8, "Is it appropriate to eat meat sacrificed to idols?"; 1 Corinthians 9, "Is the one who leaves his or her right unexercised still free?"; 1 Cor 10:23–11:1, "How do believers exercise their individual rights in freedom, and how do they respond when their right is not agreed upon by another in the community?"

46. The rhetorical pattern of "refining" is shown to stand behind Paul's maxim argumentation in this passage. See the discussion of this text in chap. 3.

47. See the discussion of 1 Corinthians 1–4 above in chap. 3; Paul integrates oblique argumentation, the use of personal examples, and maxim argumentation into the arrangement of the section.

48. All indications suggest that Paul is a creative rhetor who adapts the techniques, forms, and patterns of rhetoric to his purposes. The rhetorical handbooks are a summing up of rhetorical practices for the purpose of training. There is no indication, however, that their counsel can be synthesized into one overall pattern of argumentation that is applicable to all (or even most) texts. Quintilian, indeed, states to the contrary, "For these rules have not the formal authority of laws or decrees of the plebs, but are, with all they contain, the children of expediency. I will not deny that it is generally expedient to conform to such rules, otherwise I should not be writing now; but if our friend expediency suggests some other course to us, why, we shall disregard the authority of the professors

and follow her. . . . The orator's task covers a large ground, is extremely varied and develops some new aspect almost every day, so that the last word on the subject will never have been said" (*Institutio oratoria* 2.13.6–7, 17). Cf. the evaluation of Frank W. Hughes, "The Rhetoric of Reconciliation: 2 Corinthians 1.1–2.13 and 7.5–8.24," in *Persuasive Artistry: Studies in New Testament Rhetoric in Honor of George A. Kennedy*, ed. Duane F. Watson, JSNT Supplementary Series 50 (Sheffield, England: JSOT, 1991), 289–90.

49. In the matter of approach, then, I side with the more flexible method in Kennedy, *New Testament Interpretation*, 3–31, over the more rigid "patterns of argumentation" methodology in Mack, *Rhetoric and the New Testament*, 31–48.

50. This initial investigation of 1 Corinthians 1–10 should be helpful in identifying Paul's patterns of usage that could be profitably applied to maxim analysis in the rest of the letter and in the larger Pauline corpus.

51. See n. 5 above.

52. How Paul proceeds with his rhetorical argument and maxim argumentation indicates how he conducts his moral counsel among the Corinthians: with a high regard for the reasoning processes of his audience, with a fundamental restraint in exercising absolute authority, and with a genuine concern for both preserving the individual's freedom and promoting community sensitivity. This provides a window through which the rest of the letter should be read. See the section, "Maxims, Freedom, and Rights," in Conclusions.

Chapter 3: The Function of Maxims in Paul's Argumentation: 1 Corinthians 1–10

1. For 1 Corinthians as deliberative rhetoric, see Mitchell, *Rhetoric of Reconciliation*, 20–64, 184–86.

2. We should not posit a situation, as does Gordon D. Fee (*The First Epistle to the Corinthians*, New International Commentary on the New Testament [Grand Rapids: Eerdmans, 1987], 5–10), in which Paul stands against the entire church. Paul counsels a community who have formed divisions among themselves around a number of issues leading to pride and boasting. See William Baird, "'One against Another': Intra-church Conflict in 1 Corinthians," in *The Conversation Continues: Studies in Paul and John: In Honor of J. Louis Martyn*, ed. Robert T. Fortna and Beverly R. Gaventa (Nashville: Abingdon, 1990), 116–36, esp. 130–31.

3. This marks chaps. 1–4 as a unified section of the larger letter. See Nils A. Dahl, "Paul and the Church at Corinth according to 1 Corinthians 1:10–4:21," in *Studies in Paul: Theology for the Early Christian Mission* (Minneapolis: Augsburg, 1977), 46. Wuellner has noted further that the restatement of 1:10 in 16:13–14 holds the letter together in its entirety and demonstrates a clear theme throughout: be of the same mind (see Wuellner, "Pauline Argumentation," 182–83).

4. Dahl, "Paul and the Church at Corinth," 52, 55; cf. Mitchell, *Rhetoric of Reconciliation*, 207–13, for a more deliberative than apologetic perspective on this point.

There is general agreement concerning the overall structure of 1 Corinthians 1–4. The section forms a portion of 1:1–6:20 — typically noted as Paul's response to oral news from Corinth. The subdivisions of 1–4 are made up of well-defined units on which most commentators agree with minor variations. Cf. C. K. Barrett, *The First Epistle to the Corinthians*, Harper's NT Commentaries (New York: Harper and Row, 1968), 28; Fee, *First Corinthians*, 21; F. W. Grosheide, *Commentary on the First Epistle to the Corinthians*, New

International Commentary on the New Testament (Grand Rapids: Eerdmans, 1953), 9; Charles H. Talbert, *Reading Corinthians: A Literary and Theological Commentary on 1 and 2 Corinthians* (New York: Crossroad, 1987), 3–11; Conzelmann, *1 Corinthians*, vii.

Benjamin Fiore's division is followed here: 1:4–17 (thanksgiving and exhortation); 1:18–2:5, 2:6–3:4, 3:5–4:5 (paradigmatic sections); 4:6–13 (direct charge against status and its apostolic contrast); 4:14–21 (reiteration of Paul's exhortation and a challenge to the arrogant) (Benjamin Fiore, "'Covert Allusion' in 1 Corinthians 1–4," *Catholic Biblical Quarterly* 47 [1985]: 87). Nearly identical in division is Archibald Robertson and Alfred Plummer, *A Critical and Exegetical Commentary on the First Epistle of Paul to the Corinthians*, International Critical Commentary, 2d ed. (Edinburgh: T. and T. Clark, 1978), 1–93. Fiore's division distinguishes sections based on Paul's use of examples, thereby giving attention to a partition based on rhetorical technique and argumentation. A fuller discussion of the use of examples in hortatory letters can be found in Benjamin Fiore, *Personal Example in the Socratic and Pastoral Epistles*, Analecta Biblica 105 (Rome: Biblical Institute, 1986), esp. 164–90.

5. "I have applied [*metaschēmatisa*] all this [these things] to myself and Apollos for your benefit" (1 Cor 4:6). For *metaschēmatizein* as covert allusion as depicted in the rhetorical handbooks, see Fiore, "Covert Allusion," 87–93, and Peter Lampe, "Theological Wisdom and the 'Word of the Cross,'" *Interpretation* 44 (1990): 128–31. Cf. John T. Fitzgerald, *Cracks in an Earthen Vessel: An Examination of the Catalogues of Hardships in the Corinthian Correspondence*, SBL Dissertation Series 99 (Atlanta: Scholars Press, 1988), 119–22. I follow Fiore ("Covert Allusion," 93–95) in taking *tauta* (these things) in 4:6 as referring to all of 1 Corinthians 1–4. The suggestion of covert allusion, with short but pertinent elaboration, was made as early as Robertson and Plummer, *1 Corinthians*, 80–81. For a contrary interpretation based on works that do not consider the rhetorical nature of the term *metaschēmatizein*, see Fee, *First Corinthians*, 166–67. On figurative oblique speech in general, see Frederick Ahl, "The Art of Safe Criticism in Greece and Rome," *American Journal of Philology* 105 (1984): 174–208.

6. "The *metaschēmatismos*, therefore, consists in putting forward the names of those not really responsible for the *staseis* instead of the names of others who were more to blame" (Robertson and Plummer, *1 Corinthians*, 81).

7. I am in agreement with a number of modern commentators who see no actual parties gathered around Apollos, Peter, Paul, or Christ (this latter case as a Pauline *reductio ad absurdum*). See Fee, *First Corinthians*, 59–60. The illustrations and examples for emulation are primarily concerned with Paul himself or Paul and Apollos together (2:1–5; 3:1–4; 3:5–4:5). It is not evident from the information available that the community is divided over differences between Paul's and Apollos's teaching content (for a penetrating critique of this position as advanced in various forms by Pearson, Horsley, and Davis, see Fee, *First Corinthians*, 13–14, 49) or between their rhetorical styles (a hypothetical reconstruction advanced by Pogoloff, *Logos and Sophia*, 173–96). Richard A. Horsley ("Wisdom of Word and Words of Wisdom in Corinth," *Catholic Biblical Quarterly* 39 [1977]: 224–39) is right to point out that the Corinthian wisdom is derived from eloquence and salvific knowledge and that these two elements combined easily in the philosophic culture of the Hellenistic world. That the Corinthian wisdom derives from a specifically Hellenistic-Jewish tradition such as Philo or Wisdom of Solomon, however, cannot be established without speculating on the content of Apollos's teaching.

What is clear from Paul's depiction of the situation at Corinth is that divisions have sprung up around moral positions with their respective proponents only obliquely identified (3:21 — "let no one boast about human leaders"). These positions connect in some ways to rhetoric, status, and prideful boasting.

I grant that Paul's or Apollos's rhetorical patterns, especially those advancing moral counsel, may have been imitated by the Corinthians. These rhetorical conventions, however, were widely available from general education and spoken example (see chap. 2 above) and need not be attributed directly to Paul or Apollos. That the Corinthian positions were advanced with maxims is demonstrated below.

8. Cf. Hans Dieter Betz, "The Problem of Rhetoric and Theology according to the Apostle Paul," in *L'Apôtre Paul: Personalité, style et conception du ministère*, ed. A. Vanhoye, Bibliotheca ephemeridum theologicarum lovaniensium (Louvain: Louvain University Press, 1986), 25–26. It should be granted that Paul could have indicated both people and positions, but this would have negated the positive effects of his argumentation through covert allusion.

9. See Wuellner, "Pauline Argumentation," 182–83, for Paul's employment of the *genos endoxon* (an agreeable approach) to govern his approach in 1 Corinthians 1–4.

10. Paul's employment of covert allusion is more concerned with maintaining a hearing than with fear of reprisal for speaking out. As Paul employs it, the covert allusion is not strictly kept; Paul openly censures and exhorts the community (2:5; 3:1–4, 18, 21; 4:1–2, 6–13). See Fiore, "Covert Allusion," 91–93, 95–96.

11. Ibid., 87–88, 95–96. Cf. idem, *Personal Example*, 169–71. See also the comprehensive evidence offered by Mitchell, *Rhetoric of Reconciliation*, 39–60.

12. Fiore, *Personal Example*, 168–78, esp. 173–74.

13. "My study, in calling attention to the use of example in chaps. 1–4 as a feature in the 'covert allusion,' finds a conceptual and rhetorical element which can be shown to bridge both sections of the letter" (Fiore, "Covert Allusion," 86 n. 2). See also idem, *Personal Example*, 183–84.

14. Pogoloff (*Logos and Sophia*, 108–72) has shown that the Greek terms *logos* and *sophia* (1:17; 2:4, 13) are to be closely associated with rhetoric and its attendant indications of status.

The high profile given rhetoric and its worldly status in 1 Corinthians 1–4 is not only attributable to its identification of the wise person but also attributable to its usage by the Corinthians as a vehicle of expression for other status-seeking positions or endeavors. See Mitchell, *Rhetoric of Reconciliation*, 211 n. 132.

15. "[T]he Corinthians did not simply accept the gospel Paul gave them, but went ahead and interpreted that gospel in terms of their hellenistic religiosity." They claimed "every form of eloquence and every form of knowledge" (1:5) that warranted "excesses and abuses of freedom" (Betz, "Rhetoric and Theology," 24–28).

16. Such behavior no doubt is connected in part to status distinctions based on social position and economic disparity. For a discussion of the status terms in 1:26 (cf. 4:8) and the more concrete differentiations indicated by lawsuits, the ability to buy meat, and excessive dinners, see the studies in Theissen, *Social Setting*, 69–174. The study of Dale B. Martin, "Tongues of Angels and Other Status Indicators," *Journal of the American Academy of Religion* 59 (1991): 547–89, should now be added to this discussion.

17. This "challenge" may be indirect rather than overt. There is very little evidence that the Corinthians felt censured by Paul and are now responding in kind (contra Hurd, *Origin of I Corinthians*). There are indications that the Corinthians have misunderstand-

ings about the ongoing correspondence between themselves and Paul (5:9–13). How one "mirror reads" the text in 1 Corinthians 1–4 generally determines how much and how strong an opposition against Paul is posited.

It is possible to read the text up to 4:18 without positing contentious opposition to Paul. In 1 Cor 2:6–16, Paul asserts that there is a wisdom of God beyond the worldly wisdom the Corinthians have settled for. Paul exemplifies one who has access to God's wisdom; the Corinthians are too immature to receive it because of their divisions! (3:1–4). In 4:1–5, Paul continues the theme of judgment of leaders and offers himself as an example of one who self-tests in anticipation of God's judgment. Paul's hypothetical allusion to the Corinthians judging him (4:3; or taking him to the law court) shows his knowledge of their character and anticipates discussion in 6:1–8. Thus 4:6–13 is ironic and intended (indirectly—Paul denies it in 4:14) to shame the Corinthians.

Creative mirror reading often posits opposition and direct challenge to Paul by finding "quotations" of the Corinthian opponents in the text; see, for example, A. C. Thiselton, "Realized Eschatology at Corinth," *New Testament Studies* 24 (1978): 510–26 (1 Cor 2:16–17); and Talbert, *Reading Corinthians*, 8 (1 Cor 4:2). Note the pertinent caution on such mirror-reading endeavors in 1 Corinthians in Baird, "One against Another," 119. On the constraints of mirror-reading in general, see George Lyons, *Pauline Autobiography: Toward a New Understanding*, SBL Dissertation Series 73 (Atlanta: Scholars Press, 1985), 76–83, and John M. G. Barclay, "Mirror-Reading a Polemical Letter: Galatians as a Test Case," *Journal of the Study of the New Testament* 31 (1987): 73–93.

18. Fiore, "Covert Allusion," 97–101; cf. Mitchell, *Rhetoric of Reconciliation*, 209.

19. Cf. Fee, *First Corinthians*, 53, who posits an *A, B, A'* structure on grammatical rather than conceptual grounds.

20. The idea of spoken expression (*en tē autē gnōmē*) is veiled in this case by the RSV translation "judgment" and the NRSV translation "purpose." Cf. Barrett, *First Epistle*, 41–42; Grosheide, *First Corinthians*, 34; Fiore, "Covert Allusion," 87.

21. *Gnōmē* may be apposite to *nous* in 1:10d, either as an equivalent term (Conzelmann, *1 Corinthians*, 32) or as restatement with slight refinement (that is, final state of a mental process = RSV "judgment"). For parallel examples in the ancient literature, see L. L. Welborn, "A Conciliatory Principle in 1 Cor. 4:6," *Novum Testamentum* 29 (1987): 335–36 and n. 81. Or *gnōmē* (*A'*) as "maxim" may be intended to hark back and draw together Paul's appeal to the unity of spoken expression in 1:10b (*A*).

22. That Paul employs such an argumentative scheme has been noted by Brendan Byrne, "Ministry and Maturity in 1 Corinthians 3," *Australian Biblical Review* 35 (1987): 84–85, and Mitchell, *Rhetoric of Reconciliation*, 93–94.

23. A complete exegesis of 1 Corinthians 1–4 is not possible here. The more immediate context of the maxims is investigated with the larger context of 1–4 in view.

24. On the value of using a digression to advance an argument, see Wuellner, "Pauline Argumentation," 179–81. I mark the digression from 1:18 to 1:31 because 2:1 picks up the major thrust of 1:17. Cf. ibid., 185 (1:19–3:21) and Lampe, "Theological Wisdom," 119 (1:18–2:16).

25. Fiore, *Personal Example*, 170.

26. We can assume that this word of the cross (with a "demonstration of the Spirit and of power" [2:4–5]) is quite familiar to the Corinthians as the foundation of their coming-to-faith.

27. Paul's concept of the wisdom of God, now closely associated with Christ Jesus

(1:30), is informed by Hellenistic-Jewish apocalyptic ideas such as mystery, reversal of values (informed by the prophetic critique of God's stance with the less fortunate; cf. 1:26–28), and the unfolding of God's plan and purposes for God's people. For a recent and important discussion, see E. Elizabeth Johnson, *The Function of Apocalyptic and Wisdom Traditions in Romans 9–11*, SBL Dissertation Series 109 (Atlanta: Scholars Press, 1989), 4–109. Cf. James A. Davis, *Wisdom and Spirit: An Investigation of 1 Corinthians 1.18–3.20 against the Background of Jewish Sapiential Traditions in the Greco-Roman Period* (New York: University Press of America, 1984). Paul elaborates on this true wisdom of God in 2:6–16 and then admonishes the Corinthians in 3:1–4 for not being able to receive it in full (but note 15:51). See Conzelmann, *1 Corinthians*, 59.

28. See Lampe, "Theological Wisdom," 120–25, for an assessment of Greek wisdom aspirations and the seeking of signs by the Jews. Lampe sees 1:18–25 as a covert reproach of the Corinthians who have redefined the word of the cross into a vehicle for proud boasting in power and freedom. Such a boast is on par with the vain seeking after wisdom found in the world.

29. Conzelmann, *1 Corinthians*, 48 and n. 91, adequately explains the formal elements and usage as a maxim in terms that correspond to what has been advanced in this study as a gnomic-sentence form.

30. While Paul has the entire community in mind here, his thrust is to the many called by God in their lowly status. They should not attain to worldly standards and status through an attachment to persons or positions. The low-status members must learn to say no to higher-status members who would run the community according to worldly ways. On Paul's recognition of a small minority of higher status members in the Corinthian community based on the terms *sophoi, dynatoi,* and *eugeneis,* see Theissen, *Social Setting*, 69–119.

31. Ibid. and n. 28.

32. What has not been given adequate attention in these verses is the logic of Paul's argumentation. Paul argues for *continuity* in the lives of his converts based on their *conversion experience.* Paul's logic in 1:26–31 is similar to that pivotal question in Gal 3:2 — "The only thing I want to learn from you is this: Did you receive the Spirit by doing the works of the law or by believing what you heard?" According to Paul, what was adequate at the beginning remains adequate (and advantageous) in the continuing believer's life. In Galatians, faith working through love is sufficient; in 1 Corinthians, one's state of weakness that prohibits boasting in anything but the Lord is ample. In each problem situation there is an offering of something more: in Galatians, it is a "full" or "complete" conversion by adherence to the law; in 1 Corinthians, it is increased power, status, or freedom through alliance with human leaders. The adequacy of one's calling establishes a fundamental position from which Paul will base his moral counsel in 1 Corinthians 7.

33. "Jeremiah expresses a general truth in 9:23 which is valid for all times. It does not refer to a particular occurrence in his prophecy of doom, but he describes that quality which God most desires in man, and in which a man may legitimately take pride, that is to boast of the Lord's love, justice, and righteousness" (F. S. Malan, "The Use of the Old Testament in 1 Corinthians," *Neotestamentica* 14 (1981): 141).

34. Rearrangement and substitution by Paul can be noted by comparison:

all' ē toutō kauchasthō ho kauchōmenos (Jer 9:22, LXX)
ho kauchōmenos en kuriō kauchasthō (1 Cor 1:31)

No doubt Jer 9:23 (and 1 Sam 2:10, LXX) has also influenced the content of 1:30 in Paul's mind. But that such an echo would be perceived by the Corinthian audience remains unclear. For full discussion, see ibid., 140–42.

35. On the use of example for the elaboration of the *gnōmē*, see chap. 1, pp. 7–8. Cf. Fiore, *Personal Example*, 42–44, 179–80.

36. "And I came to you in weakness and in fear and in much trembling. My speech and my proclamation were not with plausible words of wisdom, but with a demonstration of the Spirit and of power" (2:3–4). What constituted "a demonstration of the Spirit and of power" in Paul's initial preaching remains unclear, though explanations have been advanced. Cf. the discussion in Fee, *First Corinthians*, 95–96.

37. Pogoloff, *Logos and Sophia*, 108–19.

38. On the nature of Paul's counterwisdom, see n. 27 above.

39. On the rhetorical strategy of these growth metaphors, see Mitchell, *Rhetoric of Reconciliation*, 99–111, 212–13.

40. Fee makes a connection at 3:14 with 3:8b (*First Corinthians*, 143). Paul makes a point of his foundation-laying in 3:10–11 (pointing forward to 4:14–16), but the thrust of 3:10–15 as a whole is summed up in the conclusion drawn in 3:14–15.

41. Robertson and Plummer, *First Corinthians*, 61.

42. Most commentators expand Paul's counsel in 3:10–17 to the broader Corinthian community. While this holds true, the analogy of Paul and Apollos as cooperative leaders within the community in 3:5–9 (reiterated in 4:1) tends incorrectly to fall from view in 3:10–17. Cf. Barrett, *First Epistle*, 86–92; Conzelmann, *1 Corinthians*, 75–78; Grosheide, *First Corinthians*, 83–90; Robertson and Plummer, *First Corinthians*, 59–68. The illustration of Paul and Apollos (and Peter) as a covert allusion, however, has an element of reproach throughout for leaders who advance positions around which followers boast and exclude others.

Paul's shift to "if anyone" or "if any man" (see RSV) in 3:10–17 is first a generalization from Apollos and himself to community leaders and then secondarily a generalization to the community at large. The illustration, then, remains both (1) an example for proper action and assessment by community leaders and (2) an example for how the community as a whole should perceive these leaders and make assessment of them (and indirectly themselves) as well. Cf. the position of Fee, *First Corinthians*, 135, and Gregory W. Dawes, "'But If You Can Gain Your Freedom' (1 Corinthians 7:17–24)," *Catholic Biblical Quarterly* 52 (1990): 686–87, for a similar audience in mind.

43. Apart from the stern warning, 3:16–17 anticipates the purity issues of chaps. 5–6 in general and the concluding verses at 6:19–20 in particular.

44. Conzelmann (*1 Corinthians*, 79) speaks of a "cycle" from 1:18ff. to 3:23.

45. Ibid.

46. To this point in the letter only Paul's maxim in 1:31 and the injunction to leaders (builders) in 3:10 have been imperatival. "Let no one deceive himself or herself" (1 Cor 3:18; my trans. based on RSV) should be taken with both what precedes and what follows it. As Paul addresses the wider community directly he breaks from the covert allusion (cf. 3:1–4) and gives less cover to the community leaders ("So let no one boast about human leaders" [3:21]). "It seems to involve an abrupt change from the *oratio obliqua* to the *oratio recta*. It marks the transition from explanation to exhortation" (Robertson and Plummer, *First Corinthians*, 71).

47. This injunction is thought to be the proper conclusion to the larger section from

1:18 to 3:23. See Conzelmann, *1 Corinthians*, 80; Grosheide, *First Corinthians*, 93–94; Fee, *First Corinthians*, 152–53.

48. According to Diogenes Laertius 6.72, the Cynic Diogenes of Sinope argued in syllogistic fashion that "all things belong to the gods"; "the gods are friends to the wise, and friends share all things in common"; therefore, "all things are the property of the wise." The Stoic sage is the one "to whom all things are permissible" (Dio Chrysostom *Orationes* 3:10) because the sage correctly distinguishes virtue from vice, uses indifferents (*adiaphora*) to virtuous ends, and exercises rigorous self-discipline. For a discussion of these maxims and their moral posturing of unbridled freedom for the Cynic and of more restrained freedom for the Stoic, see Stanley K. Stowers, "A 'Debate' over Freedom: 1 Corinthians 6:12–20," in *Christian Teaching: Studies in Honor of LeMoine G. Lewis*, ed. Everett Ferguson (Abilene, Tex.: Abilene Christian University, 1981), 62–68. For a full treatment on the freedom of the sage as related to the Stoic and Cynic maxims, see James L. Jaquette, *Discerning What Counts: The Function of the Adiaphora Topos in Paul's Letters*, SBL Dissertation Series 146 (Atlanta: Scholars Press, 1995), 84–91. For references to Stoic and Cynic freedom maxims in *Stoicorum verterum fragmenta*, see Robert M. Grant, "The Wisdom of the Corinthians," in *The Joy of Study: Papers on New Testament and Related Subjects Presented to Honor F. C. Grant*, ed. S. E. Johnson (New York: Macmillan, 1951), 52.

As compact, concluding statements of a strikingly expansive moral claim, these Stoic and Cynic freedom maxims are best described as moral *sententiae*. As shall be noted, Paul is not content to state his maxim formulation so generally. Instead, he crafts an elaborate gnomic sentence.

49. Constructed in the form of a doxology according to Grosheide, *First Corinthians*, 91; cf. Fee, *First Corinthians*, 154. For rhetorical description apart from rhetorical function, see Conzelmann, *1 Corinthians*, 80, and Robertson and Plummer, *First Corinthians*, 72–73.

50. The maxim's supplement, "whether Paul or Apollos or Cephas or the world or life or death or the present or the future" (3:22), draws out and enumerates "all things" to the limit. It is inclusive of all persons, things, and events and, therefore, leads to freedom. See Conzelmann, *1 Corinthians*, 80–81.

51. The question, of course, is whether this benefit is for the individual or the community or both. And if the interests of the individual and the community are in tension, how does one proceed? Paul has offered two growth metaphors (God's field, God's building) and one with respect to holiness (God's temple) in an effort to view individuals as equals and the community as based on concord. But he must take the rest of the letter to counsel appropriate freedom in specific moral matters.

52. The syntax of the phrase, *hymeis de Christou*, is significant. It is parallel to the slogans in 1:11 and 3:4 in its use of the nominative pronoun with the genitive of possession. It is antithetical to these slogans with its referent as Christ (assuming *egō Christou* was *ad absurdum*) and with its plurality of address representing a community rather than an individual perspective ("you, the community"; cf. 3:9, 16–17).

53. "Origen points out that the Greeks have a saying, *Panta tou sophou estin*, but St Paul was the first to say, *Panta tou hagiou estin*" (Robertson and Plummer, *First Corinthians*, 72).

54. The form of the gnomic sentence is maxim, supplement explicating "all things,"

restatement of maxim, and further supplement qualifying possession of all things by virtue of being possessed by Christ and God.

55. The catalyst for this overestimation is the identification with leaders or positions for pride in social standing (cf. 4:10). Fee (*First Corinthians,* 166) reads far too much specificity into Paul's statement with "they are in fact 'puffed up' in favor of 'the one' (probably Apollos, as we shall note momentarily) and over against 'the other' (Paul)." Cf. Robertson and Plummer, *1 Corinthians,* 79, 82; and Barrett, *First Epistle,* 107. For a more adequate view see Baird, "'One against the Other,'" 116, 130–31; cf. Grosheide, *First Corinthians,* 104.

56. Grosheide correctly connects Paul's contrast of *logos* and *dynamis* in 4:18–20 with the earlier contrasts of *sophia logou* and *dynamis* in 1:17ff. and 2:1–5 (Grosheide, *First Corinthians,* 115).

57. That Paul is attempting to enhance his *ēthos* in 1 Corinthians 4 is also a perspective of Mitchell, *Rhetoric of Reconciliation,* 209 (without reference to maxim usage).

58. For full discussion of maxims and *ēthos,* see the section "Speaker and Audience" in chap. 1.

59. Clearly, 1 Cor 4:1–5 is a transitional section. It functions as a concluding example-pattern for the community's perception of leaders and for community leaders' perception of themselves (3:5–4:5; and see n. 33 above) as drawn from Paul's metaphorical illustrations of the community as God's field and God's building with Paul and Apollos as co-workers, the injunction not to boast in human beings in 3:21, and his maxim in 3:21–23. But the section also begins an affirmation of Paul's own character as trustworthy before the community and God (4:1–21) — an affirmation directly appealed to again in 1 Cor 7:25. The section is viewed from both perspectives here, but its consideration as part of 1 Corinthians 4 as a whole seeks to elucidate the latter perspective more fully.

60. The *oikonomos* designates a steward (often a slave) responsible for managing the household. The steward directed the duties of others and was entrusted with the supplies but was accountable to the master of the house as slave. See Fee, *First Corinthians,* 159; and Robertson and Plummer, *1 Corinthians,* 74–75.

61. "*Zēteitai en tois oikonomois, hina pistos tis heurethē.*" According to Fee (*First Corinthians,* 160), the Greek word *zēteitai* (required) carries a "proverbial sense." *Pistos* is emphasized by position in the second clause, and the use of *tis* (anyone) rather than *pantes* (all) or simply *heurethēsan* ("that they be found," as the NRSV translates) provides a degree of more general reflection. Fee (ibid.) recognizes 4:2 as a "general maxim."

62. Paul continually emphasizes the eschatological nature of God's purposes in progress: the present age moves toward an end marked by judgment (1:7–8; 2:1; 3:12–15; 4:4–5).

63. I am in agreement with Mitchell, *Rhetoric of Reconciliation,* and Fiore, "Covert Allusion," that 4:1–5 is deliberative rhetoric built on Paul's example and not the beginning of an overt polemical defense. See n. 17 above. Paul's maxim usage in 4:2 supports his example.

That Paul is defending himself against an attack of judgment by the Corinthians is upheld by Fee, *First Corinthians,* 4–16 (who takes up this point as his pivotal interpretive guideline); Barrett, *First Epistle,* 101; and Grosheide, *First Corinthians,* 100. The position of Conzelmann and that of Robertson and Plummer remain neutral.

64. Robertson and Plummer, *1 Corinthians*, 76.

65. "For who sees anything different in you?" (4:7).

66. "What have you that you did not receive? If then you received it, why do you boast as if it were not a gift?" (4:7).

67. As indicated by the enigmatic proverbial phrase *to mē ha gegraptai* (nothing beyond what is written; NRSV). The *to* is undoubtedly a quotation indicator, so it can be assumed that the Corinthians knew exactly what Paul meant. Conzelmann's assessment of the phrase is that it is "unintelligible" (*1 Corinthians*, 86). For a thorough review of interpretation, see Welborn, "A Conciliatory Principle," 320–33. Welborn (333–46) advances an interpretation that places the phrase in the context of deliberative speeches on concord. He finds an allusion to the phrase in references to the arbitrator's written agreement that was to be held to by previously factional parties. If this is true, Paul's usage of the phrase "not to go beyond what is written" is proleptic and at least one step removed from the actual situation. For there is no agreement yet in Corinth, and Paul appeals from his privileged position of community founder and not as selected arbitrator.

Fiore advances a more convincing suggestion. In 4:6, Paul and Apollos have become a "figure" for the community. They function as an illustration of cooperation, a guide for patterning community relationships. By tracing the pattern of their cooperative conduct as any school boy traced the letters of the schoolmaster without going beyond what was written, the Corinthians might learn behavioral patterns of unity and avoid being arrogant with one another. See Fiore, *Personal Example*, 173–74 and n. 24. Also see Fitzgerald, *Cracks in an Earthen Vessel*, 122–27.

68. The twice-repeated *ēdē* ("Already you have all you want! Already you have become rich") followed by *chōris* ("Quite apart from us you have become kings [are reigning]!") in 4:8 gives every indication that some Corinthians believe they have obtained the fullness of wisdom and its resulting freedom. Again, the background is most likely connected to Stoic and Cynic ideals concerning the freedom of the wise man. "Every virtue was ascribed to the wise man, who alone led his life in accordance with reason. He was not deceived and did not deceive; he did all things well; he was not affected by evil; he was happy, rich, handsome, free, the only true king. Since reason instructed him, he was the only good man" (Grant, "Wisdom of the Corinthians," 51). Cf. *Stoicorum Veterum Fragmenta* (ed. von Arnim) 3:85–89, 150–57, and Diogenes Laertius 7.117–25. These philosophical themes were common property of the day (Grant, "Wisdom of the Corinthians," 53), so they need not have been transmitted through Hellenistic Judaism by way of Apollos, as suggested by Horsley, "Wisdom of Word," 232–36, and idem, " 'How Can Some of You Say That There Is No Resurrection of the Dead?' Spiritual Elitism in Corinth," *Novum Testamentum* 20 (1978): 207–12.

69. Barrett, *First Epistle*, 108–9; Conzelmann, *1 Corinthians*, 87–88; Fee, *First Corinthians*, 172–73; Thiselton, "Realized Eschatology," 510–26. These commentators assume that Paul's portrayal accurately reflects the mind-set of those Corinthians who claim to be wise. See, however, the next note.

70. The term is Horsley's, and he advances an appropriate caution about assuming that the Corinthians believed they were already resurrected and living in the new age (Horsley, "Spiritual Elitism in Corinth," 203–7). More probably, some had ascribed to a Hellenistic dualism that emphasized the perfection and immortality of the soul through wisdom over bodily existence. In such a case, the spiritual inspiration of some Corinthians reinforced their recognition of being wise to a point that they began to interpret

their faith in terms of Hellenistic culture — wise, rich, and reigning in status (1 Corinthians 1–4); freedom from constraints in the world and worship (1 Corinthians 5–14); and continued immortality without bodily existence (1 Corinthians 15).

71. This perspective should not discount other factors, such as higher- and lower-status distinctions among community members, contributing to Corinthian divisiveness. See n. 16 above and Baird, "'One against the Other,'" 130–31.

72. For a detailed analysis of this *peristasis* catalog, see Fitzgerald, *Cracks in an Earthen Vessel*, 117–48.

73. In the latter case, Paul would have substituted "in Christ" for (a hypothetically posited) "in life."

74. *Myrious paidagōgous echēte en christō all' ou pollous pateras.*

75. For further background and a penetrating description of the Roman father's ideal of administration through love, moderation, and justice, see Eva Maria Lassen, "The Use of the Father Image in Imperial Propaganda and 1 Corinthians 4:14–21," *Tyndale Bulletin* 42 (1991): 125–36.

76. The analogy is not of strict correspondence. Paul provides a model of imitation not based on the cultivation of his own virtue but based on imitating Christ (cf. 11:1). Paul does not "employ" other guardians in the believing community. He lays a foundation and functions as co-worker with others who together with him are all accountable to God (cf. 3:5–17). Paul does not disparage the *paidagogos* here. The neutral term describes the slave who had been entrusted with the care and oversight of the child. See Robertson and Plummer, *1 Corinthians*, 89–90. What could Timothy be in relationship to the community but a *paidagogos*? He is mentioned by Paul highly as *pistos* and one who imitates Paul's ways (4:17). See Fiore, *Personal Example*, 180.

77. Fiore, *Personal Example*, 178–79. On Pauline imitation, see W. Michaelis, *Theological Dictionary of the New Testament*, s.v. "Mimeomai," 666–73; D. M. Stanley, "'Become Imitators of Me': The Pauline Conception of Apostolic Tradition," *Biblica* 40 (1959): 859–77; and other works cited and commented upon in Fiore, *Personal Example*, 164–90. Also the recent work of Elizabeth A. Castelli, *Imitating Paul: A Discourse on Power* (Louisville: Westminster/John Knox, 1991), examines both the concept of mimesis in antiquity and the discourses of imitation in Paul through a "Foucaultian" interpretation of power. Her conclusion that Paul demands, through his example, "sameness" from community members at the expense of all "differences" does not fully engage the complexity of the community situations, Paul's thought, or texts that recognize and affirm diversity among members (for example, 1 Cor 7:36–40; 12:4–26).

78. The core statement: *"hē basileia tou theou en dynamei."* Paul's antithetical construction in 4:20: *"ou gar en logō hē basileia tou theou all' en dynamei."* The core statement as a moral *sententia* is compact with ellipsis of the verb, makes a striking claim that power is located in the social community of believers, and stands alone as self-evident. In addition, Paul's antithetical formulation provides a foundation and concluding summary to his point in 4:19 — the kingdom of God and power are important; speech and status are not.

79. Conzelmann notes the aphoristic nature of this statement in its developed form in 4:20 (Conzelmann, *1 Corinthians*, 93).

80. Horsley correctly notes (1) the connection between Paul's use of "power" in 4:20 and his earlier definitions of power as connected with the crucified Christ and (2) the connection between "talk" and the earlier descriptions of the Corinthians' "wise speech"

(see "Wisdom of Word," 237–39). Also see John Howard Schütz, "The Cross as a Symbol of Power: 1:10–4:21," in *Paul and the Anatomy of Apostolic Authority*, Society for New Testament Studies Monograph Series 26 (Cambridge: Cambridge University Press, 1975), 187–203. Cf. Conzelmann, *1 Corinthians*, 93, and (less convincingly) Fee, *First Corinthians*, 191–92.

81. A rhetorician would appreciate this move as an appropriate and interesting "color" (subtle and unusual twist of circumstance and argumentation). It is characteristic of the *sententia*. See Sussman, *Elder Seneca*, 41.

82. Paul may have picked up the moral *sententia* in 4:20 from early tradition rather than creating it himself, though undoubtedly he has crafted it to fit the situation in 1 Corinthians 4. Note, however, that Rom 14:17 describes the kingdom of God with three important Pauline words — "righteousness," "peace," and "joy." It is possible that Paul both knew kingdom sayings and crafted them based on analogy.

83. For the coexistence of the two aeons in Paul's thought-world, see Sampley, *Walking between the Times*, 7–24.

84. See Mitchell, *Rhetoric of Reconciliation*, 225–34, for the deliberative function of 1 Corinthians 5–6 as it pertains to promoting unity within the Corinthian community.

85. "Do you not know that the unrighteous will not inherit the kingdom of God? Neither the immoral, nor idolaters, nor adulterers . . . " (6:9–10). The first two cases, the man with his father's wife and believers taking other believers to the law courts, are structurally parallel in that each case is presented with a vice-list following it.

My position is contra Peter S. Zaas ("Catalogues and Context: 1 Corinthians 5 and 6," *New Testament Studies* 34 [1988]: 626–27), who argues that the vice-lists are "extension[s]" of the general paraenesis given not previously but in 1 Corinthians. His argument turns on accepting *egrapha* (which I do) as an epistolary aorist in 5:11. Zaas's argument is unconvincing, however, because the contrast represented by *nyn de* most naturally refers to the content of *egrapha hymin* and not the time of writing.

86. The sociological issues concerning "the lines dividing 'inside' from 'outside' " within the community in 1 Corinthians 5–6 have been investigated by Meeks, *First Urban Christians*, 127–31.

87. Meeks (ibid., 129) makes the connection between the Corinthian boasting on the part of some and the moral position advanced through the maxim in 6:12.

88. The strong implication is that what they are doing violates the following vice-list on interpersonal relationships.

89. "It was a commonplace of the times . . . that civil courts were not to be trusted for justice. . . . Wealth, position, and standing — in the Roman world the three were inseparable — were the best assurance of favorable judgment in the courts" (J. Paul Sampley, *Pauline Partnership in Christ: Christian Community and Commitment in Light of Roman Law* [Philadelphia: Fortress, 1980], 3).

90. Hence, holiness is threatened for the entire community from the inside by a member being allowed or encouraged to transgress the boundary markers.

91. Hence, the world (the outside) is running the believing community (the inside), and the boundaries are defiled. Holiness is threatened from the outside because the Corinthians allow it.

92. The use of this Corinthian moral *sententia* is examined in the section on 1 Corinthians 10 that begins on p. 56 above. For a provocative examination of 6:12–20 as

diatribe by Paul against a Corinthian Cynic-type moral freedom, see Stowers, "'Debate' over Freedom," 59–71.

Exestin (it is allowed, it is permissible) does not carry the connotation of "law." Therefore, the NRSV has been modified.

93. With his choice of wording (*sympherei*), Paul is consistent in his deliberative oratory (Mitchell, *Rhetoric of Reconciliation*, 33–36) and informed by moral reasoning patterns of the time (Stowers, "'Debate' over Freedom," 62–68).

94. Mitchell, *Rhetoric of Reconciliation*, 185. Cf. Luke T. Johnson (*The Writings of the New Testament: An Interpretation* [Philadelphia: Fortress, 1986], 277–83), who argues that the Corinthians must learn to think through moral matters that arise in the world.

95. "*Peri de hōn egraphate*" ("Now concerning the matters about which you wrote...").

96. The second *peri de* at 7:25 need not indicate a "new" subject. It can indicate a division of the argument as shown by Margaret M. Mitchell, "Concerning *PERI DE* in 1 Corinthians," *Novum Testamentum* 31 (1989): 229–56.

97. In making this claim I do not intend to underestimate a notable development of the Greek word *gnōmē* from stated "opinion" (usually in political assemblies) to formalized maxim. It is fair to say that along a continuum from opinion to maxim (in between, for example, might be "purpose," "decision," "counsel") each definition originates in a concrete, thoughtful situation of reflection with the reception of this *gnōmē* being tightly bound up with either the *ēthos* of received tradition or the speaker. Such is not always the case with the modern usage of "opinion." The use of maxims and the use of the opinion of the speaker (*doksa tou legontos*) are part of two different categories of "proof" and have entirely separate sections in *Rhetorica ad Alexandrum* (1430b.1–25, 1431b.9–15, respectively). This indicates that rhetorically competent audiences would be able to make distinctions. For a discussion of the development of the *gnōmē* as a rhetorical device, see chap. 1 above, especially n. 77.

98. Barrett, *First Epistle*, 174–75; John W. Drane, "Tradition, Law and Ethics in Pauline Theology," *Novum Testamentum* 16 (1974): 173; K. G. E. Dolfe, "1 Cor 7,25 Reconsidered (Paul a Supposed Advisor)," *Zeitschrift für die neutestamentliche Wissenschaft* 83 (1992): 115–18; Peter Richardson, "'I Say, Not the Lord': Personal Opinion, Apostolic Authority and the Development of Early Christian Halakah," *Tyndale Bulletin* 31 (1980): 65–86; Peter J. Tomson, *Paul and the Jewish Law: Halakha in the Letters of the Apostle to the Gentiles* (Minneapolis: Fortress, 1990), 68–87, 103–24.

99. A position now further supported for Paul's correspondence in 1 Corinthians by our analysis of 1 Corinthians 1–4, where *gnōmē* in 1:10 referred to actual maxims in 1:31 and 3:21–23. See that section and n. 21 above.

100. See chap. 1 above.

101. The status of 1 Cor 7:26 as a maxim is further confirmed below through (1) its relationship to a context of *ēthos* and (2) its use by Paul in accord with the counsel for maxims in the rhetorical handbooks.

That Paul is capable of stating a rhetorical maxim directly after using the word *gnōmē* is substantiated by H. Betz's analysis of 2 Cor 8:10–12. There, Betz more or less assumes what I am trying to make explicit here. For the 2 Corinthians context he translates *gnōmē* as "judgment" (8:10, cf. "advice," RSV), though his commentary on the verse would seem to support a translation of "maxim" (see Betz, *2 Corinthians 8 and 9*, 37, 63–67). While "judgment" is preferable to "opinion" (cf. the different renderings of *gnōmē* in 1 Cor

7:25 ["opinion," RSV] and 7:40 ["judgment," RSV]), if I am correct in arguing for an exigence in 1 Corinthians in which Paul must match maxims with those with whom he disagreed, then a translation of "maxim" in 1 Cor 7:25 and 40 would be more appropriate. On this line of argumentation see pp. 45–46 above.

102. See Snyder, "'Tobspruch' in the New Testament," 119. Barrett (*First Epistle*, 174–75, following Jeremias) considers 7:26b as a quotation of the Corinthian position. Fee (*First Corinthians*, 330) argues for a Corinthian quotation on the grounds that the Greek repetition of *kalon* in 7:25–26 is awkward. The basis of 7:26b is, however, already to be established in the socially conservative exhortation, "in whatever state each was called, there let him remain with God" (7:24; cf. 7:17, 20). This fits Paul's position far better than it fits the position of the status-seeking Corinthians. It is surely Pauline argumentation — and a pattern of argumentation already used as early as 1 Cor 1:26–29.

103. At the time of Paul, *kalon esti* was an established, formulaic, introductory phrase for maxims. Evidence abounds from early Greek literature, the LXX, NT Synoptic sayings, as well as the wider Hellenistic corpus. As an expression occurring "in every age and in all Gk. usage," see Walter Grundmann, *Theological Dictionary of the New Testament*, s.v. "Kalos," 536–50. For an analysis of its usage in the LXX, the Synoptic sources (Mk 9:42, 43, 45, 47 ‖ Mt 18:8, 9; Mk 14:21 ‖ Mt 24:24), and Paul, see Snyder, "'Tobspruch' in the New Testament," 117–20. For an occurrence of *kalon esti* in Plutarch *Moralia* 384E and a discussion of its relationship to the Pauline texts (1 Cor 7:1, 8, 26; 9:15; Gal 4:18) and the Synoptic texts (add Mk 7:27 ‖ Mt 15:26), see Hans Dieter Betz and Edgar W. Smith Jr., "*De e apud Delphos* (*Moralia* 384C–394C)," in *Plutarch's Ethical Writings and Early Christian Literature*, ed. H. D. Betz, Studia ad corpus hellenisticum novi testamenti 4 (Leiden: Brill, 1978), 86.

Rather than saying with Barrett (*First Epistle*, 155) that *kalon* is not used in a moral sense in 1 Cor 7:1, 8, and 26, it might be more accurate to say that *kalon esti* is a rhetorical formulation of a deliberative quality offered by Paul in support of his moral counsel. On *kalon* as a rhetorically important word in the epideictic type of speech, see James L. Bailey and Lyle D. Vander Broek, *Literary Forms in the New Testament: A Handbook* (Louisville: Westminster/John Knox, 1992), 120. For the use of *kalon* as a "head" topic in deliberative rhetoric, see Mitchell, *Rhetoric of Reconciliation*, 26 n. 20, 29 n. 37.

With regard to 1 Cor 7:26b, Paul has taken up a commonly available — and, I would argue, a commonly recognizable — pattern from which to signal his maxim.

104. The antecedent of *houtōs* must be established from Paul's instruction and illustration in 7:17–24. Fully expressed this antecedent is "to remain in the state in which one was called" (7:17, 24).

105. This is not unusual. A goal of rhetoric is to be as natural as possible. Drawing attention to technique or figures is not desirable unless it becomes rhetorically beneficial due to contextual reasons such as debate, contest, or challenge. Such reasons confront Paul in 1 Corinthians, but apparently not in Romans. For further discussion on the Corinthian situation, see pp. 45–46 above.

106. The syntax is parallel for the string of articular infinitives, and therefore ellipsis occurs regarding the infinitives themselves in the last (third) clause.

107. The only other beatitude in Paul occurs in the very same context and passage as the *kalon* maxim previously discussed in Rom 14:21! It is Rom 14:22b — "Blessed are those who have no reason to condemn themselves because of what they approve." This

suggests that in both 1 Corinthians 7 and Romans 14 we have a good basis for believing that Paul is purposely advancing argumentation built on traditional sayings of the maxim type. The function of Paul's maxim argumentation in each passage is, however, different. In 1 Corinthians 7, Paul uses the elaboration of a maxim to form the basis of his ethical counsel on issues of marriage and the single life. In Romans 14, Paul's use of maxims is in support of and functioning in concert with his use of "oblique speech" as an argumentative strategy to produce "common ground" among ethnic groups in the Roman community. See James C. Walters, *Ethnic Issues in Paul's Letter to the Romans: Changing Self-Definitions in Earliest Roman Christianity* (Valley Forge, Pa.: Trinity, 1993), 84–94. Paul's argumentative strategy (including maxim usage) is always shaped to the particular needs and concerns of each community.

108. So argued convincingly by Hurd, who provides a chart of older scholarship both for and against a quotation in 7:1b in *Origin of 1 Corinthians,* 65–68, 158–63. Briefly, the main problems for 7:1b representing a Pauline principle are (1) the section is left without a subject heading after the vague "now concerning matters about which you wrote," and (2) Paul modifies and disagrees with the statement as he continues. Among modern critical commentators, it appears that only Conzelmann (*1 Corinthians,* 115 n. 10) considers this Paul's own slogan. Cf. Omanson, "Acknowledging Paul's Quotations," 207–8.

109. *Kalon anthrōpō gunaikos mē haptesthai* (literally, "The not touching a woman for a man (is) good").

110. For example, abdication of control over one's body; celibacy and marriage as God's gifts; the sanctity of marriage and any exceptions for dissolution; viability of mixed marriages; holiness of children. Cf., among others, David R. Cartlidge, "1 Corinthians 7 as a Foundation for a Christian Sex Ethic," *Journal of Religion* 55 (1975): 220–34; William E. Phipps, "Is Paul's Attitude toward Sexual Relations Contained in 1 Cor. 7:1?" *New Testament Studies* 28 (1981): 125–31; Jerome Murphy-O'Connor, "The Divorced Woman in 1 Cor 7:10–11," *Journal of Biblical Literature* 100 (1981): 601–6; James A. Fischer, "1 Cor 7:8–24 — Marriage and Divorce," *Biblical Research* 23 (1978): 26–36.

111. For example, David L. Dungan, *The Sayings of Jesus in the Churches of Paul* (Philadelphia: Fortress, 1971), 81–101, 132–35.

112. *Haptesthai* (to touch) is euphemistic for "having sexual relations." See the discussion and wide range of references in Fee, *First Corinthians,* 275. He suggests a comparable English usage of "It is good for a man not to have relations with a woman."

113. The impulse for this may have come from one or (most likely) a combination of readily accessible options in urban Greco-Roman society or the traditioning processes of the nascent Christian communities. Among these options were: (1) The moralist debates about the advisability of marriage. See David L. Balch, "1 Cor. 7:32–35 and Stoic Debates about Marriage, Anxiety, and Distraction," *Journal of Biblical Literature* 102 (1983): 429–39; O. Larry Yarbrough, *Not Like the Gentiles: Marriage Rules in the Letters of Paul,* SBL Dissertation Series 80 (Atlanta: Scholars Press, 1985), 31–63; Vincent L. Wimbush, *Paul: The Worldly Ascetic: Response to the World and Self-Understanding according to 1 Corinthians 7* (Macon, Ga.: Mercer University Press, 1987), 56–69. (2) The sacral celibacy connected with Greco-Roman religions of one kind or another. See Richard E. Oster Jr., "Use, Misuse, and Neglect of Archaeological Evidence in Some Modern Works on 1 Corinthians (1 Cor 7,1–5; 8,10; 11,2–16; 12,14–26)," *Zeitschrift für die neutestamentliche Wissenschaft* 83 (1992): 58–64, with special attention to Isis; Wimbush, *Worldly*

Ascetic, 55–56. Oster seems unaware of Richard A. Horsley, "Spiritual Marriage with Sophia," *Vigiliae Christiannae* 33 (1979): 30–54, who acknowledges an ascetic devotional pattern based on Isis as well, but thinks the influence in Corinth comes through Hellenistic Judaism similar to Philo, Wisdom of Solomon, and especially the Therapeutae. Similar to Horsley is David L. Balch, "Backgrounds of I Cor. VII: Sayings of the Lord in Q; Moses as an Ascetic *THEIOS ANĒR* in II Cor. III," *New Testament Studies* 18 (1971): 358–64. (3) The oral tradition about and including sayings of Jesus. See Dungan, *Sayings of Jesus,* 80–150; Richardson, "'I Say, Not the Lord,'" 69–72; Balch, "Backgrounds of I Cor. VII," 351–58, and the literature cited there. (4) Paul's own example (7:7; 9:4–7) and possibly some misunderstanding of his previous teaching such as the baptismal formula now preserved in Gal 3:28 (cf. 1 Cor 12:13). See Dennis R. MacDonald, *There Is No Male and Female: The Fate of a Dominical Saying in Paul and Gnosticism* (Philadelphia: Fortress, 1987), 65–111 and n. 114 below.

114. Strongly argued in the recent study of Wire, *Corinthian Women Prophets,* 72–97, who, in addition to this passage, 1 Cor 11:2–16, and 14:34–36, finds a liberated group of women prophets being addressed covertly throughout the letter. I find the study of Margaret Y. MacDonald ("Women Holy in Body and Spirit: The Social Setting of 1 Corinthians 7," *New Testament Studies* 36 [1990]: 161–81) more balanced in perspective. MacDonald shows Paul's particular concern for the behavior of women but acknowledges that the moral position represented in 7:1b most likely extended to both men and women in the community. Cf. Oster, "Use, Misuse, and Neglect," 62–63. Equally important in the discussion is MacDonald, *There is No Male and Female,* 65–111.

115. Apparently the matters being referred to are the denial of conjugal rights to marriage partners, the outright divorce of believing spouses by believers, or the divorce of unbelieving spouses for fear of purity violations (cf. the Corinthian misunderstanding concerning the immoral of the world in 5:9–13). See the discussion in Fee, *First Corinthians,* 267–309.

116. As the argument unfolds, Paul gives careful attention to the perspective of both male and female partners in an attempt to promote concord. See Mitchell, *Rhetoric of Reconciliation,* 236.

117. Ibid., 235. To say that Paul views marriage with *only* a regard toward preventing *porneia* is to devalue the social obligation of marriage before God that informs Paul's Jewish cultural heritage. Wire (*Corinthian Women Prophets,* 72–97) goes too far in viewing Paul's counsel in 1 Corinthians 7 as a "program of marriage to prevent immorality" (82).

118. Exercising self-control or its lack (on the part of both parties) determines proper and advantageous relationships for an individual's freedom (see 7:5, 9, 37; 8:9; 9:12b; and esp. 9:25–27).

119. I am not arguing that v. 7 is unconnected to 7:1–6. It connects the measure of the married's ability to have periods of abstinence with Paul's example and his giftedness to exercise self-control. But v. 7 is equally connected to vv. 8–9, or else it is not possible to determine the import of Paul's example for the unmarried. Verse 7 is connected to v. 8 by Paul's example, and v. 9 indicates what constitutes the applicability and measurement of Paul's example (the ability to exercise self-control).

My division is not supported by the modern critical commentaries (see Conzelmann; Grosheide; Barrett; Fee; Robertson and Plummer), but in recent rhetorical studies, where the role of Paul's example is highlighted, vv. 7–8 are connected together (cf. Mitchell, *Rhetoric of Reconciliation*, 237; Fiore, *Personal Example*, 167–68). The issue for all commentators is what to do with vv. 8–9. Why is this counsel to the unmarried inserted as a parenthesis in the larger section (vv. 1–24) addressing issues of the married? I propose an answer to these questions based on a rhetorical consideration of 7:7–9 as a digression.

120. There are terminological distinctions between 7:8–9 and 7:25–40. *Agamoi* in 7:8 may be restricted to unmarried men such as bachelors and widowers (if it is thought that virgin women would have no say in matters of choice). Such is the view of Robertson and Plummer, *1 Corinthians*, 138. Fee (*First Corinthians*, 287–88) unnecessarily restricts the reference to widowers. Although the term *chērai* (widows; cf. 7:8) does not occur in 7:39, it is certainly implied. While 7:25 begins the section by addressing the *parthenoi* (virgins), the discussion is enlarged to include both unmarried men and women (cf. vv. 32–35).

121. Paul's rhetorical move is subtly subversive: he agrees with the Corinthian position with regard to the unmarried (with an exception provided), but he also introduces the concept of "remaining" from which he will support his own maxim in 7:26.

122. Here, there is good indication that some women stand behind the ascetic position of 7:1b, and Paul does not expect them to heed his counsel in 7:2–5.

123. *En eipēnē keklēken hymas ho theos.* The maxim is a commonplace with Paul in matters of order within community relationships, as evidenced in the recurrent usage in 14:33a: *ou estin akatastasias ho theos alla eipēnēs* ("God is a God not of disorder but of peace"). On Paul's antithetical construction from a core *sententia*, see the discussion of 1 Cor 4:20 and Rom 14:17 above. This recurrent usage demonstrates the moral *sententia*'s ability to be moved from one context to the next. Fee (*First Corinthians*, 307) recognizes 1 Cor 7:15b as a "general maxim."

124. This section has yet to be adequately related to Paul's example in 1 Cor 9:19–23. Both sections demonstrate a freedom from purity restrictions so that some might be saved and the gospel advanced in the world (cf. 5:9–10).

125. To enter into the full discussion of this passage is beyond the scope of the study. Important examinations have been made by S. Scott Bartchy, *MALLON CHRĒSAI: First-Century Slavery and the Interpretation of 1 Corinthians 7:21*, SBL Dissertation Series 11 (Missoula, Mont.: Scholars Press, 1973), and Fee, *First Corinthians*, 306–22. I am very much in agreement with the recent position taken by Dawes, "But If You Can Gain Your Freedom," 681–97.

Bartchy has noted the *A B A'* pattern to 1 Corinthians 7 as a whole, with 7:17–24 representing the *B* section (161–62). Dawes has called attention to this section as a rhetorical digression (683–84).

126. The imperative is *peripateitō* (Let each one walk). The metaphor represents how a person is to conduct his or her life in the world. For the "walking metaphor" in Paul's letters, and in 1 Cor 3:4 and 7:17 in particular, see Joseph O. Holloway, *PERIPATEŌ as a Thematic Marker for Pauline Ethics* (San Francisco: Mellon Research University Press, 1992).

127. Fee, *First Corinthians*, 306–22, with an appropriate qualification: "Paul's concern, therefore, is not that they *retain* their present social setting, but that they *recognize* it as the proper one in which to live out God's call" (309).

128. For Paul's use of *adiaphora*, see Sampley, *Walking between the Times*, 77–82. For a full study of *adiaphora* among the Greco-Roman moralists and a discussion of this passage, see Jaquette, *Discerning What Counts*, 37–96, 165–81.

129. *Hē peritomē ouden estin kai hē akrobustia ouden estin, alla tērēsis entolōn theou.* A gnomic sentence (maxim with supplement), undoubtedly constructed by Paul from his believing symbolic universe. The maxim could easily be lifted from context to context, but it is shaped here to a particular context because doing God's commandments includes honoring marital obligations. This compact maxim has: (1) no introductory particles, (2) parallel balance with emphatic *estin*, anaphora, and antistrophe marking the core maxim, and (3) ellipsis of the verb in the supplementary clause.

130. Note the emphatic use of *hekastos* in 7:17, 20, and 24. How does the individual work out moral counsel within the believing community? The question must be put this way in order for Paul to counsel the unmarried concerning the choice between celibacy and marriage.

131. Freedom from worldly or human standards and values is implied in the call of God that found the Corinthians in weakness (1:26) and in God's graciousness (contra any worldly status) that underlies their self-definition (1:27–28; 4:7). Further, the worthy walk of the Corinthians is opposite to the improper and immature "walking according to worldly standards" in 3:4 (*kata anthrōpon peripateite*). See Holloway, *PERIPATEŌ*, 64–70.

132. As one who belongs to God (6:19–20), the individual has his or her freedom constrained by covenant obligations. Some Corinthians have not understood this as indicated by their immorality (5:1–2; 6:12–20), false scales of justice (6:1–11; 11:20–22), dissolution of marriage obligations (7:1–24), and idolatry that leads to the destruction of community members (8:10–11; 10:1–22). Also cf. Zaas, "Catalogues and Context," 628–29, for an echo of the Decalogue in 1 Cor 6:9.

133. The maxim in 1 Cor 7:19 is attested to by recurrence in Gal 5:6 and 6:15. Gal 5:6: *oute peritomē ti ischyei oute akrobystia alla pistis di' agapēs energoumenē* ("Neither circumcision avails anything nor uncircumcision, but faith working through love" [my trans.]). Gal 6:15: *oute gar peritomē ti estin oute akrobystia alla kainē ktisis* ("For neither circumcision is anything nor uncircumcision [is anything], but [what is something] is a new creation" [my trans.]). Gal 6:15 is almost exactly parallel in structure, and 5:6 is less so but clearly recognizable. The rhetorician formulates a gnomic sentence with strong attention to the particular situation being addressed. The context of Gal 5:6 is amid Paul's polemic; 6:15 is a final reason and summary of one's status based on the cross of Christ that crucifies the world's values and standards.

134. Dawes, "But If You Can Gain Your Freedom," 696.

135. Ibid., 686–89, 694–97.

136. The Stoic doctrine of *adiaphora* gave serious consideration to the use of "preferreds." Preferreds are items of *adiaphora* that can be used profitably to advance the goal of "moral virtue." For Paul the goal was to conduct one's life according to the gospel; for the Stoic the goal was to live in accord with nature or reason. If choosing freedom can enhance one's living out the gospel, by all means use it. See Jaquette, "Why Choose Preferred Indifferents and Reject Their Opposites?" in *Discerning What Counts*, 65–70 for an analysis of this subject in the Greco-Roman moralists. Unfortunately, Jaquette does not apply the insights there to this section of the text.

137. With Dawes, who argues that a slave could influence decisions regarding his or her freedom and that a correct reading of *dynasai* (you are able) in 7:21 indicates this capacity ("But If You Can Gain Your Freedom," 693–94); contra Bartchy (*MALLON*

CHRĒSAI, 173–83), who argues that the slave would have no input into whether or not manumission was granted.

138. Aristotle *Rhetorica* 2.21.9; Quintilian *Institutio oratoria* 8.5.8. I view *ēthos* as a positioning by the rhetor in relationship to the entire speech situation and not something that the rhetor simply has. There is some debate on how the concept of *ēthos* may have changed from the classical to imperial periods. See Dale L. Sullivan, "The Ethos of Epideictic Encounter," *Philosophy and Rhetoric* 26 (1993): 113–14, 126–28, 130 n. 11; and S. Michael Halloran, "Aristotle's Concept of Ethos; or, If Not His Somebody Else's," *Rhetoric Review* 1 (1982): 58–63.

139. Concerning the importance of maxims to the rhetorician's *ēthos* at the time of Paul, the evidence from Seneca the Elder's *Controversiae* and *Suasoriae* is illuminating. See Sussman, *Elder Seneca*, 1–17, 94–136. For the measurement of a moralist's character based on the ability to create maxims, see Seneca *Epistulae Morales* 33.5–9. See also the section "Speaker and Audience" in chap. 1 of this study.

140. Aristotle *Rhetorica* 2.21.2–7; *Ad Herennium* 4.17.24–25; Quintilian *Institutio oratoria* 8.5.4. And also note Seneca *Epistulae Morales* 95.61–64. For an illustration of this point in a number of gnomic texts, see Wilson, *Love without Pretense*, 43–45. Contextual analysis can be applied to maxims by analogy to studies on proverbial lore. See Seitel, "Proverbs," 122–39; Abrahams, "Introductory Remarks," 143–58.

141. Aristotle *Rhetorica* 2.21.2–9; Quintilian *Institutio oratoria* 8.5.3–14. On the use of a maxim as a thesis statement, see Wilson, *Love without Pretense*, 48–49, and Sampley, *Walking between the Times*, 95–96. Cf. Demetrius *On Style* 2.109–11.

142. Sampley, *Walking between the Times*, 95.

143. For the various identifications of the "virgins" (*parthenoi*) throughout 7:25–40, see Barrett, *First Epistle*, 173–87, and Fee, *First Corinthians*, 322–57. For the purposes of this study I identify a general group of unmarried men and women (7:25–35), engaged couples (7:36–38), and widows (7:39–40). All of these are viable options within the scholarly discussion.

144. The effect of the polysyndeton is to slow down and draw out the idea. This is very appropriate to a description of "distress."

145. Rhetorically the "center point [of a chiasm] often functions in one of two ways; it may stand as the interpretive focal point of the passage, or it may mark an important transition in the movement or thought of the chiasm" (Bailey and Vander Broek, *Literary Forms*, 53). In the present case it is the latter function. The *C* component (7:28) anticipates and prepares for the exceptions introduced by the best/better refinement that follows in 7:36–40. Paul's illustration of the slave in 7:21–24 has, in turn, anticipated and prepared for his counsel here in 7:28 (see pp. 42–43 above and n. 158 below).

146. That Paul makes an unexpected shift to *adelphoi* (brothers and sisters) indicates that this perspective on living out one's life in the world is applicable to the entire community. See Fee, *First Corinthians*, 337.

147. Cf. ibid., 341–42.

148. For an overall consideration of 7:29–31, its traditioning process, and other models of life in the world with which it interacts, see Wimbush, *Worldly Ascetic*, 1–98.

149. With respect to marriage, weeping, rejoicing, buying, and (the all-inclusive) using the world. For an explanation of these concerns and their order, see ibid., 28.

150. According to Wimbush (ibid., 21–22), this stance is "an inner-worldly detachment."

151. Since the idea of marriage leading to sin is far from Paul's counsel throughout the chapter, it seems to represent the ascetic position of those in Corinth who advance the maxim in 7:1b. See Fee, *First Corinthians,* 352.

152. The classic discussion from which many of the issues were set is Hurd, *Origin of 1 Corinthians,* 114–209, 273–96.

153. This application is on analogy to studies examining proverbs, taunts, boasts, and other traditional sayings with regard to the appropriateness of their performative contexts. See Arewa and Dundes, "Proverbs," 70–73; Roger D. Abrahams, "A Rhetoric of Everyday Life: Traditional Conversational Genres," *Southern Folklore Quarterly* 32 (1968): 44–59. Aristotle (*Rhetorica,* 2.21.12–14) provides us with the only extant counsel on maxim disagreement. Given the refutation of maxims in the *progymnasmata* (preliminary exercises) of Greco-Roman education, it is surprising that the rhetorical handbooks do not provide additional counsel. We must continue to ask how rhetorical maxims function, how they are expected to be used, including *what limitations may apply,* in the social contexts of debate or *agōnes logōn* (contests of speech). For these social contexts, see Pogoloff, *Logos and Sophia,* 153–56, 158–60, 173–78.

154. Cf. Hermogenes' *Progymnasmata* (Baldwin, *Medieval Rhetoric and Poetic,* 36–37), where the thesis is discussed in the context of general debate. The question of the viability of marriage marks a prime example. When the discussion of the thesis is twofold, it examines whether or not something is better (that is, advantageous, expedient, just, profitable, etc.).

155. See Martin, *Antike Rhetorik,* 124–33. Refutation played a key role in the secondary preliminary exercises, and its instruction routinely combined with exercises for the maxim. See the discussion in chap. 1, pp. 8, 19.

156. See Cicero *De Inventione* 1.78–96: "[T]he fourth method of refutation is to counter a strong argument with one equally strong or stronger. This kind will be used particularly in speaking before a deliberative body, when we grant that something said on the other side is fair, but prove that the position we are defending is necessary; or when we acknowledge that the course of action which they defend is advantageous, but prove that ours is honourable."

157. For a review of the background of Paul's sources in 1 Corinthians 7 and additional discussion concerning the issues for and against marriage in the moral traditions of Jewish and Greco-Roman culture, see Yarbrough, *Not Like the Gentiles,* 7–63.

158. Dawes, "But If You Can Gain Your Freedom," 681–97. Dawes has brilliantly explained the function of Paul's illustration in 1 Cor 7:17–24. The case of circumcision illustrates the general exhortation (remain in the state of one's calling), but the application is more complex. Therefore, the "second example [slavery] illustrates both the ultimate indifference of one's state of life (v. 21a) *and* the possibility of having a preference where circumstances allow (v. 21b)" (697). See pp. 42–43 above.

159. Sampley, *Walking between the Times,* 97.

160. 1 Cor 7:37: *hos de hestēke en tē kardia autou hedraios, mē echōn anagkēn, exousian de echei peri tou idiou thelēmatos*... ("But whoever stands firm in his heart without necessity, but he has authority over his will..." [my trans.]).

161. For this paradigm of the individual's moral reasoning, see Sampley, *Walking between the Times,* 57–60.

162. Living uncontaminated does not mean withdrawal of the community and its members from the world (1 Cor 5:10). Reckoning rightly the will of God and properly

placed within the believing community, members need not fear contact with the world (cf. 7:14).

163. On Paul's concern to balance the individual's concerns with those of the community as a whole, see J. Paul Sampley, "Faith and Its Moral Life: A Study of Individuation in the Thought World of the Apostle Paul," in *Faith and History: Essays in Honor of Paul W. Meyer,* ed. John T. Carroll, Charles H. Cosgrove, and E. Elizabeth Johnson (Atlanta: Scholars Press, 1990), 221–38, esp. 232.

164. Although the term "strong" is not used in 1 Corinthians 8–10, the postulation of a "strong" position is reasonable based on the mention of the person with a "weak consciousness" (*hē syneidēsis autou asthenous* [8:10]). The strong, who advocate the position "we all have knowledge" with its attendant "right" (*exousia* [8:9]) to partake freely of meat having been offered to idols, are most likely located among the wealthy and prominent members of the believing community. These members are socially connected by a variety of civic, cultic, and patronal eating opportunities involving meat sacrificed to idols. In addition, the more prominent members have access to philosophical freedom positions that sanction their moral behavior and rhetorical education that shapes the expression of these positions as maxims. On the social level of the strong in 1 Corinthians 8–10, see Gerd Theissen, "Strong and Weak in Corinth: A Sociological Analysis of a Theological Quarrel," in *Social Setting of Pauline Christianity,* 121–43; Meeks, *Urban Christians,* 97–100; John K. Chow, *Patronage and Power: A Study of Social Networks in Corinth,* JSNT Supplement Series 75 (Sheffield, England: JSOT, 1992), 38–112, 141–57. On the varieties of eating occasions at Corinth in Paul's time, see Wendell Lee Willis, *Idol Meat in Corinth: The Pauline Argument in 1 Corinthians 8 and 10,* SBL Dissertation Series 68 (Chico, Calif.: Scholars Press, 1985), 7–64.

Not only have the strong found a following in their moral position, but there is some indication that they actively promote it by example to the weak. Those who are weak are being "built up" (*oikodomēthēsetai* [8:10]) by the strong to eat food offered to idols to their destruction. See Jerome Murphy-O'Connor, "Freedom or the Ghetto (1 Cor. 8:1–13; 10:23–11:1)," *Revue Biblique* 85 (1978): 548–49. Cf. Fee, *First Corinthians, 359.*

165. In describing argument, Quintilian states: "Consequently, since an argument is a process of reasoning which provides proof and enables one thing to be inferred from another and confirms facts which are uncertain by reference to facts which are certain, there must needs be something in every case which requires no proof. Otherwise there will be nothing by which we can prove anything; there must be something which either is or is believed to be true, by means of which doubtful things may be rendered credible. We may regard as certainties, first, those things which we perceive by the senses, things for instance that we hear or see, such as signs or indications; secondly, those things about which there is general agreement, such as the existence of the gods or the duty of loving one's parents; thirdly, those things which are established by law or have passed into current usage . . . ; finally, there are the things which are admitted by either party, and whatever has already been proved or is not disputed by our adversary" (*Institutio oratoria* 5.10.12–14). While maxims fit the second, third, and fourth categories, it is precisely the fourth category that is indicated in Paul's use of *oidamen hoti.*

166. Hurd, *Origin of 1 Corinthians,* 68–70, 115–25. Almost all modern commentators since Hurd attribute these three statements to the Corinthians. See Omanson, "Acknowledging Paul's Quotations," 208–9. The repetitious first plural in 8:1 (*oidamen*

hoti . . . echomen) and the double *hoti* in 8:4 (*oidamen hoti . . . kai hoti*) almost assuredly indicate direct discourse. See Fee, *First Corinthians*, 365 with nn. 30 and 31.

167. How do these maxims function for those Corinthians who employ them? Johnson indicates that some Corinthians did not want to engage in thought: "[These tendencies were] to avoid ambiguity and thought, by reducing norms to slogans" (*Writings of the New Testament*, 278). The position of Murphy-O'Connor ("Freedom or the Ghetto," 547–51) is more tenable. The Corinthian strong with their freedom statement in 6:12a ("All things are permissible for me") had no need to defend their eating of meat offered to idols. The positions represented by these Corinthian maxims are a formulation by the strong in response to the accusations of the weak. If an extended defense was the case, then Paul is probably abridging their argument.

The maxim in 8:1 is a concluding moral *sententia: pantes gnōsin echomen* ("We all have knowledge"). It is brief, emphatic (with *pantes* in first position), balanced, and generalized as a truth applicable within every believer's symbolic universe. A concluding *sententia* usually is a summation statement. In most cases, Paul presents the Corinthians' maxims as summary positions (see 6:12; 7:1; 10:23) from which he launches his own argumentation. The same strategy appears here in 8:1.

The other two maxims in 8:4 appear to be supporting argumentation for 8:1. Paul is echoing the position of the strong by using (broadly) their argumentation to strengthen a point with which he partially agrees. What I am suggesting, then, is that Paul's presentation of the Corinthian position is possibly reversed from how the strong might have advanced their argumentation before the weak.

The Corinthian maxims in 8:4 are in the form of moral *sententiae*. They are brief and occur with ellipsis of the verb:

> *Ouden eidōlon en kosmō.* ("No idol in the world really exists.")
> *Oudeis theos ei mē heis.* ("There is no God but one.")

In relation to each other, the maxims demonstrate a parallel structure with *ouden eidōlon* and *oudeis theos*. This forms the basis for the translation "No idol in the world really exists" over the alternative of "An idol is nothing in the world." On this point, see Fee, *First Corinthians*, 371 n. 8. Cf. Murphy-O'Connor, "Freedom or the Ghetto," 546.

Cf. Stanley K. Stowers ("Paul on the Use and Abuse of Reason," in *Greeks, Romans, and Christians: Essays in Honor of Abraham J. Malherbe*, ed. David L. Balch, Everett Ferguson, and Wayne A. Meeks [Minneapolis: Fortress, 1990], 275), who, with reference to Epicurus and Musonius Rufus, suggests that the Corinthian quotations in 8:1 and 4 may be "[r]easonings (*logismoi*) [which] often took the form of brief nuggets of thought that those seeking to become wise employed as spiritual exercises."

168. Most scholars believe the concentrated use of the term *gnōsis* and its verbal forms in 1 Corinthians 8 (8:1, 2, 3, 7, 11) indicates a Corinthian catchword that Paul is taking up in his argumentation. Of course, *gnōsis* is not a term unknown across the Pauline corpus, and it holds a rather positive place in Paul's thought-world — even in 1 Corinthians (see 1 Cor 1:5; 12:8; 13:2, 8, 9; 14:6; 15:34). See Rudolf Bultmann, *Theology of the New Testament*, trans. Kendrick Grobel (New York: Scribner's, 1951–55), 2:326.

Having scruples over eating meat sacrificed to idols was most likely a problem for gentiles in the Corinthian community who had turned from their previous ways of idolatry and were now fearful of any temptation to return. Hence, the monotheistic positions represented in the maxims of 8:4 were probably based in Paul's earlier preaching and teaching, which in turn are firmly based in the tenets of Hellenistic Judaism (see 1 Thess 1:9; Gal 4:8).

169. Surely the Corinthian maxim argumentation is abbreviated. See the discussion in n. 167 above.

170. The maxim is recognized as Paul's qualification and correction of the Corinthian position: the basis for moral reasoning about eating meat sacrificed to idols is not based on cognitive or theological truths only, but care in human relations. See Robertson and Plummer, *1 Corinthians*, 164; Grosheide, *First Corinthians*, 188–89; Barrett, *First Epistle*, 189; Conzelmann, *1 Corinthians*, 140–41; Fee, *First Corinthians*, 363–67. The moral *sententia* in 8:1b is antithetical, balanced, and brief; with anaphora; and with *homoeoteleuton* in the concluding verbs of each clause ("those lacking cases close with like terminations" [*Ad Herennium* 4.20.28]): *hē gnōsis physioi, hē de agapē oikodomei* ("Knowledge puffs up, but love builds up"). For Paul's use of antithetical moral *sententiae*, see the discussion of 1 Cor 4:20 above.

171. A number of commentators attribute this entire statement or at least the first part to the Corinthians (and cf. NRSV). See the chart of older scholarship in Hurd, *Origin of 1 Corinthians*, 68; Fee, *First Corinthians*, 381–84 (somewhat tentatively); Barrett, *First Epistle*, 195; Grosheide, *First Corinthians*, 194; Jerome Murphy-O'Connor, "Food and Spiritual Gifts in 1 Cor 8:8," *Catholic Biblical Quarterly* 41 (1979): 292–98 (with textual emendation). However, 1 Cor 8:8 fits the more careful maxim *adiaphora* reasoning of Paul (cf. our discussion of 1 Cor 7:19 and parallels with that of the ambiguously presented formulation of the Corinthians in 6:13: "Food is for the stomach, and the stomach for food"). Paul's formulation in 8:8 carefully *mediates* between both the stance of the weak and that of the strong. See our full discussion of Paul's argumentation in the text. Commentators who see 1 Cor 8:8 as Paul's own statement include, among others, Hurd, *Origin of 1 Corinthians*, 123; Conzelmann, *1 Corinthians*, 147–48; Robertson and Plummer, *First Corinthians*, 170; Willis, *Idol Meat in Corinth*, 97–98 (Willis argues that the second half is Paul's adaptation of the Corinthian position).

The maxim is a gnomic sentence with the supplement (here, a reason; 8:8a) preceding the maxim core (8:8b). The relation of supplement to maxim core is comparable to 7:26 and the opposite of 7:19. The maxim is particularized through the use of the first plural in both parts. The maxim core is marked by anaphora, the repeated phrase *oute ean phagōmen*, an internal negated antithesis, and formulation as an *isocolon:*

Reason: *Brōma de hēmas ou parastēsei tō theō*

Maxim core: *oute ean mē phagōmen hysteroumetha*
            oute ean phagōmen perisseuomen.

A "proverbial" and "aphoristic" quality is attributed to 8:8 by Willis, *Idol Meat in Corinth*, 97, and Fee, *First Corinthians*, 382, respectively.

172. My divisions and subdivisions of 1 Corinthians 8 as a whole have been stimulated by the analysis in H. Van Dyke Parunak, "Transitional Techniques in the Bible," *Journal of Biblical Literature* 102 (1983): 539–40.

173. Cf. the above analysis of Paul's argumentation in 1 Cor 7:25–40 as structured on the reason and maxim core in 7:26.

174. On the elaboration patterns for maxim argumentation, see chap. 1, pp. 18–20.

175. Fiore's attempt to relate the pattern of argumentation in 1 Corinthians 8–11 to the counsel of the rhetorical exercise handbooks is a worthy consideration. He is

fundamentally misguided, however, in his attempt to analyze the section as a *chreia* elaboration. Does Paul write a *chreia* about himself? Do other writers? Surely he is not writing a *chreia* about the Corinthian strong. Fiore is forced to admit that "the development here [of 1 Corinthians 8–11 as a *chreia*] is much more diffuse than what has been encountered above [his previous analyses of Socratic *chreiai*]" (Fiore, *Personal Example,* 189 with n. 78).

What is elaborated in 1 Corinthians 8 is Paul's maxim in 1 Cor 8:1b (a restatement with qualification of the Corinthian maxim in 8:1a), not a *chreia.* Paul uses the standard techniques of elaboration (shared by the *chreia* and maxim alike) for his maxim argumentation, not in a fixed pattern, but as he deems necessary for making his case.

176. Again, see the discussion and analysis of 1 Corinthians 7 above.

177. The ambiguous "we" becomes the common voice of the strong Corinthians and Paul. It is an identification from which Paul can refine or correct the strong Corinthians' position through either the voice of his maxim rejoinders (see 8:1b; 8:7–8) or his personal voice that states his example (8:13). For a provocative examination of the various "voices" represented in 1 Corinthians 8–10, see Wayne A. Meeks, "The Polyphonic Ethics of the Apostle Paul," *Annual of the Society of Christian Ethics* (1988): 17–24.

178. Above, n. 165.

179. Aristotle had counseled that a supplement or reason be added to a maxim in instances where the moral purpose might be ambiguous, unclear, or misunderstood (*Rhetorica* 2.21.3–7). See chap. 2, pp. 27–28.

180. Conzelmann, *1 Corinthians,* 141–42. Cf. Fee, *First Corinthians,* 368.

181. Cf. Fee, *First Corinthians,* 368–69, who also makes an extended connection to the relationship of love and knowledge in 1 Cor 13:2.

182. See n. 179 above.

183. For a brief account of the historical and archeological sources for establishing religious pluralism in Corinth, see Bruce W. Winter, "Theological and Ethical Responses to Religious Pluralism — 1 Corinthians 8–10," *Tyndale Bulletin* 41 (1990): 209–15. The most recent major treatment is Donald Engels, *Roman Corinth: An Alternative Model for the Classical City* (Chicago: University of Chicago Press, 1990), 92–120.

184. Murphy-O'Connor provides a thorough analysis of the tradition history and meaning of 8:6. Most insightful is his suggestion that the function of this reworked baptismal material is to remind the strong Corinthians of their foundational beginning *in community.* See Jerome Murphy-O'Connor, "1 Cor 8:6: Cosmology or Soteriology?" *Revue Biblique* 85 (1978): 253–67. Cf. Richard A. Horsley, "The Background of the Confessional Formula in 1 Kor 8.6," *Zeitschrift für die neutestamentliche Wissenschaft* 69 (1978): 130–35.

185. In this way, the hymnic material in 8:6 strongly echoes (and functions like) Paul's earlier counsel in 1:28–30 and 3:21–23. See the discussion of 1 Corinthians 1–4 above.

186. Furnish, "Belonging to Christ," 154; James A. Davis, "The Interaction between Individual Ethical Conscience and Community Ethical Consciousness in 1 Corinthians," *Horizons in Biblical Theology* 10 (1988): 12; Fee, *First Corinthians,* 363.

187. There has been much discussion concerning the possible meanings of *syneidēsis:* among others, C. A. Pierce, *Conscience in the New Testament,* Studies in Biblical Theology 1.15 (London: SCM, 1955); M. E. Thrall, "The Pauline Uses of *SYNEIDĒSIS,*" *New Testament Studies* 14 (1968): 118–25; Richard A. Horsley, "Consciousness and Freedom among the Corinthians: 1 Corinthians 8–10," *Catholic Biblical Quarterly* 40

(1978): 581–89; Willis, *Idol Meat in Corinth*, 89–96; Paul W. Gooch, " 'Conscience' in 1 Corinthians 8 and 10," *New Testament Studies* 33 (1987): 244–54.

The term "moral consciousness" is Fee's (*First Corinthians*, 380–81 with notes). *Syneidēsis* seems to indicate both recognition of past experiences and a prompting to consider future moral actions. As a whole, Paul's moral reasoning takes into account doubts and waverings that signal the *syneidēsis* and prove helpful in the evaluation of one's measure of faith (see Rom 14:1–22). See Sampley, *Walking between the Times*, 57–60. This paradigm of being able to stand firm without wavering in regard to moral options has been counseled by Paul in 1 Cor 7:37.

The Corinthian situation concerning eating meat sacrificed to idols does not appear to be one in which the weak simply fall into destruction unaware. The strong have counseled maturity and growth for the weak through the acceptance of the strong's moral position and example. Some weak have attempted such moral reckoning, but it is beyond their capacity, and they experience moral dissonance and hurt. See n. 167 above and Willis, *Idol Meat in Corinth*, 75–78.

188. "In this way Paul makes room for a second voice, one that does not in fact ever speak for itself: the voice of those who have been excluded from the 'all' of the self-defined 'knowing' Christians (8:7), the voice of those who are 'weak' (8:7, 9, 11), but whom Paul immediately personifies and individualizes as 'the brother for whom Christ died' (8:11). . . . Would it not be better if he had quoted slogans of the 'weak' as well as the 'gnostics'? Does he not by speaking *about* them and *for* them, connive in their continued weakness? Or is it the case that the 'weak in conscience' were also weak in eloquence? Did those who 'knew' so much, and who most likely commanded the greater resources of wealth and influence, also possess the skills of rhetoric the Corinthian Christians seem to have admired so much?" (Meeks, "Polyphonic Ethics," 20). This is precisely the case: the strong advance their position with maxims, and Paul responds (in behalf of the weak) with refinement, correction, and refutation.

189. "Food will not commend us to God. We are no worse off if we do not eat, and no better off if we do" (RSV).

190. The use of the term *exousia* is most likely based in the background of popular Hellenistic philosophy. See Murphy-O'Connor, "Freedom or the Ghetto," 550 and Willis, *Idol Meat in Corinth*, 101–2. It is probable that *exousia* was introduced into the discussion by the Corinthians, and Paul has taken up their term. See Horsley, "Consciousness and Freedom," 579–80; Barrett, *First Epistle*, 195; Willis, *Idol Meat in Corinth*, 99; Fee, *First Corinthians*, 385.

191. This position would find some acceptance with the strong (see 6:13). Paul, however, shapes the *adiaphoron* to guard the position of the weak ("We are no worse off if we do not eat") as viable. In making their position defensible, the strong apparently advocate an education of the weak to their position. See Willis, *Idol Meat in Corinth*, 97–98, and n. 167 above.

192. The term *parastēsei* indicates the presentation of oneself before a judge. See Conzelmann, *1 Corinthians*, 148 and n. 21. Paul's moral reasoning envisions an apocalyptic presentation of each believer before God for judgment or approval. Paul's hope is that all believers will stand worthy of commendation at that time (1 Cor 1:8; 3:13–15; 4:5). Cf. Sampley, *Walking between the Times*, 70–76.

193. Maxims are not commands or formal directives and rules. Maxims are the basis for moral reasoning in which the hearer is invited to enter into the maxim and consider

one of many possible behavioral applications. Moving hearers to make their own self-application has a very powerful rhetorical effect.

194. For the moralists' views on *adiaphora* and the doctrine of "preferreds," see n. 136 above.

195. See the discussion of these *adiaphora* maxims on pp. 42–43 above.

196. See Sampley, "Faith and Its Moral Life," 233–38, and idem., *Walking between the Times*, 77–83. Cf. Furnish, "Belonging to Christ," 154–56.

197. Paul's hyperbole (*ou mē phagō... eis ton aiōna*) is for emphasis. His declaration is conditional: in situations where Paul is aware that a fellow believer may fall due to his eating of meat, Paul does not eat. That Paul will never eat meat again (ever) goes against his conduct in the gospel ("all things to all people" [1 Cor 9:19–23]) and his argumentation in 10:23–11:1. See Robertson and Plummer, *1 Corinthians*, 173.

198. Fee argues that Paul's reference to eating in an "idol's temple" here in 8:10 must refer to participation in idolatrous cultic rituals that Paul strictly forbids in 1 Cor 10:14–22 (see Fee, *First Corinthians*, 378). Fee's position seems untenable. See the critique of B. N. Fisk, "Eating Meat Offered to Idols: Corinthian Behavior and Pauline Response in 1 Corinthians 8–10 (A Response to Gordon Fee)," *Trinity Journal* 10 (1989): 49–70. Surely the reference is more probably to the dining halls attached to pagan temples in which a variety of social occasions took place. For this position as an alternative to Fee, along with a review of the archeological evidence, and with attention to the judgment of classical scholars, see Oster ("Use, Misuse, and Neglect," 64–67), who concludes, "In light of the explicit Pauline encouragement for Christians to associate with pagan idolaters (1 Cor 5,9f.12), it takes little imagination to realize that believers would have been invited by pagan friends and would have attended numerous social and cultural events (for example, meals, birthday parties) associated with temple sites.... The dining facilities at Corinth provide architectural evidence for a situation in which 'monotheistic' believers... could attend and participate in activities indigenous to their religio-cultural matrix but which did not require overt participation in the central *cultus* and sacrifices of the religion itself" (66–67). Cf. Willis, *Idol Meat in Corinth*, 62–64.

199. The death of Christ forms the self-definition and worth of every believer (see Rom 3:21–26). This tenet is part of every believer's "common story." See Sampley, "Faith and Its Moral Life," 224.

200. Furnish, "Belonging to Christ," 154–56.

201. Murphy-O'Connor ("Freedom or the Ghetto," 364) makes a reasonable argument that the reference to "Christ" in 8:12 is interchangeable with "the body of Christ," that is, the believing community.

202. This becomes increasingly apparent as the argument continues through 1 Corinthians 10. It is important, however, even at this point, to remind ourselves that Paul is attempting to bring concord into the community and not draw further lines of separation. In addition, he wishes to do nothing that would jeopardize his own hearing by all parties involved. See Mitchell, *Rhetoric of Reconciliation*, 237–38.

203. Sampley, *Walking between the Times*, 50–52.

204. Furnish, "Belonging to Christ," 150. In agreement is Meeks, "Polyphonic Ethics," 24: "What Paul is undertaking to do in this part of his letter is not merely to secure a particular outcome in the case under discussion. It is rather to help the participants to become more competent moral agents, that is, to help them to achieve a peculiar form of moral confidence that befits their status as believers in Jesus Christ and

members of his 'body.' To have moral confidence is to know what one is doing." Cf. Willis, *Idol Meat in Corinth*, 118–20, who insists that Paul has no apparent interest in educating the weak, as evidenced in his reading of 1 Corinthians 8. It is true that Paul is not concerned to build up the weak to the strong's position, but he certainly has an interest in building up the entire community in the area of "ethical accommodation" (see n. 239 below), as the argument in 1 Corinthians 8–10 in its totality demonstrates.

205. See Sampley, "Faith and Its Moral Life," 232–33, with an extended example from Paul's relationship to Philemon. With regard to 1 Corinthians 8–10 specifically, the same point is made by Christopher M. Tuckett, "Paul, Tradition and Freedom," *Theologische Zeitschrift* 47 (1991): 321–22.

206. See the extended discussion and review of the issues in Mitchell, *Rhetoric of Reconciliation*, 243–47 with notes. Also see Wendell Willis, "An Apostolic Apology?: The Form and Function of 1 Corinthians 9," *Journal for the Study of the New Testament* 24 (1985): 3–48; Dale B. Martin, *Slavery as Salvation: The Metaphor of Slavery in Pauline Christianity* (New Haven, Conn.: Yale University Press, 1990), 68–80.

207. Mitchell, *Rhetoric of Reconciliation*, 130, 246–47. On the equation between *exousia* (right) and *eleutheria* (liberty) in 1 Corinthians 8–10, see Fee, *First Corinthians*, 384 n. 46; Conzelmann, *1 Corinthians*, 154 n. 27.

208. Mitchell, *Rhetoric of Reconciliation*, 247 and literature in n. 338.

209. Victor C. Pfitzner, *Paul and the Agon Motif: Traditional Athletic Imagery in the Pauline Literature*, Supplements to Novum Testamentum 16 (Leiden: Brill, 1967), 30, 21–35.

210. Cf. ibid., 97–98 (though I do not share Pfitzner's view that 9:24–27 is primarily Paul's defense and secondarily paraenetic).

211. That is, one who need not prove his or her freedom, but who can freely refuse to exercise freedom when doing so might harm another person.

212. For example, the theme of self-control through love resurfaces in 1 Corinthians 13 as a response to some in the community who are scrambling for recognition through their exercise of spiritual gifts. In a similar manner, this response is in the form of Paul's personal example. See Carl R. Holladay, "1 Corinthians 13: Paul as Apostolic Paradigm," in *Greeks, Romans, Christians*, ed. David L. Balch, Everett Ferguson, and Wayne A. Meeks (Minneapolis: Fortress, 1990), 80–98.

213. On the fluidity of the diatribe style, see George L. Kustas, "Diatribe in Ancient Rhetorical Theory," in *Protocol of the Colloquy of the Center for Hermeneutical Studies in Hellenistic and Modern Culture* (Berkeley: Center for Hermeneutical Studies in Hellenistic and Modern Culture, 1976), 1–15; Stowers, *Diatribe and Paul's Letter to the Romans*, 48–78; Malherbe, "Hellenistic Moralists," 313–20.

214. In agreement is Mitchell (*Rhetoric of Reconciliation*, 247), though she does not attribute her observation to Paul's diatribe style.

215. The apostrophe is "a response to an immediately preceding objection," here "an indicting rhetorical question" (Stowers, *Diatribe and Paul's Letter to the Romans*, 86–87). The fictitious interlocutor is not identified directly.

216. "It is also characteristic that after turning to address the interlocutor *one or a series of rhetorical questions* in an indicting or didactic tone *follow*" (ibid., 88).

217. Ibid., 89. A characteristic marker such as *ouk oidate* is missing, but the response of "Am I not an apostle?" by the self-proclaimed apostle (1 Cor 1:1) carries the same freight. The *ouk oidate* shows up in 9:13 and 24.

218. In using these rhetorical questions Paul can also count on the Corinthians' past experiences of having him in their midst.

219. If it is accepted that 9:1–14 is written in diatribe style, then the examination has been alluded to already. Those who examine Paul are those who question his freedom based on his personal example given in 8:13. Cf. Mitchell (*Rhetoric of Reconciliation*, 247), who makes this determination on the basis of the inner logic of the section. Cf. Willis ("Apostolic Apologia?" 34), who argues that 9:3 is a transition verse connecting vv. 1–2 to vv. 4–14. However, his attempt to render *tois anakrinousin* as a future participle (to those who would examine me) is unwarranted and unnecessary. See Fee, *First Corinthians*, 401 n. 24.

220. Techniques listed by Stowers (*Diatribe and Paul's Letter to the Romans*, 130–32) include abrupt rejection; dialogical exchange; counter question; example or *chreia*; author's own example or situation; analogies or comparisons; quotations from poets, dramatists, and philosophers; maxims ("apophthegms" or "sayings of the sages"); and exhortations. Paul's overall style continues as a barrage of rhetorical questions.

221. Paul's use of rhetorical questions in 1 Corinthians 9 is educational, as governed by the diatribe style, the advancement of his personal example, and his choice of deliberative oratory. The rhetorical questions function to persuade by common assent to shared values through apparent analogy. In 1 Corinthians 9, there is an affective element (central to diatribe in general [see Kustas, "Diatribe in Ancient Rhetorical Theory," 12–13]) at work as Paul's insistence and emphasis that he is a free person are established with over sixteen questions. For a study of rhetorical questions and their function in 1 Corinthians, see Wuellner, "Paul as Pastor," 49–77.

222. "Very often the immediate response to an objection or false conclusion is a *counter question*" (Stowers, *Diatribe and Paul's Letter to the Romans*, 131). This accounts for the interrogative form of the gnomic maxims.

223. On the connection of the maxim to diatribe style, see Appendix A n. 24 and n. 220 above.

224. Paul has composed conventional wisdom in a poetic format. The indefinite *tis* provides a general nature to each gnomic maxim. The truth of each is not in dispute; together they clinch the point, and no elaboration is needed. The stylistic qualities of Paul's composition are more easily recognized when the three interrogative statements are taken and compared as a whole:

> *Tis strateuetai idiois opsōniois pote?*
>
> *Tis phyteuei ampelōna kai ton karpon autou ouk esthiei?*
>
> *Tis poimainei poimnēn kai ek tou galaktos tēs poimnēs ouk esthiei?*

Viewed as three consecutive lines, anaphora (*Tis;* 1–3), antistrophe (*ouk esthiei;* 2–3), symploce (*Tis...ouk esthiei;* 2–3), and polyptoton (*poimn-;* 3) are identifiable as stylistic features. The needless repetition of *tēs poimnēs* (pleonasm) seems to draw out the incredulity: "not to eat [drink] of the milk *of the same flock tended?*" The "straightforward and incontestable nature" of much of what Paul presents in 9:4–14 has been noted by Willis, "Apostolic Apologia?" 35.

225. Paul substitutes the synonym *kēmōseis* for the LXX *phimōseis*. See Malan, "Use of the Old Testament," 151.

226. Generally if *hoti* is taken in a causal sense (because) related to the Deut 25:4 quotation in v. 9, then there are no quotation marks indicated for v. 10 (as in the RSV;

cf. NRSV). If *hoti* is taken as a quotation marker, then a quotation is indicated for the latter half of v. 10 (as in the Nestle-Aland 26). In the second case the quotation is thought to be from an unknown apocryphal writing (Conzelmann, *1 Corinthians*, 155). It is possible, however, that *hoti* is causal *and* a quotation is given. This is because the quotation in 9:10b can be determined on the stylistic grounds of *parallelismus membrorum* alone (ibid.):

> *opheilei ep elpidi ho apotriōn apotrian*
> *kai ho aloōn ep elpidi tou metechein*

Malan suggests that this quotation may be either Paul's composition or from an unknown source. Either way it conforms to what we have defined as a gnomic maxim. See the full discussion of 9:9–10 and their grammatical points in Malan, "Use of the Old Testament," 150–52.

227. "The heart of Paul's argument is to be found in 12b, 15a, and 18b, all three of which sentences say the exact same thing.... Paul has not exercised his *exousia*, though he surely had the right to" (Mitchell, *Rhetoric of Reconciliation*, 248).

228. If Paul's rhetorical strategy is to build himself up as a free individual who is equal to the Corinthian strong, only to impress those same strong with his reversal of values and renunciation of his rights (for example, Willis, "Apostolic Apologia?" 34–35), then why does he "play his hand," so to speak, in v. 12 prior to the crescendo of his demonstrated freedom in v. 14? Paul's boast (*kauchēma*) and reward (*misthos*) are not from the *renunciation* of his *exousia* (he never renounces his rights), but from his proper use of it (which at times means leaving it unexercised)!

229. Martin, *Slavery as Salvation*, 120–21.

230. Barrett, *First Epistle*, 207; Conzelmann, *1 Corinthians*, 157; Fee, *First Corinthians*, 412.

231. "Paul is multiplying arguments" (Conzelmann, *1 Corinthians*, 157).

232. Strongly argued by Dungan, *Sayings of Jesus*, 27. More cautiously allowed by Fee, *First Corinthians*, 413.

233. For a study of the tradition history of this proverb (Luke 10:7) and its relationship to 1 Cor 9:14, see A. E. Harvey, "'The Workman Is Worthy of His Hire': Fortunes of a Proverb in the Early Church," *Novum Testamentum* 24 (1982): 209–21.

234. Moral decisions by contrast are without *anagkē* and with *exousia* (see 1 Cor 7:37).

235. A believer's boasting is carefully circumscribed by Paul. There is always the knowledge that one's work is ultimately a result of God's working (see 1:31). Expressed from the perspective of human responsibility, one's boast is always the proper use of one's measure of faith to produce works of love, and it is not in the works of others. Through proper self-testing, the works done by a believer will, one may hope, be deemed appropriate to God. "But let each one test his own work, and then his reason to boast will be in himself alone and not in his neighbor" (Gal 6:4). See Sampley, *Walking between the Times*, 44–76, esp. 72–73.

236. The patron-client relationship seems like the best conjecture for Paul's claim in 9:12b that exercising his right to support from the Corinthians would produce an *egkopēn* (obstacle). Given the social stratification and influence of high-status individuals in the Corinthian community, Paul's identification with the weak, not to mention his freedom, would be undermined by a client relationship to high-status Corinthian patrons. Peter Marshall (*Enmity in Corinth: Social Conventions in Paul's Relations with the Corinthians*, Wissenschaftliche Untersuchungen zum Neuen Testament 2/23 [Tübingen: Mohr/

Siebeck, 1987], 1–129) has detailed the social relations of the patron-client situation in terms of friendship norms. Marshall's attempt, however, to read back the situation reflected in 2 Cor 11:7–15 and 12:11–15 as the basis for a charge against Paul as a flatterer who has spurned higher-status patrons in Corinth is misguided. See the review of Marshall's work by Dale B. Martin, *Journal of Biblical Literature* 108 (1989): 542–44. Also cf. Ronald F. Hock ("Paul's Tentmaking and the Problem of His Social Class," *Journal of Biblical Literature* 97 [1978]: 555–64), who sees in 1 Corinthians 9 Paul defending his choice to be a servile working philosopher rather than the household philosopher of a patron. For a study of patronage in Roman Corinth, see Chow, *Patronage and Power,* 38–82.

Paul is surely aware of the restrictions and complications that surround worldly patron-client relationships in their variety of forms. He wants to stay clear of all obstacles to the gospel and counsels the Corinthians, as well, not to walk according to human status-seeking ways in the community. When Paul does enter into a relationship in which he receives support from the more mature Philippians, it is not as a client but as an equal in partnership. See Sampley, *Pauline Partnership,* 51–72, 85–87, 109. Cf. Bengt Holmberg, *Paul and Power: The Structure of Authority in the Primitive Church as Reflected in the Pauline Epistles* (Philadelphia: Fortress, 1978), 89–93.

237. See n. 235 above.

238. Noteworthy is the insightful treatment by Martin in which he suggests that Paul's metaphor of self-enslavement is heard and accepted differently along the social scale. Lower-status members of the community would respond positively to Paul as an "enslaved leader" (an ancient topos). Higher-status members of the community would find Paul's slavery claim to be somewhat distressing. Paul's argument in chapter 9 (a "fictitious defense" to the strong), however, attempts to persuade these high-status individuals to accept and follow Paul's example as one whose leadership role is more appropriate to the gospel (see *Slavery as Salvation,* 117–24). Martin has further suggested that Paul's rhetoric through much of 1 Corinthians is to pattern himself as one of the strong who then renounces rights and privileges in behalf of the weak. The strong are encouraged to follow Paul in this example (ibid., 140–42, and idem, "Tongues of Angels," 578–80). Paul, however, never *renounces* his rights: he leaves them unexercised in *certain* instances when not to do so could harm a weaker member.

239. Gooch has appropriately analyzed the ethics of accommodation, noting its three forms: theological, epistemological, and ethical. Paul does not accommodate theologically and he is careful in 1 Cor 9:20–22 to give parameters for his beliefs ("not myself being under the law"; "not being without law"). Paul accommodates epistemologically in the sense that he is willing to take up the arguments and terms of others into discussion. He, however, qualifies, refines, and corrects these positions based on his understanding of the gospel. Ethical accommodation is the goal of Paul's discussion in 1 Corinthians 9. Gooch rightly indicates that Paul's point is made from his personal conduct, his behavior. Paul's new identity (in Christ) leaves him free from maintaining old identities and allows him self-identification with others. See Peter Richardson and Paul W. Gooch, "Accommodation Ethics," *Tyndale Bulletin* 29 (1978): 93–117. Cf. Mitchell, *Rhetoric of Reconciliation,* 248, who stresses the role of accommodation (or compromise) for the sake of concord.

240. See the analysis in Fee, *First Corinthians,* 423 n. 9; Barbara Hall, "All Things to All People: A Study of 1 Corinthians 9:19–23," in *The Conversation Continues: Studies*

in Paul and John, ed. Robert T. Fortna and Beverly R. Gaventa (Nashville: Abingdon, 1990), 139.

241. The identification and relationship of the groups cited are not my central concern here. See the discussion in Fee, *First Corinthians,* 422–33. Willis ("Apostolic Apologia?" 37–38) notes that Paul seems to have no specific occasions in mind. Hall ("All Things to All People," 144–54) tries to connect 1 Cor 9:19–23 to the echo of Gal 3:28 found in 1 Cor 7:17–24.

242. Barrett, *First Epistle,* 215; Conzelmann, *1 Corinthians,* 161; Grosheide, *First Corinthians,* 213–14; Willis, "Apostolic Apologia?" 36–38; Furnish, "Belonging to Christ," 155. Fee (*First Corinthians,* 430–31) disagrees, opting for an apologetic function.

243. Hall, "All Things to All People," 138.

244. *Hoi en stadiō trechontes pantes men trechousin, eis de lambanei to brabeion.* The interrogative form is influenced by the diatribe style; the form is antithetical with a common wisdom claim analogous to the three maxims in 1 Cor 9:7.

245. The emphasis is on focusing oneself to obtain "the prize" and not the limited number of victors. See Pfitzner, *Paul and the Agon Motif,* 87; Conzelmann, *1 Corinthians,* 162; Fee, *First Corinthians,* 435.

246. Paul's use of the diatribe is pedagogical; therefore, the use of exhortation as he begins to draw his conclusion is appropriate. See Stowers, *Diatribe and Paul's Letter to the Romans,* 132–33.

247. The maxim core (9:25a) would function as a gnomic maxim in any contextual situation. Paul, however, has attached an explanation that particularizes the application to the believing community. Since the explanation (9:25b) lacks a finite verb, it must be taken as an extension of the maxim core. Paul has composed what we have referred to as a gnomic sentence.

Maxim core (9:25a):
 Pas de ho agōnizomenos panta egkrateuetai.
 "Every athlete exercises self-control in all things."
Maxim supplement (9:25b):
 Ekeinoi men oun hina phtharton stephanon labōsin, hēmeis de aphtharton.
 "They do it to receive a perishable wreath, but we an imperishable one."

In the flow of Paul's usage this maxim is notable and emphasized by virtue of *not* being in the interrogative form. The *de* is surely consecutive and to be rendered as "now" or simply left untranslated (Fee, *First Corinthians,* 436 n. 15). The maxim core (9:25a) is a compact piece of common wisdom, straightforwardly presented, but carefully shaped. For the emphasis falls on *panta egkrateuetai,* which undoubtedly signaled the hearer to compare previously exchanged maxims from 1 Cor 3:23 (*panta hymōn estin*) and 6:12 (*panta exestin moi*).

248. Here *soma* is to be equated with the whole person. Paul's use of *dolagōgō* with *soma* certainly echoes *emauton edoulōsa* in 1 Cor 9:19. See Pfitzner, *Paul and the Agon Motif,* 92–93. For the use of the runner, boxer, and wrestler as a moral metaphor among the Hellenistic philosophers, see ibid., 31–32.

249. See the discussion of 1 Cor 6:12 in relation to 10:23 below.

250. Limits of space and time do not allow a full exegesis of 1 Corinthians 10 to be undertaken here. The flow of Paul's argument is maintained, and maxim usage is examined in particular. Detailed studies on 1 Corinthians 10 include Fee, *First Corinthians,* 441–91; Wayne A. Meeks, "'And Rose Up to Play': Midrash and Paraenesis in 1 Cor

10:1–22," *Journal for the Society of the New Testament* 16 (1982): 64–78; Willis, *Idol Meat in Corinth*, 123–263.

251. Conzelmann, *1 Corinthians*, 166; Willis, *Idol Meat in Corinth*, 127–32; Mitchell, *Rhetoric of Reconciliation*, 251.

252. The contours of Paul's illustration suggest that they knew the story in some detail.

253. *Tauta de typikōs synebainen ekeinois, egraphē de pros nouthesian hēmōn* ("Now these things happened to them in a patterned fashion, and they were written for our instruction" [my trans.]).

254. See Willis, *Idol Meat in Corinth*, 147–53, for an analysis of the structure of 1 Cor 10:7–10 and the textual issues connected with these verses.

255. Ibid., 147–48.

256. Contra Willis, *Idol Meat in Corinth*, 148–53, who argues that the listing after idolatry represents general paraenesis rather than specific occasions in Corinth. On the other hand, Mitchell, *Rhetoric of Reconciliation*, 250–51, sees the entire list as representative of "specific behaviors that divide" the Corinthians.

257. For a discussion concerning whether 10:13 continues the warning in v. 12 or provides a word of comfort, see Willis, *Idol Meat in Corinth*, 157–59.

258. That some Corinthians believed they were protected from contamination or punishment of sins by baptism and the eating of the Lord's supper is not a necessary conjecture from this section. The warning in 10:12 may be directed to the consequences of divisions within the community as based on these examples from the Hebrew scriptures. See Mitchell, *Rhetoric of Reconciliation*, 251–52; cf. Willis, *Idol Meat in Corinth*, 155–57, 159–61.

259. Of course, this freedom position of some Corinthians is the attitude or stance of walking in a humanly way that Paul has attempted to adjust with his reminder of cruciform freedom in 1 Corinthians 1–4. Cf. 1 Cor 1:19, 30–31; 3:18–23; 4:7.

260. The list in 1 Cor 10:7–10 functions in a manner similar to the vice-lists in 1 Corinthians 5–6. See pp. 38–39 above.

261. Mitchell, *Rhetoric of Reconciliation*, 254–55: "[In antiquity] [c]ultic ties are commonly appealed to in attempts to get divided groups back together again."

262. Cf. Willis, *Idol Meat in Corinth*, 182–84.

263. See ibid., 165–222, for the identification and background of *koinōnia* as well as a discussion of its various interpretations. I am in general agreement with Willis's conclusions: "Therefore, in 1 Cor 10:16f. *koinōnia* does not mean 'participate in the Lord,' either understood as the ingesting of Christ, or as being incorporated into a Risen Lord. Nor does it mean comradeship, the association among people of similar beliefs and sentiments. Rather, *koinōnia* means the relationship established among members of a covenant and the obligations ensuing from it."

264. Mitchell, *Rhetoric of Reconciliation*, 255–56. Or possibly the partnership is to a community of members that is perceived as being connected to demonic powers. Cf. Willis, *Idol Meat in Corinth*, 188–92.

265. Mitchell, *Rhetoric of Reconciliation*, 256, and the literature cited in n. 388.

266. See Furnish, "Belonging to Christ," 145–57, who argues that "belonging to Christ" is the pivotal foundation in Paul's ethical argumentation in 1 Corinthians — a position based on "Christ crucified" that encompasses love for oneself and others.

267. Cf. Gooch (Richardson and Gooch, "Accommodation Ethics," 111), who states:

"As Christ's slave the Christian is freed from all else and everyone else; but he must have regard for his own good and the preservation of his freedom; and above all he must look to the good of others rather than to his own advantage. Paul puts it nicely in 7:35: in what he says he doesn't want to put a rein on the Corinthians with regulations; instead he is thinking of their own good, of what will promote good order, and of their ability to wait without distraction on the Lord. Thus the context of Christian behaviour includes freedom, and love for Christ, for others, and for self."

268. Paul has taken the Corinthians' moral *sententia* and added a supplement in antithetical form (cf. the discussion of 1 Cor 4:20 and 8:1b above). The initial maxim in 6:12a reads:

> Maxim core: *panta moi exestin*
> Supplement: *all' ou panta sympherei*

The resulting maxim employs (1) a concise form, (2) an antithetical structure, (3) repetition of *panta,* and (4) a nicely balanced syllabic rhythm on both sides of the *alla.* In 1 Cor 10:23a, Paul drops the *moi* in the maxim core, but little, if anything, is lost with regard to its maxim features. Cf. Stowers, "Debate over Freedom," 62, who has noted the "compact and aphoristic" style.

269. Ibid., 62–63, 66–69.

270. *Sympherein:* to be advantageous, profitable, helpful, beneficial. See the discussion in Mitchell, *Rhetoric of Reconciliation,* 33–39. Cf. Stanley K. Stowers, *Letter-Writing in Greco-Roman Antiquity,* Library of Early Christianity (Philadelphia: Westminster, 1986), 108–9.

271. Noted early by Grant, "Hellenistic Elements," 61. A fuller treatment with texts from Musonius Rufus, Epictetus, and Marcus Aurelius can be found in Stowers, "Debate over Freedom," 64–65.

272. This is a gnomic sentence of Paul's composition. It is particularized with its reference to "eating" and with its use of the second plural.

> *Eite oun esthiete eite pinete eite ti poieite,*
> *panta eis doksan theou poieite.*

> "So whether you eat or drink, or whatever you do,
> do all things to the glory of God."

Stylistic features have been analyzed by Watson, "1 Corinthians 10:23–11:1," 307: the maxim (Watson simply calls it a "restatement" that is "rhetorically sophisticated") as a whole employs the figures of polysyndeton (*eite... eite... eite*), antistrophe (*poieite... poieite*), homoeoptoton (*esthiete, pinete, poieite*), and amplification by accumulation (*esthiete, pinete, ti poieite = panta*). Cf. Willis, *Idol Meat in Corinth,* 251; Conzelmann, *1 Corinthians,* 171.

273. Murphy-O'Connor, "Freedom or the Ghetto," 571–73.

274. Detailed discussion of these and other issues can be found in Fee, *First Corinthians,* 475–91; Willis, *Idol Meat in Corinth,* 223–57.

275. This aspect has been the focus of Watson's study, "1 Corinthians 10:23–11:1," 301–18. Also see Omanson, "Acknowledging Paul's Quotations," 210–11.

276. For the refining of a maxim as an elaboration pattern, see chap. 1, pp. 19–20.

277. "We shall not repeat the same thing precisely — for that, to be sure, would weary the hearer and not refine the idea — but with changes."

278. *Mēdeis to heautou zēteitō alla to tou heterou.* Each *to* in 10:24 remains unspecified: "the [thing]." The referent must be supplied, and the RSV inserts "good" (although *agathon* does not appear in the text). The NRSV has recently substituted "advantage" for "good." *To* with a neuter adjective can represent an abstract idea in Greek. According to Blass, Debrunner, and Funk (*A Greek Grammar of the New Testament and Other Early Christian Literature* [Chicago: University of Chicago Press, 1961], 138), "[p]eculiar to Paul (Heb) is the use of a neuter singular adjective like an abstract, mostly with a dependent genitive." Taking Paul's refinement seriously, we should expect 10:24 to incorporate his qualifications from 10:23ab. Thus I have supplied "advantage" in the first instance and "what builds up" in the second instance. Another rendering that highlights the appropriateness of the dependent genitives might be: "Let each not seek the advantage of him/herself only, but the upbuilding of the other."

279. Paul does not demand that the believer abandon seeking after his or her own advantage — as our discussion of the rest of this passage bears out. So also Robertson and Plummer, *1 Corinthians*, 220. What Paul seeks is a balance between individuation and sensitivity to community members.

280. See n. 278 above.

281. Paul's quotation corresponds exactly to the LXX Ps 23:1 (Masoretic text 24:1): *Tou kuriou hē gē kai to plērōma autēs.* The Corinthians may well have recognized it as a scriptural text taught them by Paul. If not, the statement represents a gnomic maxim. Either way, the function as supporting proof is the same. For scripture used as a gnomic maxim, see the discussion of 1 Cor 1:31 above. In the case of 1:31, maxim identification is aided by Paul's reformulation of the LXX and recurrence in 2 Cor 10:17. Cf. the discussion in Malan, "Use of the Old Testament," 153–54.

282. The *Ad Herennium* examples are also in the interrogative form. For example: "How can I adequately repay her from whom I have received these blessings?" (4.55).

283. Only in these final four verses (10:31–11:1) of the section does Watson ("1 Corinthians 10:23–11:1," 311) see the rhetorical move of refining (*expolitio*) at work. As we have shown, however, refining structures 1 Cor 10:23–11:1 throughout.

284. Paul uses the techniques of refining (restatement with variation, dialogue, arousal) and some of the elaborating forms such as reasons, illustration, example, and conclusion in developing his pattern of maxim argumentation in 10:23–11:1. It, however, does not read like a fully and systematically developed *progymnasmata* exercise. Cf. the developed example of maxim refinement in *Ad Herennium* 4.43.56–44.58.

285. See *Ad Alexandrum* 33.1439b.12–14. for recapitulation in deliberative rhetoric. The various forms of recapitulation are discussed in Watson, "1 Corinthians 10:23–11:1," 311. In 1 Corinthians 10:23–11:1, recapitulation takes the form of an enumeration of points already considered (*apologismos*).

286. Hurd (*Origin of 1 Corinthians*, 129–30) is entirely right on this point, and his chart of parallel relationships between 1 Corinthians 8–9 and 1 Cor 10:23–11:1 remains valuable. Compare the chart in Fisk, "Eating Meat Offered to Idols," 66.

287. So Gooch, "Conscience in 1 Corinthians," 251–52. Cf. Fee, *First Corinthians*, 481; Willis, *Idol Meat in Corinth*, 229–34.

288. An accepted position by a number of scholars, for example, Barrett, *First Epistle*, 242; Robertson and Plummer, *1 Corinthians*, 221; Grosheide, *First Corinthians*, 242. Fee (*First Corinthians*, 483–85), however, rejects the view of a weak Christian and argues for a pagan informant. See a full discussion of the issues in Willis, *Idol Meat in Corinth*,

240–45. If Paul is (1) recapitulating his argumentation from 1 Corinthians 6, 8, and 9 and (2) proceeding with an *expolitio* pattern of restatement, why would he advance a new situation (concern for a pagan's conscience) with so little detail? Would the Corinthians have noticed such a sharp turn?

289. According to the pattern of refining described above, these verses make up *one* illustration developed in three ways: restatement (twice, the second with more specificity), dialogue, and arousal.

290. For example, see nn. 288 and 289 above. The emphasis in *Ad Herennium* 4.42.54 is on equivalency (*eadem*).

291. Willis (*Idol Meat in Corinth*, 244) rightly rejects this catalog of Robertson and Plummer, commonly followed by others, in favor of the two situations that follow now in our discussion.

292. Willis, *Idol Meat in Corinth*, 244.

293. Willis (ibid., 242–45) advances the same function for vv. 28–29a (a general restriction based on v. 24 and posited to both v. 25 and v. 27) but finds it necessary to argue that Paul begins a new subsection and has shifted the argument to general paraenesis. Hence, Fee (*First Corinthians*, 483, n. 40) takes him to task for ignoring the "clear grammatical tie" between v. 27 and v. 28 as indicated by the adversative *de* (but). The pattern of refining explicated here supports Willis's position while removing the need to divide the argument or discount the grammatical link between vv. 27 and 28.

294. That Paul has changed his address to the weak is argued by some in order to explain *mēden anakrinontes dia tēn syneidēsin* ("without raising any question on the ground of conscience") in v. 25. See Grosheide, *First Corinthians*, 241; Robertson and Plummer, *1 Corinthians*, 220. Robert Jewett (*Paul's Anthropological Terms*, AGJU 10 [Leiden: Brill, 1971], 478) even proposes that those with weak consciences introduced the term *anakrinein* and the phrase *dia syneidēsin*. See the review of positions in Willis, *Idol Meat in Corinth*, 229–34.

295. For example, Hall ("All Things to All People," 155, n. 19) suggests this pattern: to the strong, v. 23; to both strong and weak, v. 24; to the weak, vv. 25–27; "side glance" to the strong, vv. 28–29a; to the weak, vv. 29b–30.

296. Cf. Willis, *Idol Meat in Corinth*, 232–33.

297. Ibid., 232.

298. Hence, Meeks ("Polyphonic Ethics," 20) notes that the voice of the weak is present, but it never speaks for itself. Cf. John C. Brunt, "Love, Freedom, and Moral Responsibility: The Contribution of 1 Cor 8–10 to an Understanding of Paul's Ethical Thinking," in *Society of Biblical Literature Seminar Papers 1981*, ed. Kent Harold Richards (Chico, Calif.: Scholars Press, 1981), 20.

299. It is not an education of the conscience (of the weak), as Murphy-O'Connor ("Freedom or the Ghetto," 566–68) suggests. Paul is counseling all Corinthians to treat themselves and each other well. All should be done to the glory of God. Also see n. 300 below.

300. Paul models the strong and free person who cares for the weak. But Paul's thought-world includes the notion that the faith of each believer should grow continually in strength, and this growth makes more options available. See Sampley, "Faith and Its Moral Life," 236–37. Paul's instruction in 1 Corinthians 8–10 provides guidelines, information, validation, and modeling that might increase the options of the weak. Also of note is how Paul's moral counsel in 1 Corinthians as a whole provides believers with

the ability to test options and remain faithful (see the discussion of maxim argumentation in 1 Corinthians 7 above; esp. 1 Cor 7:36–37). Cf. the discussion of 1 Cor 6:12–20 and 1 Cor 7:1–40 as "models of responsible deliberation" in Stowers, "Paul on the Use and Abuse of Reason," 262–66.

301. Cf. Sampley, *Walking between the Times*, 49.

302. On this issue see the section "Maxims, Freedom, and Rights" in the Conclusions to this book.

303. Wuellner ("Greek Rhetoric and Argumentation," 187) notes the connection of these final verses (10:31–11:1) with 1 Cor 1:10.

Conclusions

1. For example, Romans (2:11; 4:4; 8:6; 13:3; 14:17), 2 Corinthians (3:17b; 10:17; 13:11), Galatians (3:15b; 5:6; 6:7, 15), Philippians (1:21; 2:4; 4:1a, 8), 1 Thessalonians (5:14–22). This listing is not intended to be comprehensive. The reader may wish to consider nn. 8, 10, and 13 in the introduction above.

2. We need not limit the captivation of some Corinthians with rhetoric to the use of maxims alone. But given the emphasis on maxims in the letter, it seems reasonable to think maxims played some part in the *sophia tou logou* (1:17; 2:1, 4).

3. Sometimes this qualifying statement is a maxim formed from the Corinthian maxim, as in 6:12a and b; and 10:23a and b. At another time the qualifying statement is Paul's own maxim, as in 8:1b (related to the Corinthian maxim by the common term *gnōsis*). In 7:2, it is simply a qualifying statement.

4. The pattern is: (1) Corinthian maxim (6:12a), qualifying statement (6:12a and b), elaboration (6:13–19), directive (6:20); (2) Corinthian maxim (7:1), qualifying statement (7:2), elaboration (7:3–24), new maxim (7:25–26), elaboration of new maxim (7:27–40); (3) Corinthian maxim (8:1a), qualifying statement (8:1b), elaboration (8:2–7), new maxim (8:8), elaboration of new maxim (8:9–13); (4) Corinthian maxim (10:23a, without *moi*), qualifying statement (10:23a and b), elaboration (10:24–30), new maxim (10:31), elaboration of new maxim (10:32–11:1). The "new maxim" in each case does not introduce a new idea but a new maxim expression of material already qualified and elaborated on by Paul.

5. See n. 4 above.

6. *Panta moi exestin all' ou panta sympherei.* (6:12a)
   Panta moi exestin all' ouk egō exousiasthēsomai hypo tinos. (6:12b)
   Panta exestin all' ou panta sympherei. (10:23a)
   Panta exestin all' ou panta oikodomei. (10:23b)

7. *Pas de ho agōnizomenos panta egkrateuetai.* (9:25a)
   ...*panta eis doksan theou poieite.* (10:31b; maxim core)
   Ta de panta ek tou theou. (11:12; cf. 3:21–23)
   ...*panta pros oikodomēn ginesthō.* (14:26; maxim core of a gnomic
        sentence containing a supplement by accumulation)
   Panta de euschēmonōs kai kata taxin ginesthō. (14:40; concluding *sententia*)
   Panta hymōn en agapē ginesthō. (16:14; Paul's concluding exhortation in
        a maxim stack)

8. The problems in the Corinthian community most likely had a variety of sources found either separately or in combination: among others, social-class distinctions connected with rhetoric or wealth, spiritual enthusiasm, pride, conflicting notions of the

role of the corporeal body, syncretism with pagan religious customs, and low esteem among weaker members who were unable to say no to other members trying to run the community as if it were in the world.

9. On the subject of the establishment of moral communities in early Christianity, see Wayne A. Meeks, *The Origins of Christian Morality: The First Two Centuries* (New Haven, Conn.: Yale University Press, 1993).

10. Meeks, "Polyphonic Ethics," 17.

11. Paul's moral reasoning, however, is bounded by the vice-lists that appear as a given. He expects the Corinthians to know and accept these boundaries as well. See Sampley, *Walking between the Times,* 57.

12. "Maxims steadfastly keep the responsibility for direction squarely upon the believer — just as Paul, eschewing command, did with Philemon — who must determine what light refracts from that maxim onto his or her own situation" (ibid., 97).

13. That the content and possibly the form of the Corinthian maxims originated with Paul is a reasonable conjecture but not a conclusive one. Paul is only in qualified disagreement with the maxims in 6:23, 8:1, and 8:4. The concepts of freedom, knowledge, the one God, and the nonexistence of idols are evident elsewhere in Paul's letters and may very well have been taught to the Corinthians by Paul. The use of maxims both in rhetoric and in moral persuasion were, however, common traditions undoubtedly known by some Corinthians apart from the instruction and teaching of Paul.

14. In addition to maxims, Sampley (*Walking between the Times,* 87–100) notes these other resources for reasoning from what is known: the scripture, "[t]raditions derived from believers prior to and contemporary with Paul," Jesus' teachings, custom and nature, and practices in the churches.

15. A trajectory running from Plato's *Republic* and Aristotle's *Politics* to the Hellenistic philosophers of Paul's time. For examples in the Hellenistic period, see Bruce W. Winter, *Seek the Welfare of the City: Christian Benefactors and Citizens* (Grand Rapids: Eerdmans, 1994), 82–93, and Malherbe, *Moral Exhortation,* 149–50.

16. See Hans Jonas, "Epilogue," in *The Gnostic Religion,* 2d ed. (Boston: Beacon, 1963), 320–40, and Robert S. Ellwood Jr., *Religious and Spiritual Groups in Modern America* (Englewood Cliffs, N.J.: Prentice-Hall, 1973), 43–54, as noted in Luther Martin, *Hellenistic Religions: An Introduction* (New York: Oxford University Press, 1987), 3.

17. Social-political factors include: imperialism over and against the city-state structure, colonization, increased mobility, and widespread communication. Intellectual factors include: a strong sense of human rationality, a new cosmological perception of the world as a spherical body among the stars, and a perceived anthropological dualism between soul and body. Cf. Martin, *Hellenistic Religions,* 3–15.

18. I follow M. Nilsson's definition of the Hellenistic age as a revolution occurring in two stages. After the conquest of Alexander the Great in 323 B.C.E., there followed a period of about one hundred years of increased individualism and feeling of control over one's destiny — this being promoted by the expanding boundaries of the known world and colonization. The next two hundred years marked a feeling of loss of control over one's destiny, individual isolation, and abandonment to fate — this being promoted by intense fighting among Alexander's successors and the domination of Roman imperialism. See Martin Nilsson, *Greek Piety,* trans. Herbert Jennings Rose (New York:

Norton, 1948), 84–85. For intellectual factors that also belong in Nilsson's model of the Hellenistic revolution, see the previous note.

19. Paul's consistent concern in 1 Corinthians is that no members of the community become enslaved to any human being. As argued above, one reasons well and uses freedom properly when a contemplated moral action does no harm to oneself, to one's relationship to God and Christ, or to other members of the community.

20. The community as a whole or significant segments therein.

21. Members of the community who do this well become examples to follow. And Paul believes these folks, like himself, provide appropriate leadership.

22. That is, in matters *outside the vice-lists* that have been commonly agreed upon by the community. These vice-lists establish the community's boundaries and identity as a whole.

Appendix A

1. Two very early examples of maxim investigation in Paul are noted by Betz (*Galatians*, 291, n. 5) as Johannes Weiss, "Beiträge zur Paulinischen Rhetorik," in *Theologische Studien: Herrn Professor D. Bernhard Weiss au seinem 70. Geburtstag dargebracht*, ed. C. R. Gregory et al. (Göttingen: Vandenhoeck & Ruprecht, 1897), 165–247 and Rudolf Bultmann, *Der Stil der paulinischen Predigt und die kynisch-stoische Diatribe*, Forschungen zur Religion und Literatur des Alten und Neuen Testaments 13 (Göttingen: Huth, 1910). Betz also notes one other work, nearly a decade before his own contribution, as Norbert Schneider, *Die rhetorische Eigenart der paulinischen Antithese*, Hermeneutische Untersuchungen zur Theologie 11 (Tübingen: Mohr/Siebeck, 1970).

2. Rudolf Bultmann, *The History of the Synoptic Tradition*, trans. John Marsh (New York: Harper and Row, 1963), 69–179.

3. Work cited in n. 1 above.

4. William A. Beardslee, "What Is Literary Criticism?" and "The Proverb," in *Literary Criticism of the New Testament* (Philadelphia: Fortress, 1970), 30–41; idem, "Uses of the Proverb in the Synoptic Gospels," *Interpretation* 24 (1970): 61–73; and idem, "Plutarch's Use of Proverbial Forms of Speech," *Semeia* 17 (1980): 101–12.

5. John Dominic Crossan, *In Fragments: The Aphorisms of Jesus* (New York: Harper and Row, 1983) and the edited volumes of *Semeia* 17 and 43.

6. Cf. R. H. Stephenson, "On the Widespread Use of an Inappropriate and Restrictive Model of the Literary Aphorism," *Modern Language Review* 75 (1980): 1–17. Also in this category is James G. Williams, *Those Who Ponder Proverbs: Aphoristic Thinking and Biblical Literature* (Sheffield, England: Almond, 1981), though he does give some credence to the world-ordering aspect.

7. Charles E. Carlston, "Proverbs, Maxims, and the Historical Jesus," *Journal of Biblical Literature* 99 (1980): 87–105, esp. 88. Carlston, like most scholars of Jesus' sayings, doesn't differentiate between proverbs and maxims: "For our purposes, it is not necessary to define wisdom-sayings precisely or to distinguish sharply between, say, 'maxims' and 'proverbs.'" According to Carlston, the proverb is thought to develop from the maxim as wide currency of usage is obtained.

8. Winton, *Proverbs of Jesus*, 127–40. The influence of folklore studies on proverb structural description and performance had already been integrated into biblical studies with Fontaine, *Traditional Sayings*. This trajectory continues in the study of Paul's maxims with Wilson's *Love without Pretense*.

9. An important and often-overlooked study is Vernon K. Robbins, "Picking Up the Fragments: From Crossan's Analysis to Rhetorical Analysis," *Foundations and Facets Forum* 1/2 (1985): 31–64. Robbins brilliantly illustrates how the shortcomings of Crossan's work on Jesus' aphorisms can be corrected with more careful consideration of the rhetoric of the time. See idem, *Jesus the Teacher: A Socio-Rhetorical Interpretation of Mark* (Philadelphia: Fortress, 1984). It is the work of Burton L. Mack (*Rhetoric and the New Testament,* 43–47), however, that has more carefully drawn out the social-rhetorical context of maxim use within the *chreia* construction.

10. Mack, *Rhetoric,* 34–48, 56–73. Mack's argumentative patterns appear to be based on the rhetorical exercise handbooks which instruct in the usage of *progymnasmata* exercises (he illustrates with Hermogenes; see the section on these handbooks in chap. 1, pp. 7–8 above). Maxims played a very prominent role in these exercises, and it is somewhat surprising that Mack does not consider the role of maxims in his consideration of 1 Corinthians 13 and 2 Corinthians 9. His analyses of 1 Corinthians 9, 13, 15, 2 Corinthians 9, and Galatians are, however, by necessity quite abbreviated.

11. Hurd, *Origin of 1 Corinthians,* 61–94.

12. There is an implicit understanding then by those that use the word "slogan" that Paul must be encountering a group that has moved outside his authority or who are challenging it so strongly that a response is called for. By and large, I have not found the word "slogan" defined carefully, except in its political usage by L. L. Welborn, "On the Discord in Corinth: 1 Corinthians 1–4 and Ancient Politics," *Journal of Biblical Literature* 106 (1987): 90–93, and (in reaction) Mitchell, *Rhetoric of Reconciliation,* 83–86. Hurd is assuming that Paul is being challenged by a group at Corinth who have reacted with strong disagreement to his previous letter (see n. 13 below). All that can really be said about these "slogans" is that they are "moral positions" advanced by one or more groups in the Corinthian community.

13. Hurd, *Origin of 1 Corinthians,* 213–88. Hurd's work is valuable in laying out the numerous issues connected with the quotations found in 1 Corinthians and for its review of early scholarship. His underlying thesis — the Corinthians are countering Paul's conservative theological shift after (and caused by) the Apostolic Council with direct quotations of Paul's earlier teachings on freedom — is problematic.

14. Examples on 1 Corinthians, among others, would include Barrett, *First Epistle;* Fee, *First Corinthians;* Murphy-O'Connor, "Corinthian Slogans in 1 Cor 6:12–20," *Catholic Biblical Quarterly* 40 (1978): 351–67; Stowers, "'Debate' over Freedom," 59–71; Dawes, "But If You Can Gain Your Freedom," 681–97; Yarbrough, *Not Like the Gentiles;* Willis, *Idol Meat in Corinth.* Most studies, of course, formulate modified or different social and historical circumstances for Paul's interaction with the Corinthians. For a recent consideration of the matter in detail, see Omanson, "Acknowledging Paul's Quotations," 201–13.

15. For example, Byrne, "Ministry and Maturity in 1 Corinthians 3," 83–87; David Daube, "Missionary Maxims in Paul," in *The New Testament and Rabbinic Judaism* (New York: Arno, 1956), 336–51; Welborn, "On the Discord in Corinth," 85–111; Jouette M. Bassler, *Divine Impartiality: Paul and a Theological Axiom,* SBL Dissertation Series 59 (Chico, Calif.: Scholars Press, 1982); James A. Fischer, "1 Cor. 7:8–24 — Marriage and Divorce," *Biblical Research* 23 (1978): 26–36; and others. I use the term "traditional saying" to designate a recognized statement of a culture's accepted and revered common knowledge. These may then be subdivided by clarification of certain characteristics (for-

mal, structural, functional) into proverb, maxim, aphorism, epigram, and so forth. See G. B. Milner, "Quadripartite Structures," *Proverbium* 14 (1969): 379–80.

16. Conzelmann, *1 Corinthians*, 8, 48, 80, 93, 98, 104, 105–6, 108–10, 110–11, 115, 116, 139–40, 155, 168, 176, 268.

17. For Betz's contribution discussed here, see literature cited in the introduction above, nn. 3 and 7.

18. Betz's discussion of Gal 4:12–20 with respect to Paul's appropriation, re-statement, and creative formulation of *sententiae* based on the topos of friendship is illuminating. See also his discussion of Gal 5:25–6:10. I find Betz's suggestion that in 2 Cor 9:6, Paul has combined a proverb with a composed *sententia* to produce a "maxim" most curious, and certainly indicative of the difficulty in terminological issues.

19. Wilson, *Love without Pretense*. See nn. 9, 10, and 13 to the introduction above.

20. For example, the apothegm concluded a *chreia* in which the narrative description is determinative of meaning; the epigram was a more developed literary form designed to please and entertain a reader; the aphorism in earlier times was connected to summariz-ing scientific observations; the proverb was attributed to anonymous common tradition and not to specific individuals. For a more detailed discussion of these distinctions, see Wilson, *Love without Pretense*, 12–24.

21. "One way that an author could accommodate gnomic sayings to a particular setting or audience was to somehow personalize their communication.... An author could make the intended message seem more immediate and familiar by representing the sayings as being spoken by or addressed to specific figures [ex. "my son" or "my brothers"].... Another, more sophisticated, strategy was to express gnomic sayings in the first or second person, or in the form of a rhetorical question, or to employ terms within the sayings that refer to either the speaker or the reader [Quintilian 8.5.6–7]" (see *Love without Pretense*, 41). I will argue that "personalization" is a development from the gnomic maxim to the gnomic sentence, evidenced as early as Aristotle and Anaximenes and of importance to Isocrates. See pp. 10–12 above.

22. Wilson, *Love without Pretense*, 41.

23. See introduction n. 8 above. For Malherbe's extensive contribution to our under-standing of Paul as a moral philosopher, see the essays in Abraham J. Malherbe, *Paul and the Popular Philosophers* (Minneapolis: Fortress, 1989), and the more recent idem, "Hellenistic Moralists and the New Testament," 267–333.

24. Stowers, *Diatribe and Paul's Letter to the Romans*, 132–33. On the use of maxims in diatribe style, also see Betz, "De laude ipsius (Moralia 539A–547F)," 379–80; idem, *Galatians*, 291–311; and Wilson, *Love without Pretense*, 54–55.

25. Wilson, *Love without Pretense*, 55.

26. For detailed consideration of Paul's use of the rhetorical handbooks, see J. Paul Sampley, "Paul, His Opponents in 2 Corinthians 10–13 and the Rhetorical Handbooks," in *The Social World of Formative Christianity and Judaism: In Honor of Howard Clark Kee*, ed. Jacob Neusner et al. (Philadelphia: Fortress, 1988), 162–77.

27. See Sampley, *Walking between the Times*, 94–98, and introduction above n. 8.

Appendix B

1. For a list of the rhetorical handbooks most germane to this study, see chap. 1, n. 44.

2. These points are argued in detail in chap. 1.

3. Simply reading the later extant rhetorical handbooks might lead one to believe that judicial rhetoric had completely eclipsed deliberative and epideictic forms. That assumption, of course, would be in error.

4. An emphasis established by Isocrates and a resilient factor in the development of rhetoric and education into the Greco-Roman period. See chap. 1, n. 3 above. Proper preparation for social life was extremely important because it was the means by which status was obtained and maintained in the culture.

5. Kennedy, "Earliest Rhetorical Handbooks," 169–78.

6. Ibid. The imitative tradition went in two directions: sophistic rhetoric and philosophic rhetoric. See Kennedy, *Classical Rhetoric,* 25–35. On rhetoric as the goal of *paideia,* see chap. 1, p. 5 above. On imitation theory, see chap. 1, n. 7.

7. Marrou, *Education in Antiquity,* 197–203.

8. All knowledge is socially constructed, and all analysis must be dynamic; transformations have occurred and ongoing transformations continue to be at work within a group or between groups. See Kee, *Knowing the Truth,* 7–64; see Berger and Luckmann, *Social Construction of Reality.*

9. This type of approach, while not only being the most helpful in my opinion, seems best to explain the differences in counsel that can sometimes be found among the handbooks themselves. The handbooks are responding to and adapting counsel to fit changing social situations and present concerns as well. Rather than diminishing the scope of the rhetorical handbook tradition as Mitchell (*Paul and the Rhetoric of Reconciliation,* 8–11) does, it seems better to view it in wider historical and social perspective.

10. A growing perspective in both sociological and cultural anthropological theory is that the analysis of cultural particulars must take precedence over mere "fixed categorization" and the cataloguing of presumably similar social factors and movements. See Kee, *Knowing the Truth,* esp. 37–50. Cf. Clifford Geertz, "Thick Description: Toward an Interpretive Theory of Culture," in *The Interpretation of Cultures* (New York: Basic Books, 1973), 3–30.

11. Within the fields of folklore and anthropology, the genre description of traditional sayings is analyzed with either a supercultural (that is, cross-cultural) or ethnographic method (or some combination of both). See Neal R. Norrick, *How Proverbs Mean: Semantic Studies in English Proverbs,* Trends in Linguistics, Studies and Monographs 27 (New York: Mouton, 1985), 58 and Daniel Ben-Amos, "Analytical Categories and Ethnic Genres," *Genre* 2 (1969): 286.

To examine Paul's maxim usage in a supercultural manner would be to ask how Greco-Roman maxim usage is illuminated by a defined "maxim type" constructed through a comparison of wide-ranging cross-cultural materials and observations. Or to quote Norrick (*How Proverbs Mean,* 58): "on genre interculturally versus genre in a given culture." Supercultural genre definition generally imposes the investigator's own cross-cultural categories on ethnic descriptions. See Ben-Amos ("Analytical Categories," 286), who does not deny the place of either the supercultural or ethnographic approach, but who stresses, and I think rightly, separate investigations into each prior to integration.

To examine Paul's maxim usage in an ethnographical manner would be to identify: "the conception a culture [here, Greco-Roman] has of its own folkloric communication [here, the maxim in particular] as it is represented in the distinction of forms, the attribution of names to them, and the sense of the social appropriateness of their application in various cultural situations" (Ben-Amos, "Analytical Categories," 286).

12. Here, we are fortunate that in some instances the terms and structures of the Greco-Roman educational system have been passed down to our time. See Marrou, *Education in Antiquity*, xi–xii.

13. By and large, noted scholars in the field of Greco-Roman education and rhetoric take this position. See Marrou, *Education in Antiquity*, 242; Harry Caplan, "Introduction to *Rhetorica ad Herennium*," in *On Eloquence: Studies in Ancient and Mediaeval Rhetoric* (Ithaca, N.Y.: Cornell University Press, 1970), 1–2. This is presumed to be true in Bonner's treatment of Quintilian's *Institutio oratoria* with respect to primary, secondary, and rhetorical training as well (see Bonner, *Education in Rome*, 165–327). While this position assumes a remarkably uniform foundation for rhetorical instruction traced to Greek influence, the point in no way advocates the perception of some kind of "mono-rhetoric." Debated issues (for example, Asianism versus Atticism, usage of declamation exercises, and numbers of more minor points) within the rhetorical handbooks themselves mitigate against such a stance. We need to be aware of the rhetorical choices that are available at any given historical period and then evaluate particular authors in light of them.

14. The literacy level of Paul and his congregations continues to be debated. For a positive evaluation of rhetorical influence, see Edwin A. Judge, "St. Paul and Classical Society," *Jahrbüch Für Antike und Christentum* 15 (1972): 19–36, Pogoloff, *Logos and Sophia*, 2, 15–26; and F. Gerald Downing, "*A bas les aristos:* The Relevance of Higher Literature for the Understanding of the Earliest Christian Writings," *Novum Testamentum* 30 (1988): 212–30. Cf. Paul J. Achtemeier, "*Omne verbum sonat:* The New Testament and the Oral Environment of Late Western Antiquity," *Journal of Biblical Literature* 109 (1990): 3–27. For a contrary position and complete bibliography, see P. J. J. Botha, "Greco-Roman Literacy as Setting for New Testament Writings," *Neotestamentica* 26 (1992): 195–215.

I believe that Judge ("Classical Society," 31) is right in calling for an investigation of the still-unexplored urban middle ground between high literacy and lower or non-literacy. It is true that such an undertaking would be precarious because of our shortage of sources. But if Judge is right, then investigation rather than neglect of what we do have is the way forward: "[P]roviding the New Testament writers with their lost intellectual milieu must be regarded as one [an interest] of much wider importance still. The work needs to be done not only with careful attention to periods, places and types of writing, but with an overall eye to the way the intellectual life of the age as a whole was carried forward." On the use of the New Testament texts as appropriate and unique sources for this type of investigation, see Wayne A. Meeks, "Understanding Early Christian Ethics," *Journal of Biblical Literature* 105 (1986): 9. What seems apparent from the number of convincing rhetorical studies on Paul is that however this "middle ground" be conceived, rhetoric played a vital part in it.

It seems many scholars can entertain the idea of Paul's gentile converts being more acquainted with a broad spectrum of Greco-Roman cultural tradition than Paul ("the Jew"). It is not our intent to try to make Paul more Greek or more Roman than he was Jewish. To put the issue that way is, indeed, inappropriate. It is clear that Greco-Roman culture, and more particularly Greco-Roman educational patterns, interacted freely with the urban Palestinian and urban Jewish Diaspora centers. Paul may have received rhetorical instruction in a Hellenistic school, an urban Diaspora school, or a special Jewish training academy of whatever kind. For evidence on this kind of cultural interaction and the available opportunities, see James L. Kinneavy, *Greek Rhetorical Origins of Christian Faith: An Inquiry* (New York: Oxford University Press, 1987), 56–100. With the situation as it is, Judge's counsel again rings true: "We need a living picture of the scholarly industry and of its outworkings in the [Greco-Roman] community at large — the textbooks, manuals, digests, encyclopedias and libraries through which information is available. Not that St Paul should be thought of as working directly from such resources, let alone from the classical authors themselves. But if these are the effective sources of knowledge at the time, we should begin there before trying to decide how it may have reached him" ("Classical Society," 31–32). Finally, as a self-proclaimed Jew (Phil 3:5–6; Rom 11:1), Paul continued to choose Greco-Roman cultural patterns to serve as mediums of persuasion for his gospel to gentiles.

15. Though all of the ancient audiences were not rhetorically trained, all were rhetorically competent in the sense that they were able to follow an argument and to be persuaded by a good one. This issue is of course tied up with the rhetorical competence we attribute to Paul. For the evidence pertaining to constituents of the Corinthian community, see Pogoloff, *Logos and Sophia*, 99–172, and Betz, "Rhetoric and Theology," 24–39.

16. Lausberg, *Handbuch der literarischen Rhetorik*; Martin, *Antike Rhetorik*.

17. Delarue, "La sententia chez Quintilien," 97.

18. This also may be accomplished when we construct our own generalizations from an examination of the extant rhetorical handbooks without consideration to historical, social, and rhetorical developments through time.

19. This perspective is developed from a consideration of Quintilian's *Institutio oratoria* 8.5, where three types of maxims can be detected: the gnomic maxim, the gnomic sentence, and the moral *sententia*. See chap. 1 above.

Selected Bibliography

Primary Texts and Translations

Aphthonius. *See* Nadeau, Ray.

Aristotle. *The "Art" of Rhetoric.* Trans. John Henry Freese. Loeb Classical Library. Cambridge, Mass.: Harvard University Press, 1976.

———. *Rhetoric.* Trans. W. Rhys Roberts. Modern Library. New York: Random House, 1954.

Baldwin, Charles S. "The *Progymnasmata* of Hermogenes." In *Medieval Rhetoric and Poetic,* 23–38. New York: Macmillan, 1928.

Butts, James R. "The *Progymnasmata* of Theon: A New Text with Translation and Commentary." Ph.D. diss., Claremont Graduate School, 1987.

Cicero. *De inventione.* Trans. H. M. Hubbell. Loeb Classical Library. Cambridge, Mass.: Harvard University Press, 1949. In the volume with Cicero, *De optimo genere oratorum, topica.*

———. *Orator.* Trans. H. M. Hubbell. Loeb Classical Library. Cambridge, Mass.: Harvard University Press, 1939. In the volume with Cicero, *Brutus.*

———. *De oratore, Partitione oratoriae.* Trans. E. W. Sutton and H. Rackham. Loeb Classical Library. 2 vols. Cambridge, Mass.: Harvard University Press, 1942. In the volumes with Cicero, *De fato, Paradoxa stoicorum.*

Demetrius. *On Style.* Trans. W. Rhys Roberts. Loeb Classical Library. Cambridge, Mass.: Harvard University Press, 1932. In the volume with Aristotle, *Poetics,* and Longinus, *On the Sublime.*

Hermogenes. *See* Baldwin, Charles S.

Homer. *See* Lattimore, Richard.

Isocrates. Trans. G. Norlin and La Rue Van Hook. Loeb Classical Library. 3 vols. Cambridge, Mass.: Harvard University Press, 1928–45.

Lattimore, Richard. *The Iliad of Homer.* Chicago: University of Chicago Press, 1951.

———. *The Odyssey of Homer.* New York: Harper and Row, 1965.

Longinus, *On the Sublime.* Trans. Hamilton Fyfe. Loeb Classical Library. Cambridge, Mass.: Harvard University Press, 1932. In the volume with Aristotle, *Poetics,* and Demetrius, *On Style.*

Nadeau, Ray. "The *Progymnasmata* of Aphthonius in Translation." *Speech Monographs* 19 (1952): 264–85.

Plutarch. *Moralia.* Trans. F. C. Babbitt et al. Loeb Classical Library. 16 vols. Cambridge, Mass.: Harvard University Press, 1927–69.

Quintilian. *Institutio oratoria.* Trans. H. E. Butler. Loeb Classical Library. 4 vols. Cambridge, Mass.: Harvard University Press, 1920–22.

Rhetorica ad Alexandrum. Trans. H. Rackham. Loeb Classical Library. Cambridge, Mass.: Harvard University Press, 1983. In the volume with Aristotle, *Problems.*

Rhetorica ad Herennium. Trans. Harry Caplan. Loeb Classical Library. Cambridge, Mass.: Harvard University Press, 1954.

Seneca the Elder. *Controversiae* and *Suasoriae*. Trans. Michael Winterbottom. Loeb Classical Library. 2 vols. Cambridge, Mass.: Harvard University Press, 1974.

Seneca the Younger. *Epistulae Morales*. Trans. R. M. Gummere. Loeb Classical Library. 3 vols. Cambridge, Mass.: Harvard University Press, 1917–25.

Secondary Texts

Abrahams, Roger D. "The Complex Relation of Simple Forms." *Genre* 2 (1969): 104–28.

———. "Introductory Remarks to a Rhetorical Theory of Folklore." *Journal of American Folklore* 81 (1968): 143–58.

———. "A Rhetoric of Everyday Life: Traditional Conversational Genres." *Southern Folklore Quarterly* 32 (1968): 44–59.

Achtemeier, Paul J. *"Omne verbum sonat:* The New Testament and the Oral Environment of Late Western Antiquity." *Journal of Biblical Literature* 109 (1990): 3–27.

Ahl, Frederick. "The Art of Safe Criticism in Greece and Rome." *American Journal of Philology* 105 (1984): 174–208.

Arewa, E. Ojo, and Alan Dundes. "Proverbs and the Ethnography of Speaking Folklore." *American Anthropologist* 66 (1964): 70–85.

Bailey, James L., and Lyle D. Vander Broek. *Literary Forms in the New Testament: A Handbook*. Louisville: Westminster/John Knox, 1992.

Baird, William. "'One against the Another': Intra-church Conflict in 1 Corinthians." In *The Conversation Continues: Studies in Paul and John: In Honor of J. Louis Martyn*, ed. Robert T. Fortna and Beverly R. Gaventa, 116–35. Nashville: Abingdon, 1990.

Balch, David L. "Backgrounds of I Cor. VII: Sayings of the Lord in Q; Moses as an Ascetic *THEIOS ANĒR* in II Cor. III." *New Testament Studies* 18 (1971): 351–64.

———. "1 Cor. 7:32–35 and Stoic Debates about Marriage, Anxiety, and Distraction." *Journal of Biblical Literature* 102 (1983): 429–39.

Barclay, John M. G. "Mirror-Reading a Polemical Letter: Galatians as a Test Case." *Journal of the Study of the New Testament* 31 (1987): 73–93.

Barrett, C. K. *The First Epistle to the Corinthians*. Harper's NT Commentaries. New York: Harper and Row, 1968.

Bartchy, S. Scott. *MALLON CHRĒSAI: First-Century Slavery and the Interpretation of 1 Corinthians 7:21*. SBL Dissertation Series 11. Missoula, Mont.: Scholars Press, 1973.

Bassler, Jouette M. *Divine Impartiality: Paul and a Theological Axiom*. SBL Dissertation Series 59. Chico, Calif.: Scholars Press, 1982.

Beardslee, William A. *Literary Criticism of the New Testament*. Philadelphia: Fortress, 1970.

———. "Plutarch's Use of Proverbial Forms of Speech." *Semeia* 17 (1980): 101–12.

———. "Uses of the Proverb in the Synoptic Gospels." *Interpretation* 24 (1970): 61–73.

Ben-Amos, Daniel. "Analytical Categories and Ethnic Genres." *Genre* 2 (1969): 275–301.

Berger, Peter L., and Thomas Luckmann. *The Social Construction of Reality: A Treatise in the Sociology of Knowledge*. New York: Doubleday, 1966.

Betz, Hans Dieter. "De laude ipsius (Moralia 539A–547F)." In *Plutarch's Ethical Writings and Early Christian Literature*, ed. H. D. Betz, 379–93. Studia ad corpus hellenisticum novi testamenti 4. Leiden: Brill, 1978.

———. *Galatians: A Commentary on Paul's Letter to the Churches in Galatia*. Hermeneia. Philadelphia: Fortress, 1979.

———. "The Problem of Rhetoric and Theology according to the Apostle Paul." In *L'Apôtre Paul: Personalité, style et conception du ministère,* ed. A. Vanhoye, 24–39. Bibliotheca Ephemeridum Theologicarum Lovaniensium. Louvain: Louvain University Press, 1986.

———. *2 Corinthians 8 and 9: A Commentary on Two Administrative Letters of the Apostle Paul.* Hermeneia. Philadelphia: Fortress, 1985.

Betz, Hans Dieter, and Edgar W. Smith. "De e apud Delphos (Moralia 384C-394C)." In *Plutarch's Ethical Writings and Early Christian Literature,* ed. H. D. Betz, 85–102. Studia ad corpus hellenisticum novi testamenti 4. Leiden: Brill, 1978.

Bitzer, Lloyd. "The Rhetorical Situation." *Philosophy and Rhetoric* 1 (1968): 1–14.

Bonner, Stanley F. *Education in Ancient Rome: From the Elder Cato to the Younger Pliny.* Los Angeles: University of California Press, 1977.

———. *Roman Declamation in the Late Republic and Early Empire.* Berkeley: University of California Press, 1949.

Botha, P. J. J. "Greco-Roman Literacy as Setting for New Testament Writings." *Neotestamentica* 26 (1992): 195–215.

Brunt, John C. "Love, Freedom, and Moral Responsibility: The Contribution of 1 Cor 8–10 to an Understanding of Paul's Ethical Thinking." In *Society of Biblical Literature Seminar Papers 1981,* ed. Kent Harold Richards, 19–33. Chico, Calif.: Scholars Press, 1981.

Bultmann, Rudolf. *Der Stil der paulinischen Predigt und die kynisch-stoische Diatribe.* Forschungen zur Religion und Literatur des Alten und Neuen Testaments 13. Göttingen: Huth, 1910.

———. *The History of the Synoptic Tradition.* Trans. John Marsh. New York: Harper and Row, 1963.

———. *Theology of the New Testament.* Trans. Kendrick Grobel. New York: Scribner's, 1951–55.

Byrne, Brendan. "Ministry and Maturity in 1 Corinthians 3." *Australian Biblical Review* 35 (1987): 83–87.

Canter, H. V. "Rhetorical Elements in Livy's Direct Speeches." *American Journal of Philology* 38 (1917): 125–51.

Caplan, Harry. *On Eloquence: Studies in Ancient and Mediaeval Rhetoric.* Ithaca, N.Y.: Cornell University Press, 1970.

Carlston, Charles E. "Proverbs, Maxims, and the Historical Jesus." *Journal of Biblical Literature* 99 (1980): 87–105.

Cartlidge, David R. "1 Corinthians 7 as a Foundation for a Christian Sex Ethic." *Journal of Religion* 55 (1975): 220–34.

Castelli, Elizabeth A. *Imitating Paul: A Discourse on Power.* Louisville: Westminster/John Knox, 1991.

Chow, John K. *Patronage and Power: A Study of Social Networks in Corinth.* JSNT Supplement Series 75. Sheffield, England: JSOT, 1992.

Clark, Donald Lemen. *Rhetoric in Greco-Roman Education.* New York: Columbia University Press, 1957.

Clarke, M. L. *Rhetoric at Rome: A Historical Study.* London: Cohen and West, 1953.

Cole, Thomas. *The Origins of Rhetoric in Ancient Greece.* Baltimore: Johns Hopkins University Press, 1991.

Conzelmann, Hans. *1 Corinthians: A Commentary on the First Epistle to the Corinthians.* Trans. James W. Leitch. Hermeneia. Philadelphia: Fortress, 1975.

Crossan, John Dominic. *In Fragments: The Aphorisms of Jesus.* New York: Harper and Row, 1983.

Dahl, Nils A. "Paul and the Church at Corinth according to 1 Corinthians 1:10–4:21." In *Studies in Paul: Theology for the Early Christian Mission*, 40–61. Minneapolis: Augsburg, 1977.

Daube, David. "Missionary Maxims in Paul." In *The New Testament and Rabbinic Judaism*, 336–51. New York: Arno, 1956.

Davis, James A. "The Interaction between Individual Ethical Conscience and Community Consciousness in 1 Corinthians." *Horizons in Biblical Theology* 10 (1988): 1–18.

———. *Wisdom and Spirit: An Investigation of 1 Corinthians 1.18–3.20 against the Background of Jewish Sapiential Traditions in the Greco-Roman Period*. New York: University Press of America, 1984.

Dawes, Gregory W. "'But If You Can Gain Your Freedom' (1 Corinthians 7:17–24)." *Catholic Biblical Quarterly* 52 (1990): 681–97.

Delarue, F. "La sententia chez Quintilien." *La Licorne* 3 (1979): 97–124.

Dolfe, K. G. E. "1 Cor 7, 25 Reconsidered (Paul a Supposed Advisor)." *Zeitschrift für die neutestamentliche Wissenschaft* 83 (1992): 115–18.

Downing, F. Gerald. *'A bas les aristos:* The Relevance of Higher Literature for the Understanding of the Earliest Christian Writings." *Novum Testamentum* 30 (1988): 212–30.

Drane, John W. "Tradition, Law and Ethics in Pauline Theology." *Novum Testamentum* 16 (1974): 167–78.

Duhaime, Jean, and Marc St-Jacques. "Early Christianity and the Social Sciences: A Bibliography." *Social Compass* 39 (1992): 275–90.

Dundes, Alan. "On the Structure of the Proverb." In *The Wisdom of Many: Essays on the Proverb*, ed. Wolfgang Mieder and Alan Dundes, 43–64. New York: Garland, 1981.

Dungan, David L. *The Sayings of Jesus in the Churches of Paul*. Philadelphia: Fortress, 1971.

Eagleton, Terry. *Literary Theory: An Introduction*. Minneapolis: University of Minneapolis Press, 1983.

Ellis, E. Earle. "Traditions in 1 Corinthians." *New Testament Studies* 32 (1986): 481–502.

Ellwood, Robert S., Jr. *Religious and Spiritual Groups in Modern America*. Englewood Cliffs, N.J.: Prentice-Hall, 1973.

Engels, Donald. *Roman Corinth: An Alternative Model for the Classical City*. Chicago: University of Chicago Press, 1990.

Evans, Craig A., and James A. Sanders, eds. *Paul and the Scriptures of Israel*. JSNT Supplement Series 83. Sheffield, England: JSOT, 1993.

Fee, Gordon D. *The First Epistle to the Corinthians*. New International Commentary on the New Testament. Grand Rapids: Eerdmans, 1987.

Fiore, Benjamin. "'Covert Allusion' in 1 Corinthians 1–4." *Catholic Biblical Quarterly* 47 (1985): 85–102.

———. *Personal Example in the Socratic and Pastoral Epistles*. Analecta Biblica 105. Rome: Biblical Institute, 1986.

Fischer, James A. "1 Cor 7:8–24 — Marriage and Divorce." *Biblical Research* 23 (1978): 26–36.

Fisk, B. N. "Eating Meat Offered to Idols: Corinthian Behavior and Pauline Response in 1 Corinthians 8–10 (A Response to Gordon Fee)." *Trinity Journal* 10 (1989): 49–70.

Fitzgerald, John T. *Cracks in an Earthen Vessel: An Examination of the Catalogues of Hardships in the Corinthian Correspondence*. SBL Dissertation Series 99. Atlanta: Scholars Press, 1988.

Fontaine, Carol R. *Traditional Sayings in the Old Testament: A Contextual Study.* Sheffield, England: Almond, 1982.

Furnish, Victor Paul. *II Corinthians.* Anchor Bible. Vol. 32A. New York: Doubleday, 1984.

Geertz, Clifford. *The Interpretation of Cultures.* New York: Basic Books, 1973.

Georgi, Dieter. *Theocracy in Paul's Praxis and Theology.* Trans. David E. Green. Minneapolis: Fortress, 1991.

Gloer, W. Hulitt. "Homologies and Hymns in the New Testament: Form, Content and Criteria for Identification." *Perspectives on Religious Studies* 11 (1984): 115–32.

Gooch, Paul W. "'Conscience' in 1 Corinthians 8 and 10." *New Testament Studies* 33 (1987): 244–54.

Goodwin, Paul D., and Joseph W. Wenzel. "Proverbs and Practical Reasoning: A Study in Socio-Logic." In *The Wisdom of Many: Essays on the Proverb,* ed. Wolfgang Mieder and Alan Dundes, 140–60. New York: Garland, 1981.

Grant, Robert M. "Hellenistic Elements in I Corinthians." In *Early Christian Origins: Studies in Honor of Harold R. Willoughby,* ed. Allan Wikgren, 60–66. Chicago: Quadrangle, 1961.

———. "The Wisdom of the Corinthians." In *The Joy of Study: Papers on New Testament and Related Subjects Presented to Honor F. C. Grant,* ed. S. E. Johnson, 51–55. New York: Macmillan, 1951.

Grosheide, F. W. *Commentary on the First Epistle to the Corinthians.* New International Commentary on the New Testament. Grand Rapids: Eerdmans, 1953.

Grundmann, Walter. "Kalos." In *Theological Dictionary of the New Testament,* ed. G. Kittel and G. Friedrich, 536–50. 1967.

Hall, Barbara. "All Things to All People: A Study of 1 Corinthians 9:19–23." In *The Conversation Continues: Studies in Paul and John,* ed. Robert T. Fortna and Beverly R. Gaventa, 137–57. Nashville: Abingdon, 1990.

Halloran, S. Michael. "Aristotle's Concept of Ethos; or, If Not His Somebody Else's." *Rhetoric Review* 1 (1982): 58–63.

Hansen, Mogens Herman. *The Athenian Assembly: In the Age of Demosthenes.* Oxford: Blackwell, 1987.

Harvey, A. E. "'The Workman Is Worthy of His Hire': Fortunes of a Proverb in the Early Church." *Novum Testamentum* 24 (1982): 209–21.

Hays, Richard. *Echoes of Scripture in the Letters of Paul.* New Haven, Conn.: Yale University Press, 1989.

Henderson, Ian H. "Quintilian and the *Progymnasmata.*" *Antike und Abendland* 37 (1991): 82–99.

Hock, Ronald F. "Paul's Tentmaking and the Problem of His Social Class." *Journal of Biblical Literature* 97 (1978): 555–64.

Hock, Ronald F., and Edward N. O'Neil. *The Chreia in Ancient Rhetoric.* Vol. 1: *The Progymnasmata.* Atlanta: Scholars Press, 1986.

Holladay, Carl R. "1 Corinthians 13: Paul as Apostolic Paradigm." In *Greeks, Romans, Christians,* ed. David L. Balch, Everett Ferguson, and Wayne A. Meeks, 80–98. Minneapolis: Fortress, 1990.

Holloway, Joseph O. *PERIPATEŌ as a Thematic Marker for Pauline Ethics.* San Francisco: Mellon Research University Press, 1992.

Holmberg, Bengt. *Paul and Power: The Structure of Authority in the Primitive Church as Reflected in the Pauline Epistles.* Philadelphia: Fortress, 1978.

Horsley, Richard A. "The Background of the Confessional Formula in 1 Kor 8.6." *Zeitschrift für die neutestamentliche Wissenschaft* 69 (1978): 130–35.

————. "Consciousness and Freedom among the Corinthians." *Catholic Biblical Quarterly* 40 (1978): 574–89.

————. "'How Can Some of You Say That There Is No Resurrection of the Dead?' Spiritual Elitism in Corinth." *Novum Testamentum* 20 (1978): 203–31.

————. "Spiritual Marriage with Sophia." *Vigiliae Christianae* 33 (1979): 30–54.

————. "Wisdom of Word and Words of Wisdom in Corinth." *Catholic Biblical Quarterly* 39 (1977): 224–39.

Hughes, Frank W. "The Rhetoric of Reconciliation: 2 Corinthians 1.1–2.13 and 7.5–8.24." In *Persuasive Artistry: Studies in New Testament Rhetoric in Honor of George A. Kennedy*, 273–90. JSNT Supplementary Series 50. Sheffield, England: JSOT, 1991.

Hurd, John C. *The Origin of 1 Corinthians*. New York: Seabury, 1965.

Jaeger, Werner. "The Rhetoric of Isocrates and Its Cultural Ideal." In *The Province of Rhetoric*, ed. Joseph Schwartz and John A. Rycenga, 84–111. New York: Ronald, 1965.

Jaquette, James L. *Discerning What Counts: The Function of the Adiaphora Topos in Paul's Letters*. SBL Dissertation Series 146. Atlanta: Scholars Press, 1995.

Jewett, Robert. *Paul's Anthropological Terms*. Arbeiten zur Geschichte des antiken Judentums und des Urchristentums 10. Leiden: Brill, 1971.

Johnson, E. Elizabeth. *The Function of Apocalyptic and Wisdom Traditions in Romans 9–11*. SBL Dissertation Series 109. Atlanta: Scholars Press, 1989.

Johnson, Luke T. *The Writings of the New Testament: An Interpretation*. Philadelphia: Fortress, 1986.

Jonas, Hans. *The Gnostic Religion*. 2d ed. Boston: Beacon, 1963.

Judge, Edwin A. "St Paul and Classical Society." *Jahrbüch für Antike und Christentum* 15 (1972): 19–36.

Karavites, Peter. "*Gnōmē*'s Nuances: From Its Beginning to the End of the Fifth Century." *Classical Bulletin* 66 (1990): 9–34.

Kee, Howard Clark. *Knowing the Truth: A Sociological Approach to New Testament Interpretation*. Minneapolis: Fortress, 1989.

Keegan, Terence J. *Interpreting the Bible: A Popular Introduction to Biblical Hermeneutics*. New York: Paulist, 1985.

Kelber, Werner H. *The Oral and the Written Gospel: The Hermeneutics of Speaking and Writing in the Synoptic Tradition, Mark, Paul, and Q*. Philadelphia: Fortress, 1983.

Kennedy, George A. *Aristotle on Rhetoric: A Theory of Civic Discourse*. New York: Oxford University Press, 1991.

————. *The Art of Rhetoric in the Roman World*. Princeton, N.J.: Princeton University Press, 1972.

————. *Classical Rhetoric and Its Christian and Secular Tradition from Ancient to Modern Times*. Chapel Hill: University of North Carolina Press, 1980.

————. "The Earliest Rhetorical Handbooks." *American Journal of Philology* 80 (1959): 169–78.

————. *New Testament Interpretation through Rhetorical Criticism*. Chapel Hill: University of North Carolina Press, 1984.

Kinneavy, James L. *Greek Rhetorical Origins of Christian Faith: An Inquiry*. New York: Oxford University Press, 1987.

Kloppenborg, John S. *The Formation of Q: Trajectories in Ancient Wisdom Collections*. Philadelphia: Fortress, 1987.

Krentz, Edgar. *The Historical-Critical Method*. Philadelphia: Fortress, 1975.

Kriel, D. M. "The Forms of the Sententia in Quintilian VIII.v.3–24." *Acta Classica* 4 (1961): 80–89.

Kustas, George L. "Diatribe in Ancient Rhetorical Theory." In *Protocol of the Colloquy of the Center for Hermeneutical Studies in Hellenistic and Modern Culture,* 1–15. Berkeley: Center for Hermeneutical Studies in Hellenistic and Modern Culture, 1976.

Lampe, Peter. "Theological Wisdom and the 'Word of the Cross.'" *Interpretation* 44 (1990): 117–31.

Lanham, Richard A. *A Handlist of Rhetorical Terms.* 2d ed. Berkeley: University of California Press, 1991.

Lassen, Eva Maria. "The Use of the Father Image in Imperial Propaganda and 1 Corinthians 4:14–21." *Tyndale Bulletin* 42 (1991): 125–36.

Lausberg, Heinrich. *Handbuch der literarischen Rhetorik.* Munich: Hueber, 1960.

Levet, J. P. *"RHĒTŌR et GNŌMĒ:* Présentation sémantique et recherches isocratiques." *La Licorne* 3 (1979): 9–40.

Levinson, John R. "Did the Spirit Inspire Rhetoric? An Exploration of George Kennedy's Definition of Early Christian Rhetoric." In *Persuasive Artistry: Studies in New Testament Rhetoric in Honor of George A. Kennedy,* ed. Duane F. Watson. JSNT Supplement Series 50. Sheffield, England: JSOT, 1991.

Lyons, George. *Pauline Autobiography: Toward a New Understanding.* SBL Dissertation Series 73. Atlanta: Scholars Press, 1985.

MacDonald, Dennis R. *There Is No Male and Female: The Fate of a Dominical Saying in Paul and Gnosticism.* Philadelphia: Fortress, 1987.

MacDonald, Margaret Y. "Women Holy in Body and Spirit: The Social Setting of 1 Corinthians 7." *New Testament Studies* 36 (1990): 161–81.

Mack, Burton L. *Rhetoric and the New Testament.* Minneapolis: Fortress, 1990.

Malan, F. S. "Hellenistic Moralists and the New Testament." In *Aufstieg und Niedergang der römischen Welt* 2.26/1, ed. H. Temporini and W. Haase, 267–333. Berlin and New York: Walter de Gruyter, 1992.

Malherbe, Abraham J. *Moral Exhortation: A Greco-Roman Sourcebook.* Library of Early Christianity. Philadelphia: Westminster, 1986.

———. *Paul and the Popular Philosophers.* Minneapolis: Fortress, 1989.

Marrou, H. I. *A History of Education in Antiquity.* 3d ed. Trans. George Lamb. Madison: University of Wisconsin Press, 1982.

Marshall, Peter. *Enmity in Corinth: Social Conventions in Paul's Relations with the Corinthians.* Wissenschaftliche Untersuchungen zum Neuen Testament 2/23. Tübingen: Mohr/Siebeck, 1987.

Martin, Dale B. *Slavery as Salvation: The Metaphor of Slavery in Pauline Christianity.* New Haven, Conn.: Yale University Press, 1990.

———. "Tongues of Angels and Other Status Indicators." *Journal of the American Academy of Religion* 59 (1991): 547–89.

Martin, Josef. *Antike Rhetorik: Technik und Methode.* Munich: Beck, 1974.

Martin, Luther. *Hellenistic Religions: An Introduction.* New York: Oxford University Press, 1987.

Meeks, Wayne A. *The First Urban Christians: The Social World of the Apostle Paul.* New Haven, Conn.: Yale University Press, 1983.

———. *The Origins of Christian Morality: The First Two Centuries.* New Haven, Conn.: Yale University Press, 1993.

———. "The Polyphonic Ethics of the Apostle Paul." *Annual of the Society of Christian Ethics* (1988): 17–29.

———. "'And Rose Up to Play': Midrash and Paraenesis in 1 Cor 10:1–22." *Journal for the Society of the New Testament* 16 (1982): 64–78.

————. "Understanding Early Christian Ethics." *Journal of Biblical Literature* 105 (1986): 3–11.

Michaelis, W. "Mimeomai." In *Theological Dictionary of the New Testament*, ed. G. Kittel and G. Friedrich, 666–73. 1967.

Miller, Arthur B. "Rhetorical Exigence." *Philosophy and Rhetoric* 5 (1972): 111–18.

Milner, G. B. "Quadripartite Structures." *Proverbium* 14 (1969): 379–83.

Mitchell, Margaret M. "Concerning *PERI DE* in 1 Corinthians." *Novum Testamentum* 31 (1989): 229–56.

————. *Paul and the Rhetoric of Reconciliation: An Exegetical Investigation of the Language and Composition of 1 Corinthians*. Hermeneutische Untersuchungen zur Theologie 28. Tübingen: Mohr/Siebeck, 1991.

Mullins, Terence Y. "Visit Talk in New Testament Letters." *Catholic Biblical Quarterly* 35 (1973): 350–58.

Murphy, James J. *Quintilian on the Teaching of Speaking and Writing: Translations from Books One, Two, and Ten of the Institutio Oratoria*. Carbondale: Southern Illinois University Press, 1987.

————. "Roman Writing Instruction as Described by Quintilian." In *A Short History of Writing Instruction: From Ancient Greece to Twentieth-Century America*, ed. James J. Murphy, 19–76. Davis, Calif.: Hermagoras, 1990.

Murphy-O'Connor, Jerome. "Corinthian Slogans in 1 Cor 6:12–20." *Catholic Biblical Quarterly* 40 (1978): 351–67.

————. "The Divorced Woman in 1 Cor 7:10–11." *Journal of Biblical Literature* 100 (1981): 601–6.

————. "Food and Spiritual Gifts in 1 Cor 8:8." *Catholic Biblical Quarterly* 41 (1979): 292–98.

————. "Freedom or the Ghetto (1 Cor. 8:1–13; 10:23–11:1)." *Revue Biblique* 85 (1978): 541–74.

————. "1 Cor. 8:6: Cosmology or Soteriology." *Revue Biblique* 85 (1978): 253–67.

Nida, E. A., et al. *Style and Discourse: With Special Reference to the Text of the Greek New Testament*. Cape Town: Bible Society of South Africa, 1983.

Nilsson, Martin. *Greek Piety*. Trans. Herbert Jennings Rose. New York: Norton, 1948.

Norrick, Neal R. *How Proverbs Mean: Semantic Studies in English Proverbs*. Trends in Linguistics, Studies and Monographs 27. New York: Mouton, 1985.

Olson, Stanley N. "Epistolary Uses of Expressions of Self-Confidence." *Journal of Biblical Literature* 103 (1984): 585–97.

————. "Pauline Expressions of Confidence in His Addressees." *Catholic Biblical Quarterly* 47 (1985): 282–95.

Omanson, Roger L. "Acknowledging Paul's Quotations." *The Bible Translator* 43 (1992): 201–13.

Oster, Richard E. "Use, Misuse and Neglect of Archaeological Evidence in Some Modern Works on 1 Corinthians (1 Cor 7,1–5; 8,10; 11,2–16; 12,14–26)." *Zeitschrift für die neutestamentliche Wissenschaft* 83 (1992): 52–73.

Outka, Gene. "On Harming Others." *Interpretation* 34 (1980): 381–93.

Painter, John. "Paul and the *Pneumatikoi* at Corinth." In *Paul and Paulinism: Essays in Honor of C. K. Barrett*, ed. M. D. Hooker and S. G. Wilson, 237–50. London: SPCK, 1982.

Parunak, H. Van Dyke. "Transitional Techniques in the Bible." *Journal of Biblical Literature* 102 (1983): 525–48.

Perelman, Ch., and L. Olbrechts-Tyteca. *The New Rhetoric: A Treatise on Argumentation*. Trans. John Wilkinson and Purcell Weaver. Notre Dame, Ind.: University of Notre Dame Press, 1969.

Pfitzner, Victor C. *Paul and the Agon Motif: Traditional Athletic Imagery in the Pauline Literature.* Supplements to Novum Testamentum 16. Leiden: Brill, 1967.

Phipps, William E. "Is Paul's Attitude toward Sexual Relations Contained in 1 Cor. 7:1?" *New Testament Studies* 28 (1981): 125–31.

Pierce, C. A. *Conscience in the New Testament.* Studies in Biblical Theology 1.15. London: SCM, 1955.

Plank, Karl A. *Paul and the Irony of Affliction.* SBL Semeia Studies. Atlanta: Scholars Press, 1987.

Pogoloff, Stephen L. *Logos and Sophia: The Rhetorical Situation of 1 Corinthians.* SBL Dissertation Series 134. Atlanta: Scholars Press, 1992.

Pugsley, Roger F. "The Sound Aspects of the Greek of the New Testament." *Westminster Theological Journal* 18 (1976): 192–94.

Richardson, Peter. "'I Say, Not the Lord': Personal Opinion, Apostolic Authority and the Development of Early Christian Halakah." *Tyndale Bulletin* 31 (1980): 65–86.

Richardson, Peter, and Paul W. Gooch. "Accommodation Ethics." *Tyndale Bulletin* 29 (1978): 89–142.

Robbins, Vernon K. *Jesus the Teacher: A Socio-Rhetorical Interpretation of Mark.* Philadelphia: Fortress, 1984.

———. "Picking Up the Fragments: From Crossan's Analysis to Rhetorical Analysis." *Foundations and Facets Forum* 1/2 (1985): 31–64.

Robertson, Archibald, and Alfred Plummer. *A Critical and Exegetical Commentary on the First Epistle of Paul to the Corinthians.* 2d ed. International Critical Commentary. Edinburgh: T. and T. Clark, 1978.

Russell, D. A. *Greek Declamation.* Cambridge: Cambridge University Press, 1983.

Sampley, J. Paul. "Faith and Its Moral Life: A Study of Individuation in the Thought World of the Apostle Paul." In *Faith and History: Essays in Honor of Paul W. Meyer,* ed. John T. Carroll, Charles H. Cosgrove, and E. Elizabeth Johnson, 223–38. Atlanta: Scholars Press, 1990.

———. "Paul, His Opponents in 2 Corinthians 10–13 and the Rhetorical Handbooks." In *The Social World of Formative Christianity and Judaism: In Honor of Howard Clark Kee,* ed. Jacob Neusner et al., 162–77. Philadelphia: Fortress, 1988.

———. *Pauline Partnership in Christ: Christian Community and Commitment in Light of Roman Law.* Philadelphia: Fortress, 1980.

———. "From Text to Thought World: The Route to Paul's Ways." In *Pauline Theology,* vol. 1, ed. Jouette Bassler, 3–14. Minneapolis: Fortress, 1991.

———. *Walking between the Times: Paul's Moral Reasoning.* Minneapolis: Fortress, 1991.

Schnabel, Eckhard J. *Law and Wisdom from Ben Sira to Paul: A Traditional Historical Inquiry into the Relation of Law, Wisdom, and Ethics.* Wissenschaftliche Untersuchungen zum Neuen Testament 2.16. Tübingen: Mohr/Siebeck, 1985.

Schneider, Norbert. *Die rhetorische Eigenart der paulinischen Antithese.* Hermeneutische Untersuchungen zur Theologie 11. Tübingen: Mohr/Siebeck, 1970.

Schütz, John H. "The Cross as a Symbol of Power: 1:10–4:21." In *Paul and the Anatomy of Apostolic Authority,* 187–203. Society for New Testament Studies Monograph Series 26. Cambridge: Cambridge University Press, 1975.

Seitel, Peter. "Proverbs: A Social Use of Metaphor." In *The Wisdom of Many: Essays on the Proverb,* ed. Wolfgang Mieder and Alan Dundes, 122–39. New York: Garland, 1981.

Snyder, Graydon F. "The 'Tobspruch' in the New Testament." *New Testament Studies* 23 (1976): 117–20.

Snyman, Andreas H. "On Studying the Figures (*schēmata*) in the New Testament." *Biblica* 69 (1988): 93–107.

————. "Style and the Rhetorical Situation in Romans 8.31–39." *New Testament Studies* 34 (1988): 218–31.

Stambaugh, John E., and David L. Balch. *The New Testament in Its Social Environment.* Philadelphia: Westminster, 1986.

Stamps, Dennis L. "Rhetorical Criticism and the Rhetoric of New Testament Criticism." *Journal of Literature and Theology* 6 (1992): 268–79.

Stanley, Christopher D. *Paul and the Language of Scripture: Citation Technique in the Pauline Epistles and Contemporary Literature.* Cambridge: Cambridge University Press, 1992.

Stanley, D. M. "'Become Imitators of Me': The Pauline Conception of Apostolic Tradition." *Biblica* 40 (1959): 859–77.

Stephenson, R. H. "On the Widespread Use of an Inappropriate and Restrictive Model of the Literary Aphorism." *Modern Language Review* 75 (1980): 1–17.

Stowers, Stanley K. "A 'Debate' over Freedom: 1 Corinthians 6:12–20." In *Christian Teaching: Studies in Honor of LeMoine G. Lewis,* ed. Everett Ferguson, 59–71. Abilene, Tex.: Abilene Christian University, 1981.

————. *The Diatribe and Paul's Letter to the Romans.* SBL Dissertation Series 57. Chico, Calif.: Scholars Press, 1981.

————. *Letter-Writing in Greco-Roman Antiquity.* Library of Early Christianity. Philadelphia: Westminster, 1986.

————. "Paul on the Use and Abuse of Reason." In *Greeks, Romans, and Christians: Essays in Honor of Abraham J. Malherbe,* ed. David L. Balch, Everett Ferguson, and Wayne A. Meeks, 253–86. Minneapolis: Fortress, 1990.

Sullivan, Dale L. "The Ethos of Epideictic Encounter." *Philosophy and Rhetoric* 26 (1993): 113–33.

Sussman, Lewis A. *The Elder Seneca.* Leiden: Brill, 1978.

Talbert, Charles H. *Reading Corinthians: A Literary and Theological Commentary on 1 and 2 Corinthians.* New York: Crossroad, 1987.

Theissen, Gerd. *The Social Setting of Pauline Christianity: Essays on Corinth.* Trans. John H. Schütz. Philadelphia: Fortress, 1982.

————. "The Sociological Interpretation of Religious Traditions: Its Methodological Problems as Exemplified in Early Christianity." In *The Social Setting of Pauline Christianity: Essays on Corinth,* trans. John H. Schütz, 175–200. Philadelphia: Fortress, 1982.

————. "Strong and Weak in Corinth: A Sociological Analysis of a Theological Quarrel." In *The Social Setting of Pauline Christianity: Essays on Corinth,* trans. John H. Schütz, 121–43. Philadelphia: Fortress, 1982.

Thiselton, A. C. "Realized Eschatology at Corinth." *New Testament Studies* 24 (1978): 510–26.

Thrall, M. E. "The Pauline Uses of SYNEIDĒSIS." *New Testament Studies* 14 (1968): 118–125.

Tomson, Peter J. *Paul and the Jewish Law: Halakha in the Letters of the Apostle to the Gentiles.* Compendia rerum iudaicarum ad novum testamentum. Minneapolis: Fortress, 1990.

Tuckett, Christopher M. "Paul, Tradition and Freedom." *Theologische Zeitschrift* 47 (1991): 307–25.

Vickers, Brian R. *In Defense of Rhetoric.* Oxford: Clarendon, 1988.

Villemonteix, J. "Remarques sur les sentences homériques." *La Licorne* 3 (1979): 83–96.

Walters, James C. *Ethnic Issues in Paul's Letter to the Romans: Changing Self-Definitions in Earliest Roman Christianity.* Valley Forge, Pa.: Trinity, 1993.

Watson, Duane F. *Invention, Arrangement, and Style: Rhetorical Criticism of Jude and 2 Peter.* SBL Dissertation Series 104. Atlanta: Scholars Press, 1988.

―――. "The New Testament and Greco-Roman Rhetoric: A Bibliographic Update." *Journal of the Evangelical Theological Society* 33 (1990): 513–24.

―――. "The New Testament and Greco-Roman Rhetoric: A Bibliography." *Journal of the Evangelical Theological Society* 31 (1988): 465–72.

―――. "1 Corinthians 10:23–11:1 in Light of Greco-Roman Rhetoric: The Role of Rhetorical Questions." *Journal of Biblical Literature* 108 (1989): 301–18.

Weiss, Johannes. "Beiträge zur Paulinischen Rhetorik." In *Theologische Studien: Herrn Professor D. Bernhard Weiss au seinem 70. Geburtstag dargebracht,* ed. C. R. Gregory et al., 165–247. Göttingen: Vandenhoeck & Ruprecht, 1897.

Welborn, L. L. "A Conciliatory Principle in 1 Cor. 4:6." *Novum Testamentum* 29 (1987): 320–46.

―――. "On the Discord in Corinth: 1 Corinthians 1–4 and Ancient Politics." *Journal of Biblical Literature* 106 (1987): 85–111.

Williams, James G. *Those Who Ponder Proverbs: Aphoristic Thinking and Biblical Literature.* Sheffield, England: Almond, 1981.

Willis, Wendell Lee. *Idol Meat in Corinth: The Pauline Argument in 1 Corinthians 8 and 10.* SBL Dissertation Series 68. Chico, Calif.: Scholars Press, 1985.

Wilson, Walter T. *Love without Pretense: Romans 12.9–21 and Hellenistic-Jewish Wisdom Literature.* Wissenschaftliche Untersuchungen zum Neuen Testament 46. Tübingen: Mohr, 1991.

Wimbush, Vincent L. *Paul: The Worldly Ascetic: Response to the World and Self-Understanding according to 1 Corinthians 7.* Macon, Ga.: Mercer University Press, 1987.

Winter, Bruce W. *Seek the Welfare of the City: Christian Benefactors and Citizens.* Grand Rapids: Eerdmans, 1994.

―――. "Theological and Ethical Responses to Religious Pluralism — 1 Corinthians 8–10." *Tyndale Bulletin* 41 (1990): 207–26.

Winton, A. P. *The Proverbs of Jesus: Issues of History and Rhetoric.* JSNT Supplement Series 35. Sheffield, England: JSOT, 1991.

Wire, Antoinette Clark. *The Corinthian Women Prophets: A Reconstruction through Paul's Rhetoric.* Minneapolis: Fortress, 1990.

Wooten, Cecil. "Le développement du style asiatique pendant l'époque hellénistique." *Revue des études grecques* 88 (1975): 94–104.

Wuellner, Wilhelm. "Greek Rhetoric and Pauline Argumentation." In *Early Christian Literature and the Classical Intellectual Tradition,* ed. William Schoedel and Robert L. Wilken, 177–88. Théologie Historique 53. Paris: Beauchesne, 1979.

―――. "Paul as Pastor: The Function of Rhetorical Questions in First Corinthians." In *L'Apôtre Paul: Personalité, style et conception du ministère,* ed. A. Vanhoye, 49–77. Bibliotheca Ephemeridum Theologicarum Lovaniensium 73. Louvain: Louvain University Press, 1986.

―――. "Where Is Rhetorical Criticism Taking Us?" *Catholic Biblical Quarterly* 49 (1987): 448–63.

Yarbrough, O. Larry. *Not Like the Gentiles: Marriage Rules in the Letters of Paul.* SBL Dissertation Series 80. Atlanta: Scholars Press, 1985.

Young, Norman H. "Paidagogos: The Social Setting of a Pauline Metaphor." *Novum Testamentum* 29 (1984): 150–76.

Zaas, Peter S. "Catalogues and Context: 1 Corinthians 5 and 6." *New Testament Studies* 34 (1988): 622–29.

Scripture Index

Index of Subjects
and Modern Authors